1784

1784

DUNCAN SPROTT

London
GEORGE ALLEN & UNWIN
Boston   Sydney

First published in 1984

**George Allen & Unwin (Publishers) Ltd,
40 Museum Street, London WC1A 1LU, UK**

George Allen & Unwin (Publishers) Ltd,
Park Lane, Hemel Hempstead, Herts HP2 4TE, UK

George Allen & Unwin Australia Pty Ltd,
8 Napier Street, North Sydney, NSW 2060, Australia

© Duncan Sprott, 1984

ISBN 0 04 808045 4

Typeset in 11 on 12 point Plantin Light by Columns of Reading
and printed in Great Britain by
Anchor Brendon Ltd, Tiptree

One of the principal amusements of the Idler is to read the works of those minute historians, the writers of news, who, though contemptuously overlooked by composers of bulky volumes, are yet necessary in a nation where much wealth produces much leisure, and one part of the people has nothing to do but observe the lives and fortunes of the other. To us, who are regaled every morning and evening with intelligence, and are supplied from day to day with materials for conversation, it is difficult to conceive how man can subsist without a newspaper, or to what entertainment companies can assemble in those wide regions of the earth that have neither "Chronicles" nor "Magazines", neither "Gazettes" nor "Advertisers", neither "Journals" nor "Evening Posts".

Samuel Johnson: The Idler
27 May 1758

The only true history of a country is to be found in the newspapers.

Macaulay

Have you noticed that life, real honest-to-goodness life, with murders and catastrophes and fabulous inheritances, happens exclusively in the newspapers?

Jean Anouilh: The Rehearsal

I read the newspaper avidly. It is my one form of continuous fiction.

Aneurin Bevan

INTRODUCTION

"Hurly, Burly Times", wrote Parson Woodforde of 1784, a year which began with "Bitter, bitter cold", snow on the ground and plenty of blood in the snow. Events were as violent as the weather – violent robbery, violent death, violent differences of opinion. The newspapers gave their readers blood in the eye in the first sentence, and managed to keep it up most of the way through as well.

Life in 1784 must have been very nasty, very brutish and very short for many, but the picture, though lurid, is not all gloom and despondency; there is much of the lighter side of life: fantastic windfalls, fairs, elopements, practical jokes, eccentrics, and a people hungry for news of it all.

The rich spent the mornings reading the news and the evening discussing it – when they were not being burgled or being attended by Mr Barrington, the prince of pickpockets. The rest of the populace were out on the streets keeping alive, gambling and making absurd wagers, making the news and breaking the law, or going "to the devil and the dogs" as fast as they could.

1784 lies in the lull between two storms: the American War of Independence was over; the French Revolution was still five years away. In politics Pitt's India Bill and the May election bulk large, but everything else is dwarfed into insignificance by the Balloon Craze. The heroes of the year were foreigners: Lunardi and Blanchard, who made the first manned balloon ascents in this country. Emulating them were countless home-made home-designed contrivances which appear for the most part to have descended or crashed into haystacks or set fire to private property, to the delight of the mob and the dismay of the owners.

There are tantalizing glimpses into the extraordinary things that happened to ordinary people, and the ordinary things that happened to the famous, but these are often sadly isolated incidents: one may search and search for more next week, but in vain. We never find out, for example, whether the brewer's servant's wife recovers her senses; whether Mrs. Seagood, the Emperor of Morocco's favourite concubine, ever escapes, or what happens to her unfortunate husband; we never discover the fate of "the noted Mrs. Hall, Mother of the still more notorious Lydia Hall" who was charged with robbery and committed for trial. But this, it seems to me, is part of the attraction: these fragments are enough to whet the appetite – we must read between the lines, guess, imagine or wonder, and finish them ourselves.

The rich and famous are better documented: George Stephenson was only 3 years old at the beginning of the year; Turner and Jane Austen were 8; Napoleon and Beethoven were 13, Wordsworth was 14, Wellington 15; the Prince of Wales, later George IV, was 21 and beginning to patronize Brighton; Nelson and Danton were 25; William Pitt the Younger was Prime Minister and only 25; Mozart was 28; Louis XVI was 30, with only 9 years left to live. Fox was 35, Parson Woodforde 44, King George III was 45, Gibbon was 47 and in the middle of *Decline and Fall*; Horace Walpole was 67, Dr. Johnson was 75 and not expected to survive the winter; Benjamin Franklin was 78 and John Wesley still going at 81. Voltaire and Rousseau were only five years dead.

Time seems to stand still in these pages but things were changing fast, or soon would. 1779 had seen the invention of Crompton's Mule; 1785 would see the introduction of the steam engine into factories and the invention of Cartwright's power loom. It was not very far from the riots in Covent Garden to the France of 1789.

Compulsive and delightful reading though the newspapers were – and are – the amount of truth contained in them is questionable and at this late date difficult to determine. Eighteenth-century journalists were not famed for their accuracy and even stories that today have a ring of truth about them were frequently disclaimed in a later edition.

Oliver Goldsmith had written in *The Citizen of the World*

in 1762: "You must not imagine that they who compile these papers have any actual knowledge of the politics or the government of state; they only collect their materials from the oracle of some coffee-house, which oracle has himself gathered them the night before from a beau at a gaming table, who has pillaged his knowledge from a great man's porter, who had his information from the great man's gentleman, who has invented the whole story for his own amusement the night preceding."

Looking back has had its disadvantages ever since Lot's wife: I can only advise that some of the extracts included here (I have my doubts about the baby born with a lamb's leg) must be taken with a pinch of salt.

I have tried to let the eighteenth century speak for itself and only reluctantly dispense with the long *s* which makes the originals so charming. By way of demonstration I have transcribed the following incident, which has no business in the present volume (coming from 1773) but is one of my favourites and would otherwise lie on a shelf at Colindale for another two centuries:

Mr. Francis of London called at an Inn at Reading, but other company coming in, and Beds running fcarce, he agreed to fhare his Bed with a young Fellow juft come from Bath. In the morning Mr. Francif's Gold Watch was miffing, and the young Man was charged on a Sufpicion of Felony; but on a Scrutiny into the Affair, it was found that the Rats had drawn the Watch into a Hole in the Wainfcot where it was difcovered by the Ribband.

Here is the news and the news only and you may draw your own conclusions and trace your own patterns, or not, as you please. I hope the result will be as much fun to read as it has been to make.

I would like to thank the following for their assistance and unfailing kindness: the staff of the British Library, Bloomsbury, particularly in the North Library Gallery; the staff of the British Library Newspaper Library, Colindale;

the staff of the London Library; the doctor who treated me when my eye turned vermilion after staring into a microfilm reader for six weeks; Michael Macgregor, Trudi Braun, and all those who made suggestions and encouraging noises.

Finally I must be grateful to the shade of the Revd Charles Burney DD (1757–1817), collector of newspapers, without whom this project would probably not have been possible.

DUNCAN SPROTT

ACKNOWLEDGEMENT

Quote from *Nineteen Eighty-Four* reproduced by kind permission of the estate of the late Sonia Brownell Orwell and Martin Secker & Warburg Ltd.

The NEWS-PAPERS! Sir, they are the most villainous – licentious – abominable – infernal – Not that I ever read them – No – I make it a rule never to look into a news-paper.

R. B. Sheridan: The Critic (1779)

Do not wonder that we do not entirely attend to things of earth; fashion has ascended to a higher element. All our views are directed to the air. *Balloons* occupy senators, philosophers, ladies, everybody . . .

Horace Walpole to Sir H. Mann
2 December 1783

Lady Middleton exerted herself to ask Mr. Palmer if there was any news in the paper. "No, none at all," he replied, and read on.

Jane Austen: Sense and Sensibility

He filled the glasses and raised his own glass by the stem.

"What shall it be this time?" he said, still with the same faint suggestion of irony.

"To the confusion of the Thought Police? To the death of Big Brother? To humanity? To the future?"

"To the past," said Winston.

"The past is more important," agreed O'Brien gravely.

George Orwell: Nineteen Eighty-Four

JANUARY

Tuesday the Dover Stage Coach was overturned this Side of Canterbury, and a Woman Passenger, who was on the Roof, was dashed to pieces by the Hardness of the Road, and expired on the Spot. The Effusion of Blood was so great as to astonish every Spectator who passed that Way.

The Public Advertiser
1 January 1784

A considerable wager was made at Brookes's the other night, that the *Frost* would endure longer than the *Ministry* – Indeed there is some analogy between *Ice* and the present *Administration*, in so far as they are a composition of materials naturally in *repulsive commotion* among each other, and which nothing but the absence of the *Sun* of *Parliament* can bring into adhesion.

Gazeteer and New Daily Advertiser
1 January 1784

Underneath is the copy of a singular letter lately received by post by Mr. Stone, Portrieve of Modbury, Devon,

"SIR,   Exeter, Nov. 12, 1783.
    The inclosed spoon was stolen out of a house on the hill, going from Modbury, I think it was the last house in Modbury, and as some of the servants, or any person who is innocent may be charged with the theft, I have sent it to you as I don't know the person's name who lost it; it was taken in the last house on the hill going from Modbury to Plympton by your humble servant

Tristram Shandy.

P.S.   I hope, Sir, you will take care that the right owner

1

has it; I am certain it will never do me any good to keep it, but at that moment I was forsaken by my just and good God, and guided by the Devil."

General Evening Post
1–3 January 1784

[The portrieve was the mayor or principal magistrate.]

Anecdote. A sailor married a woman some time since; he staid with her the first night, went to sea the next day, and did not return for three months, at which period his wife was brought to bed of a fine girl. Jack was greatly enraged, and complained of his wife's inconstancy; but the nurse undertook to appease his wrath by telling him, that women reckoned by night as well as by day. Well, replies the son of Neptune, that makes but six months, and women generally go nine. You fool, replies the old matron, you have forgot the three months you have been at sea; only recollect that three months by day, three months by night, and three months at sea, make nine months; your wife is an honest woman. Jack thought her explanation very right, and begged pardon for his unjust accusation, and at present lives very happy with his virtuous wife.

London Chronicle
1–3 January 1784

The following intelligence appeared in the York Chronicle of Friday last.

INTELLIGENCE EXTRAORDINARY!
AIR BALLOON DILIGENCES.
(Between YORK and LONDON)

Will shortly be established, carrying four persons, each of whom will be allowed 13 st. weight, including luggage of every kind.— It is recommended that any provisions taken may be of the flatulent kind, that in case of necessity proper use may be made of the gaz produced by them; for the application of which, particular directions will be given in due time.

The Balloon will be towed by a single horse, the line fixed firmly to the saddle.

To prevent the inconveniences which might arise from curiosity, before they come into general use, it is proposed that they shall not stop at any town during their flight, but descend for refreshment at the following single houses, viz. Barnby Moor, Witham Common, and Alkenbury Hill.

N.B.   To obviate any alarm in the passengers, Balloons will be raised above twice the height of St. Paul's.

The Country Papers are filled with accounts of the manufacturing and letting off Air Balloons; at Manchester, Whitehaven, Newark and Chester, they have succeeded to the admiration of thousand of spectators.

Bath Chronicle
1 January 1784

CHRISTMAS GAMBOLS

THESE periodical sports commenced this season sooner than usual, and under a more than ordinarily dignified authority. They were begun in the House of Peers, where the noble Lords, before Christmas was fairly arrived, entertained themselves with snatching away each others seats. Not John nor Molly could display more assiduity and pleasure in letting each other down upon the bare boards or stones, than did certain noble Peers in slily possessing themselves of the warm births of their fellow Patricians. . . . As to the people in general, they are not quite so frolicsome, and not having such good reasons for playing at cross-purposes as their betters, they are content with an humbler amusement, that of battledore and shuttlecock, thus at submissive distance imitating the manners of those who are called their superiors. The little boys too have caught the infection, and trip up each others heels with as much glee and artifice as their seniors kick in and out their friends in the House of Lords and St. Stephen's Chapel. It were to be wished that the gambols of the rich and powerful were as harmless as those of the young and humble, then might a face of joy be spread amongst the people in general, and Christmas prove a festival indeed.

General Evening Post
30 December 1783–
1 January 1784

[The House of Commons sat in St Stephen's Chapel.]

According to the common Cause of Things, it is expected that the *Parliament* and the *Frost* will be dissolved about the same Time; and it is feared a good deal of Damage will be done by both Events.

Public Advertiser
1 January 1784

Sunday Morning Thomas Shaftoe, a young Man, in attempting to catch a Water Hen, followed it into the River Wear, at Durham, got out of his Depth, and perished before any Assistance could be got.

The Thames, both above and below Bridge is so full of Ice, that the Craft and Boats are stopped from working.

The River is so choaked up with Ice above Maidenhead, that no Craft whatever can pass.

Wednesday Morning a poor Man who lodged in a Garret in Gray's-inn-lane, was found dead upon the Floor, supposed to have perished through the Inclemency of the Weather, and for Want of the Necessaries of Life. It is supposed he had been dead two Days.

The same Morning a poor Woman was found frozen to Death near the Adam-and-Eve Turnpike, Tottenham-court Road.

Public Advertiser
2 January 1784

London, Dec. 29.
Last night the Aurora Borealis, or Northern Lights, were seen so exceedingly vivid in many parts of the metropolis, that it was generally supposed to be a' great fire. On Shooter's Hill it was seen very awful.

Caledonian Mercury, Edinburgh
3 January 1784

London, Jan. 2.
Such is the rage for doing miraculous things, that, not satisfied with travelling in the air, a man in France has offered to walk across the Seine in shoes of his own making; and another has petitioned to be allowed to throw himself, body breeches and all into a great fire, and engages that neither he nor the breeches shall be hurt. It may be a question, however, even yet, whether St. Stephen's Chapel be not the mart of *miracles* after all.

Caledonian Mercury, Edinburgh
7 January 1784

Salisbury, Jan. 5.
Last Wednesday Morning Edward Brown was found frozen to Death on the Downs, about five Miles from this City.

The same Day the Boy who brought the Mail from Devizes to Heytesbury was just expiring when he arrived there. He was lifted from the Horse almost motionless, and it was some Hours before he totally recovered.

York Courant
13 January 1784

London, January 5.

This morning part of the luggage of his Grace the Duke of Dorset was sent off for Paris.

Caledonian Mercury, Edinburgh
10 January 1784

[The 3rd Duke of Dorset was Ambassador to the Court of France.]

Mr. B——, the preacher, being found in one of the royal apartments at Versailles, Mademoiselle, the King's eldest daughter, asked him what brought him there? "I intend, says he, Mademoiselle, in my next sermon to give a description of Paradise, and I come here for materials."

Whitehall Evening Post
3–6 January 1784

Last Sunday Night a Man who had been in London to be engaged as an Assistant in a Pastry-cook's Shop, Today being Twelfth-Day, was robbed in the Bishop's Walk, Lambeth, of a new Hat, new Coat and Waistcoat, a Silver Watch, two Guineas and some Silver, a Pair of plated Shoe buckles, and even his very Shoes, by two Footpads. He begged hard for his Shoes, but to no Purpose.

Public Advertiser
6 January 1784

The St. Clement's chop-house is a true school of morality; while on the one hand the guest beholds the cook preparing his beef steak, he observes on the other, a number of his friends put under *cover* by the sexton; so that at the same moment he sees what it is to *live*, and what it is to die!

Gazeteer and New Daily Advertiser
6 January 1784

The Roads from Newcastle to Edinburgh have been rendered so extremely difficult by the great Quantity of Snow that the Diligences and other Modes of Communication have been entirely stopped for some Days past.

On Wednesday last the Frost was very severe here, the Thermometer, at Nine in the Morning, was so low as 8, or 22 Degrees below the freezing Point. It began to thaw that Afternoon, and on Friday and Saturday there was the greatest Fall of Snow that has been known here for many Years. It began to freeze again on Sunday Evening, and still continues.

On Thursday se'nnight, about Ten in the Morning, a very strong Gale of Wind began to blow from the S.E. which almost instantly caused a higher sea upon Tinmouth Bar, and at the Mouth of Shields Harbour, than can be remembered there by the oldest Person living. A light Ship coming over the Bar, belonging to Mr. Armstrong of Culdercoats, was drove ashore on the Black Middings, where she now lays without any Possibility of her being recovered. The Crew was with Difficulty saved. The Violence of the Wind was so great, that she split a Rock against which she was drove, and was afterwards hoisted so far ashore, as to be out of the Water-Mark at the highest Spring Tides.

In the Evening, when the Violence of the Sea had abated, a set of Villains came down and plundered the Ship of the Captain's Chest, Sailor's Clothes, and every Thing of Value which they could conveniently carry off.

York Courant
6 January 1784

During the above Storm the Ship Jean, of Sunderland, drove from her Anchors in the Roads, on the Rocks betwixt Whitburn and that Harbour, and was entirely lost; but the Crew were saved.—A Sloop and a Shallop went on Shore on Seaton Sands near Hartlepool; the Sloop Bottom up, and all on board perished.—The Industry, Capt. Lamb, of Stockton, in making for Scarborough Harbour, drove behind Sunderland Pier: They had one Man wash'd overboard, and it is feared the Ship will be entirely lost.—The Aurora, belonging to Capt. Mercer of Sunderland, drove on Shore near Bridlington; the Crew were saved, but the Ship lost.—The Falkirk, Hunter, from Newcastle to Leith, with Treacle, Sugar, &c. was lost near Holy Island; the Crew and Passengers saved, except a Boy.

York Courant
6 January 1784

Lord Fortescue some time since gave Orders to his Steward to make a Deduction in the Rents of all his Tenants in Lincolnshire, who suffered by the Failure of their Crops in 1782.—A most worthy Deed, deserving the imitation of those blessed with Affluence.

The Prisoners in Ouse-Bridge Gaol return thanks to a Gentleman unknown for a Guinea.

York Courant
6 January 1784

A few days ago as the widow of Mr. Roger Thornton, of Margate, was going for her grist to Mr. Lemmon's mill, near Margate, unfortunately one of the mill sweeps caught hold of her and killed her on the spot.

Canterbury Journal
6 January 1784

Last Week a Man undertook to descend, in Imitation of flying, on a Rope, affixed to the Top of St. Andrew's Steeple, Droitwich, which he did with great Velocity over the Tops of many Houses, to the great Amazement of Hundreds of the principal Inhabitants, and alighted in the Street, about a Quarter of a Mile from the said Steeple.

Public Advertiser
7 January 1784

A Gentleman disputing the other Day with a saucy Fellow of a Coachman at Charing cross; who demanded evidently more than his Fare; People crowded about, and as they were presently convinced that the Gentleman was wronged, called the Coachman a Rascal, and bade him take what the Gentleman offered him.—"Look you there," said the Gentleman, "the very *Mob* take my Part."— "Mob!" cried the People, "d——n you Sir, who is the Mob?"—upon which they all immediately joined with the Coachman, and insisted upon his not bating the Gentleman a farthing of his Demand, for that it was no more than his Due.

Public Advertiser
7 January 1784

BAGATELLES

I have heard of a gentleman in the army whose imagination was so easily affected in sleep with impressions made on the outward senses, that his companions, by speaking softly in his ear, could cause him to dream of what they pleased. Once, in particular, they made him go through the whole procedure of a duel, from the beginning of the quarrel to the firing of a pistol, which they put into his hand for that purpose, and which, by the explosion, awaked him.

Some people contract strange habits of what may be called external association. I call it so, because the body is more concerned in it than the mind, and external things than ideas: they connect a certain action with a certain object so, that without the one they cannot easily perform the other; although, independently of habit there is no connection between them. I have heard of a clergyman who could not compose his sermon except when he held a foot-rule in his hand; and of one who, while he was employed in study, would always be rolling between his fingers a parcel of peas, whereof he constantly kept a trencher-full within reach of his arm. I knew a gentleman who would talk a great deal in company by the help of a large pin, which he held between his thumb and forefinger; but when he lost his pin, his tongue seemed at the same instant to lose its volubility; and he never was at ease till he had provided himself with another implement of the same kind. Locke speaks of a young man who, in one particular room where an old trunk stood, could dance very well; but in any other room, if it wanted such a piece of furniture, could not dance at all. The Tatler mentions a more probable instance of a lawyer, who in his pleadings always used to be twisting about his finger a piece of pack-thread; which the punsters of that time called, with some reason, the thread of his discourse. One day, a client of his had a mind to see how he would acquit himself without it, and stole it from him: the consequence was, that the orator became silent in the middle of his harangue, and the client lost his cause.

Such example may be uncommon; but many persons are to be met with who have contracted similar habits. You may see a boy, while repeating his catechism, button and unbutton his coat a dozen times; and, when learning to write, screw his features unknowingly into a variety of forms, as if he meant by the motion of those parts to imitate that of his pen. Some men there are, who no sooner bid you good morrow, than they thrust a snuff-box into your hand; and some can hardly either speak or think without gnawing their nails, scratching their head, or fumbling in their pockets.

Whitehall Evening Post
6–8 January 1784

We are assured that a gentleman from the West of England, of considerable fortune, coming to town in the Christmas week to conclude a matrimonial treaty, was inveigled into a fashionable house, at the West end of the town, where he lost at play near 5,000 l. with his ring, watch, coach and four horses. The winners *generously* gave ten guineas each to his domestics.

Bonner and Middleton's Bristol Journal
10 January 1784

The late frost was so very severe, that several Snipes were found frozen to death with their bills in the ground. Two poor men were frozen to death in Northamptonshire.

Bonner and Middleton's Bristol Journal
10 January 1784

On Tuesday the 23 of December last, Mr. S., professor of anatomy, Great Queen-street, employed a man to procure him a dead body, that he might demonstrate the muscels the day following to his young pupils, amounting to upwards of seventy. The man according to agreement brought the body in a sack the same evening to his dissecting room, but shocking to relate, on examining the body, he found it to be his own sister, that was buried at Kensington on the 14th, the sight of which threw Mr. S. into strong convulsions, and he now lies dangerously ill.

Bonner and Middleton's Bristol Journal
10 January 1784

Friday a man was found dead under a hayrick, in the Parish of Foleshill. He is supposed to have perished through the inclemency of the weather.

On Wednesday evening a countryman coming over Blackheath when it snowed extremely hard, missed the path, and fell into a hollow way, fractured his skull, and expired immediately.

On Thursday afternoon as some people were skating on a pond near Peckham-Gap, the ice suddenly gave way, when the people hastened off as fast as possible, except a lad, who being in the middle, the ice broke, and he was drowned in the sight of fifty persons, who could afford him no assistance.

Same morning as two young men were skating on the canal in St. James's Park, the ice suddenly gave way, and they were both drowned.

Bonner and Middleton's Bristol Journal
10 January 1784

The following is a fact.—A hamper, in which were a small bag, containing 11 guineas, and some elegant cups and saucers, were last week received by a gentleman in the city (London), with a letter, containing the following remarkable words:

"Sir, on the 18th of June last I robbed you of 11 guineas, and now return it to you with many thanks. I knew you well. Distress caused the act. Present to your wife and daughter these cups and saucers; they are very pretty. I am your humble servant."

Bonner and Middleton's Bristol Journal
10 January 1784

It appears that the offer made by the watch-maker at Lyons, to walk over the river Seine at Paris, without so much as wetting the soles of his shoes, was an attempt to humbug the inhabitants of the capital. . . .

Sussex Weekly Advertiser or Lewes Journal
January 1784

Yesterday morning between Two and Three o'clock, the Chester Coach was stopped between South Mimms and Ridge Hill by a single Highwayman. On his demanding the Passengers Money, a lady in the Coach with uncommon Resolution expostulated with him on the Atrociousness of his Attempt, assuring him that there were Fire Arms in the coach sufficient to destroy him on the Spot if he did not immediately retire. The Highwayman, however, with several Imprecations, declared that he must have Money. At this juncture a Gentleman in the coach presented a Pistol at him, but was prevented from firing by a lady in the coach, who at that Instant fainted away. A Collection then was made for him, and when a Gentleman gave him his Purse, on telling him it was his all, the Robber spiritedly offered to return Part of it back, which the Gentleman refused to accept; he then rode off wishing them a good Journey. He was well mounted on a Black Horse about 14 hands high, is a middle sized genteel Man, with a long dark visage, had on a blue Surtout Coat, and a round Buck Hat.

Just before the above Robbery, the same Person levied Contributions on the Passengers in the Leeds and Shropshire Coaches.

Adams's Weekly Courant, Chester
11 January 1784

The Frost was never known in the Memory of Man so severe in Worcestershire as on Tuesday and Wednesday last Week. The Severn was frozen over for Miles together; and various are the Accounts of People and Cattle that perished.

York Courant
13 January 1784

Colchester. Early on Monday morning a labouring man, at the Hythe in this town, dreaming that a deal stack was falling on him, got out of bed, and, in his fright, jumped out of a window, and unfortunately broke a leg and an arm.

Ipswich Journal
16 January 1784

London. A few days since the Lady of Sir Trevor Curry met with a similar accident to that which some time ago befel the unfortunate Miss Picket, of Ludgate-hill; for sitting near the fire, a spark caught her clothes, which were extended over a bell-hoop, and in an instant she was overpowered with the flames; a lady hearing her shrieks, ran into the room, and with great presence of mind pushed her Ladyship into the street, and rolled her into the kennel; though this extinguished the flames, Lady C. was so terribly burnt, that her life is despaired of.

Bonner and Middleton's Bristol Journal
17 January 1784

Last week as two lads, apprentices to a butcher near Painswick, were going out to shoot crows, one of them, in going out of the door with his gun cocked, struck the piece against the door case, and it went off and killed the other lad, who was just before him.

Bonner and Middleton's Bristol Journal
17 January 1784

On Monday night an elderly gentleman, having a necessary call under a gate-way in Meath-street, was in an instant touched on the shoulder by a villain, who presented a pistol to his breast, and robbed him of a gold watch, value thirty guineas; after which the robber swore if he presumed to stir from the spot for half an hour, he would shoot him. This desperado spoke with an English accent.

Magee's Weekly Packet, Dublin
17 January 1784

On the 20th ult. died, at an Inn on the road between Ostend and Rotterdam, Thomas Nelson, Esq;—He was born near Leeds in Yorkshire, went apprentice and served part of his time to a stay-maker in that neighbourhood, but being of an enterprising turn, he ran away from his master and went to sea. He had been upwards of 20 years in the slave trade, to and from the Dutch West India Settlements, by which he had made a fortune of upwards of 60,000 l. —He retired about four years since, and has chiefly resided in the neighbourhood of Rotterdam, where he lived in a very private and penurious manner.—He has left some 40,000 l. to his nephew, Mr. William Rowland, and considerable legacies to some other relations.

Rowland Nelson, a journeyman cloth-dresser, in Leeds, and nephew to the above gentleman, is already set off to lay claim to the above legacy.

Cambridge Chronicle and Journal
17 January 1784

London, January 6.

NECESSARY CAUTIONS
For January, 1784

It is particularly recommended at this season not to eat too many *Cherries* or *Strawberries*, nor let Children eat too many *green Pease*.

Parents are cautioned not to permit their children to *bathe in the River Thames*. The ladies, in particular, are advised for a few days, to desist from *going to the Rock to bathe*.

Church-wardens are recommended not to feed the poor, during this *month*, upon *House-lamb*.

It is hoped the Managers will not open Vauxhall-gardens for at least a *Fortnight*.

Gentlemen are requested not to *angle* in the Serpentine for a few days.

Orders ought to be given, that no person pluck *Roses*, Pink, Jessamine, or other flowers, from off the borders in Kensington Gardens.

It is advisable not to take the Bed-curtains *down*, or sleep with the Windows *open*.

15

Persons who regard their health should not eat too many *Cucumbers*, or too much *Raspberry-ice*, during this month.

The eating of *Mulberries*, at this season, is particularly hurtful.

City Tradesmen are advised not to sit quiet in their Gardens at Islington, Newington, &c. without their *Coats*, and their Shirt-Collars *open*.

The Bishops and Judges are recommended not to play at throwing Snow-Balls, or slide upon the *Ice* in St. James's Park.

The Inhabitants of the City of London and Westminster merit every praise for with-holding, this season, their usual contribution for the relief of the poor, as *starving* them will effectually put a period to their miseries.

Butchers and Fishmongers are advised not to sell their Meat and Fish under prime cost, while this weather continues.

Edinburgh Evening Courant
20 January 1784

London, Jan. 20.
Yesterday a young woman took a boat at Pickle-Herring-Stairs, and desired to be ferryed over; when the boat came to the middle of the river, she threw down 6d. and jumped over. The waterman with great difficulty drew her again into the boat; on which she confessed that being far gone with child by a noble lord, and being refused any assistance, [she] had determined to put a period to her existence.

Ipswich Journal
24 January 1784

PRIVATE EDUCATION

A Gentleman of a small Fortune, about 27 Years of Age, who has had a regular University Education, and who, having resided some Years abroad, is acquainted with

16

the FRENCH and ITALIAN LANGUAGES, wishes to engage himself as Tutor to some young Nobleman or Gentleman, and would have no Objection to travel.

☞ Direct for Mr. FRANKE, No. 20, Carey-street, Lincoln's-Inn-Fields, London.

The York Courant
20 January 1784

ANECDOTE OF THE LATE ADVOCATE OF STRASBOURG

The Advocate being taken ill, he sent for a Brother Lawyer to make his Will, by which he bequeathed 72,000 Florins to the Hospital for Ideots at Strasbourg.—His Brother Advocate expressing his Surprize at the Bequest, "Why not bestow that Sum upon them? (said the dying Man) You know I got my Money by Fools, and therefore to Fools it ought to return."

Adams's Weekly Courant, Chester
21 January 1784

Edinburgh. This day John Robertson, who was whipped through this city on the 24th ult. for theft, underwent a like discipline for the same crime. After which a Miss Clark was drummed, for encouraging boys in theftuous practices, and assisting in the debauchery of very young girls.

Edinburgh Evening Courant
21 January 1784

Foreign Anecdote.—The Father of a Family at Bordeaux being missed for a considerable Time, and no Tidings heard of him, two affectionate Sons, who were indefatigable in their Enquiries to know the Fate of their lost Parent, happened many Months after their Loss (and when all Hope of a Discovery was despaired of) to fall in Company with a certain Priest, to whom they were lamenting their Loss, aggravated by the additional Affliction of not knowing certainly whether Death, Imprisonment, or Assassination has deprived them of so virtuous a Parent. The Priest advised them to be resigned to the Will of God, intimating, at the same Time, that there was little or no Probability of their ever being truly satisfied on that Head. The two Brothers, on their quitting the Priest's Company, were both inclined to suspect, by the Manner in which the Priest endeavoured to console them, that he knew the Fate of their lost Father by Means of *Confession*; and the Elder of the two determined to come at the Truth, though by the most desperate Means. He got the Priest, therefore, into the Fields to walk out with him, and there, taking a Pistol from his Pocket, told him his Suspicions, and threatened him with immediate Death if he did not declare all he knew. Fear seized the Priest; he saw in the Countenance of the young Man a Determination to put him to Death if he did not speak *out*, and, therefore, informed him, that his Father had been murdered by such a Man, and the Body was buried under a certain Tree. The Place was searched, and the Body found; but, sad to relate, the Priest was broke alive on the Wheel, for discovering the Confession of his Penitent. The son of the murdered Person was broke for extorting it from him by the Fear of his Life. The Murderer, however, suffered no other Punishment than that of being left to his own Conscience!—If the Natives of a Country, and of the same Religion, are liable to such Acts of Injustice, certain it is that Strangers of a different Religion who establish themselves among them are never absolutely secure. To pass through a Catholic Country is, perhaps, safe enough; but to become a Resident, must be attended with some

18

Danger, especially as it is in the Power of any great Man, with the King of P——'s Spirit, whom a Stranger may offend, to *bastile* you *à la Linguet*.

Public Advertiser
22 January 1784

To the Printer of the Bath Chronicle,
SIR,
IF you think the following particulars relative to the Air Balloon, which was let off from Crescent Fields on Saturday the 10th of this month, will be in any degree interesting to your readers, you are very welcome to insert them.

"Thomas Urch, of the parish of Westbury, which is four miles nearly West from Wells, says, that being about half way between those two places, on Saturday the 10th instant, about one o'clock, he discovered, at a great height in the air, an object, which he at first took for a large bird, and which seemed to come in a strait line towards him, from the center of Wells horse-course. As it approached him nearer, it appeared much larger, and gradually descended as it came to the ground, at the distance, as he judged, of about a quarter of a mile from the place where he stood. It continued its course in a direct line towards him, standing erect, and seeming to sweep along the ground with its lower end, like a duck which is half walking and half flying. Believing it to be some unknown and dangerous animal, he was at first going to run away from it, but before he set out, determined to see it near enough to discover whether it had a mouth and claws; seeing it had no appearances of this kind, he stood still till it came to him, and was stopped by a hedge which was near; he then ventured to put his hand upon it, when it rose up from the ground. The man was alarmed at this new motion, and started back; but re-assuming his course, endeavoured to catch hold of it, but without success, as it yielded to his touch, and made him fancy that it raised him

19

off his feet; at last, however, he seized it, and carried it with him to Westbury, where Mr. Lane, a farmer of that place, from reading the label annexed to the balloon, understood what it was, and by his watch ascertained the time when it fell.

These particulars were communicated to me by the Rev. Mr. Bowen of Wells, who had them from the man's own mouth, and who informs me that the man blew up the balloon with a pair of bellows, and exhibited it in that state to the populace of Wells and Shepton-Mallet at 2d. each.

The balloon was not hurt, and from circumstances related, it appears, that, supposing its course to have been in a direct line, it must have travelled nearly 19 miles in a few minutes more than an hour. In all probability, however, its course was much longer, as the place where it fell is South West from Bath, and the balloon disappeared from the Crescent Fields in a direction somewhat to the North of West. C.H.P.

Bath Chronicle
22 January 1784

BATH

MASTER CROTCH, the Self-Taught MUSICAL CHILD, continues to perform on the Piano Forte and Violin, at No. 2, Savile-Row, each day from twelve till two o'clock.—Admittance Ladies and Gentlemen 2s.
☞ Master Crotch began to play when he was but two years and three weeks old, and is allowed to have the finest ear that ever was known.—
Harpsichords and Piano Fortes tuned by J. Crotch.

Bath Chronicle
22 January 1784

London, Jan. 20.
Yesterday being kept as her Majesty's birth-day, the Court was extremely brilliant. The King and Queen entered the

drawing-room about two o'clock, and retired at half after four. They were accompanied by the Prince of Wales and the Princess Royal. Not only the ministry of the day were present but the Duke of Portland, Mr. Fox, Lord North, Lord Stormont, Lord Carlisle, and the whole suit of placemen under the last administration. Hence the drawing-room was more than usually crowded, and presented a motley view of ministers and the leaders of opposition, and the adherents of both strangely commingled. There were many beautiful women present, in most rich and fanciful dress . . . The ladies were dressed in sattins and weighty silks trimmed with furs, and decorated with gold and silver spotted gauze, &c. &c. . . . His Majesty wore an elegant maroan coloured velvet coat embroidered superbly with gold; the Queen, as usual on her birth-day, was plainly dressed, but neatly and with taste. The Prince was rather gaudy than grand. His coat was of cloth of gold embroidered splendidly down the fronts and seams . . . Many of the light-fingered gentry attended as usual; they made shift to strip Sir James Harris of his insignia of the order which he wore, and lightened the pockets of many gentlemen, in their way to and from the drawing-room, of watches, handkerchiefs, &c. and where they could do no better, they carried off such arm hats as they could snatch away.

Politics were in a strange shape of uncertainty in the drawing-room yesterday. No person of either party could or would decisively say, whether the Parliament was to be dissolved or not. A general coalition was declared to be wished for by many, but expected by few.

Caledonian Mercury, Edinburgh
24 January 1784

Yesterday a man was whipt through High-street, in the Borough, for stealing dead bodies out of the Church-yard of St. George's in the East.

Whitehall Evening Post
20-22 January 1784

The week before last, a remarkable smart little fellow went to Yarm, and pretended to be Master of a ship laying then at Hull, for which he wanted to buy a large quantity of corn and timber; and actually agreed with a gentleman for drafts to the value of 600 l. for which he offered in immediate payment bills on one of the York banks for 1200 l. all of which he wished to have discounted. This the gentleman would have done, had the money been at hand; for the bills seemed true, and had been accepted; but soon thinking it extraordinary a stranger should pay him so large a sum without receiving any value, he peremptorily refused. The little Captain bore all the disappointment with great good humour, and said "He should go to Darlington, and exchange 'em at the Bank there." In the evening, he got into the company of a gentleman who had retired from the sea service, and, after lamenting that his baggage was stopped by the storm on the way from Hull, especially as he had put on his worst coat for the journey, he observed, "that they were both of the same size", and requested a suit of cloaths, for which he could pay.—The Gentleman sent immediately for a suit, but payment was deferred till his return from Darlington, when he was to dine with him. He went there on a post-horse the next day, when, without stopping at the Bank, he took on to Newcastle, and dismissed the boy who attended him, by saying the horses were paid for. He went forwards the same day to Hexham, and attended the market, took samples of corn, smattered French, and seemed quite at ease, till on Thursday he decamped. The ostler pursued him till he had got into Carlisle, where, on examination, *The Little Dapper Captain* was found to be a *Female* and the very *Lady* who behaved so genteelly in this town about a month ago. Her name is Violet Chambers, a notorious courtezan, who had the honor to stand in the pillory at Carlisle in July last, for defrauding several tradesmen in that place of considerable sums of money, under pretence of pregnancy.—She is committed to gaol.

Public Advertiser
23 January 1784

Last week died at Chester, Mr. S. Bisset, the extraordinary teacher of beasts, birds and fishes, on his journey with the learned pig.—Perhaps no nation has produced so singular a character as Bisset; tho' in this age of apathy, his merit was but little rewarded. At any former aera of time, the man who could assume a command over the dumb creation, and make them act with a docility which went far beyond mere brutal instinct, would have been looked upon as possessed of supernatural powers, according to the Pagan notions, or be burned for a wizard according to the Christian system. He first tried his hand on a horse & a dog, which succeeded beyond expectation. Two monkies were his next pupils, one of which he taught to dance and tumble on the rope, whilst the other held a candle with one paw for his companion, and while the other played the barrel organ; he also instructed them to play several fanciful tricks, such as drinking to the company, riding and tumbling on the horse's back, and going thro' several regular dances with the dog.—He taught the young cats to strike their paws in such directions on the dulcimer, as to produce several regular tunes, having music books before them, and squalling at the same time, in different keys or notes, first, second, and third, by way of concert. At the well-known cats opera in the Hay-market, he cleared near 1000 l.—He procured a leveret, and rear'd it to beat several marches on the drum with its hind legs, until it became a good stout hare. He taught canary birds, linnets and sparrows, to spell names, &c. He trained six turkey cocks to go thro' a regular country dance. In 6 months he made a turkey to fetch and carry like a dog, and by chalking the floor and blacking its claws, could direct it to trace out any given name of the company. His confidence even led him to try experiments on a gold-fish, which he did not despair of making perfectly tractable.—In 16 months he made a pig, the most obstinate and perverse animal in nature, to be under full command, and become as pliant and good-natur'd as a spaniel; it was lately seen by many persons of condition in Dublin, to spell (without any apparent direction) the names of those in company, to

23

cast up accounts, and point out even the words thought by persons present; to tell exactly the hour, minutes, and seconds; to point out the married and unmarried; to kneel, and to make his obeisance to the company, &c. &c.—Mr. Bisset was born at Perth in Scotland about the year 1721, and bred a shoe-maker; his widow is now at Belfast with these wonderful animals.

Bonner and Middleton's Bristol Journal
24 January 1784

An old Lady in the Country was lately pressed to lend some Money on the Tolls of a Turnpike: No, no (says she) who would trust Money on the Turnpikes, when all the World will shortly be travelling in Air Balloons?

Public Advertiser
24 January 1784

A banditti has been lately detected and luckily apprehended, near the town of Boyle, which for some months had carried terror and depredation all over that once peaceable country; this fortunate discovery and apprehension was effected by the vigilance and unremitting activity of the Boyle Rangers.—

Though the nation is burthened with augmented, unnecessary armies, what benefit does the public derive from them? Is it not to its Volunteers the Kingdom owes its safety in every sense?

We hear that above 60 robbers are come from England to this city—this accounts for the several robberies that happens every night.

Magee's Weekly Packet, Dublin
24 January 1784

Extract of a letter from Shaftesbury, January 24

"Tuesday afternoon last, about four o'clock, an Air-Balloon, ticketed from Bath, fell in a field in the parish of Farrington, near Sturminster-Newton in this county, to the no small consternation of the neighbouring villages, which it passed over at the height of about 40 yards. It fell in a field among a parcel of cows, who gathered round it with hideous bellowing. The farmer and his men agreed to attack it; seeing it bounding on the ground, they concluded it to be some monster come to carry off the cattle; one of his men, more courageous than the rest, went to it, and secured it by tying it to the railing of a rick. The curiosity of the country for six or eight miles round was never more raised than to see this Air-Balloon."

Bath Chronicle
29 January 1784

On Friday died in Newgate William Penn, a black, who in October was convicted of stealing a shirt and a waistcoat, the property of William Ridgeway, and sentenced to transportation for seven years to Africa.

Gazeteer and New Daily Advertiser
26 January 1784

The following Medicines, &c. are sold by Richard Bird, Printer, Bookseller and Stationer, at his Medicinal Warehouse in High-street, near Broad-gate, Coventry:

Arquebuscade Water
Antipertussis for Coughs, Colds, &c.
Beaume de Sante
Balsam of Honey for Coughs and Colds
Balsam of Canada
British Oil

Balm of Gilead
Bateman's Drops
Bostock's Cordial
Beaum de Vie
British Powder for cleaning the teeth
Balsam of Life
British Herb Snuff

25

British Herb Tobacco
Court Plaister
Carthusian Tincture
Corn Plaister
Cephalic Snuff in Bottles
Corn Salve
Crawcour's Liquid for
cleaning the Teeth
Do. Powders
Dentifrice Powder
Dalby's Carminative
Daffy's Elixir
Dentilave Tincture
Essential Salt of Lemons
Egyptian Balsam
Essence of Water-dock
Elixir of Bardana
Eau de Sans Parielle
Essence of Rosemary
Essence of Jessamine
Essence of Peppermint
Eau de Luce
Fryar's Balsam
Flugger's Drops
Franklin's Corn Salve
Gale's Spa Elixir
Greenough's Tincture for the
Teeth
Griffin's Tincture
Grant's Chymical Drops
Glasse's Magnesia
Godfrey's Cordial
Gutta Salutaris for Venereal
Complaints
Godfrey's Tooth Powder
Hatfield's Tincture
Hamilton's Tincture for the
Tooth-ach
Hooper's Female Pills
Hongrie Water
Hydropic Elixir
Henry's nervous Medicine

Hickman's Pills for Stone and
Gravel
Hypo Drops
Issue Plaisters
Imperial Oil
Jackson's Tincture
James's Fever Powder
James's Araleptic Pills
Jesuit's Drops, by Wessels
Japan Ink
Kendrick's Worm Cakes
Lavendar Water
Leake's Pills
Leake's Cleansing Drops
McHan's Antirheumatic
Drops
McHan's Universal Dentrifrice
Montpelier Drops
Maredant's Drops
Molineaux's Smelling
Medicine for the Itch
Norris's Ear Drops
Newby's Tincture
Northey's Rat Medicine
Ormskirk Medicine for the
Bite of a mad Dog by Hill
Pullen's Anticorbutic Pills
Pullen's Purging Pills
Pullen's Female Pills
Paste for destroying Rats and
Mice
Pectoral Lozenges of Tolu
Radcliff's Purging Elixir
Ruston's Pills for the
Rheumatism
Royon's Ointment for the Itch
Spilsbury's Drops
Stoughton's Elixir
Swinfen's Electuary for the
Stone and Gravel
Spirits of Scurvy Grass
Sans Parielle Powder

Storey's Worm Cakes
Smyth's Scouring Drops
Steel Preservative
Specific Purging Remedy for Venereal Diseases, by Wessels
Tasteless Ague and Fever Drops
Turlington's Balsam
Tincture of Centaury

Tincture of Valerian
Vandour's Pills, for Nervous Complaints
Velnos's Vegetable Syrup
West's Elixir
Ward's White Drops
Patent Blacking Balls
Patent Blacking Cakes

Jopson's Coventry Mercury
26 January 1784

A CERTAIN CURE FOR A SCALD OR BURN

Apply ink to the part affected. This remedy was totally discovered from the following accident: A maid servant being employed in ironing linen, and holding the iron towards her face, to ascertain the degree of heat, the heater fell into her bosom; her fellow servant seeing her distress, had the presence of mind to cut her stays, and let out the heater. A bottle of ink which stood near was immediately poured on the part affected, to cool it, which gave present ease; and on the same being often repeated, it effected a complete cure. This has been often since tried with the like happy success; it is therefore recommended in preference to any other means.

Whitehall Evening Post
27–29 January 1784

Yesterday an inquisition was taken at Walthamstow, on the body of a man unknown, who was found frozen to death in a summer-house.

Ipswich Journal
30 January 1784

Last week was committed to Leicester gaol, Thomas Henfrey and William Rider, both of Stonesby in that county, charged with a highway robbery the 16th inst. upon Richard Caunt of Plungar, whom they robbed of five guineas in gold, a half-crown piece and one shilling in silver, and some halfpence, near the eighth milestone on the road leading from Grantham to Nottingham.—They are supposed to be the same persons who on the Wednesday following stopped a horse-dealer coming from Nottingham fair, on Wilford-hill, whom they robbed of about 50 s. The dealer had considerable property in notes, which he luckily preserved.

Cambridge Chronicle and Journal
31 January 1784

Saturday evening, Mr. Stephenson, inventor of the diving machine, was stopt in the road behind the Crescent in Bath, by a Footpad, who demanded his money; he said that he had none for him, upon which he presented a pistol, saying, "By Jesus I'll do for you" and immediately fired, the ball of which went through the back part of his hat, but providentially did no further hurt.

Tuesday the celebrated Mr. Stephenson exhibited the Art of Diving in his new-invented Machine on the river Avon. He was seen to dance, and heard to sing, under water, to the surprize of a number of spectators; but the Snow was so thick on the ground, and the unluckiness of the boys pelting the company with Snow, greatly hurt the performance of that celebrated Artist.

Bonner and Middleton's Bristol Journal
31 January 1784

On Thursday evening letters from his Royal Highness the Duke of Cumberland were received at Cumberland-house, which mention, that the Hon. Miss Luttrell is perfectly recovered from her late illness, and that the whole of the family enjoys a perfect state of heatlh; but they add, that the severity of the season at Strasburg had been so great, that numbers of people have perished in the roads or streets; and that the soldiery were particular sufferers, many of them being found daily frozen to death in the sentry boxes.

Whitehall Evening Post
29–31 January 1784

Sculthorpe, Jan. 31.

A BURGLARY

WHEREAS the Dwelling-house of HANNAH BRADFIELD, widow, of Sculthorpe, near Fakenham, was broke into some Time last Night, or early this Morning, and a Bureau broke open, and five Pounds in Silver, a Silver Watch, and a Pair of Silver Buckles taken out of it; and also another Silver Watch, and one Shilling and Sixpence taken out of the Breeches Pocket of the Man Servant, as he lay asleep with his Breeches under his Pillow, there being at the same Time three Boys and two Dogs in the same Room with him, and yet the Offender or Offenders got away without being discovered.—Whoever will apprehend and prosecute to Conviction the Villain or Villains who committed the above Burglary, will be rewarded by the said Hannah Bradfield, over and above the Reward of FORTY POUNDS he will be entitled to by Act of Parliament, for each offender.

Norfolk Chronicle or Norwich Gazette
7 February 1784

Last Monday evening Edward Kelsall, house-carpenter, in Ditton, about 60 years of age, was murthered very near his own house, by a young man about 20 years of age, who calls himself John Toms, and says he is a saddler; he had followed the deceased from Liverpool, joined him in company on the road, and perpetrated the horrid act with a horse-pistol, the ball of which hit him on the back part of his head, and went through his forehead; he then robbed him of his watch and some halfpence, and afterwards put the pistol under the body of the deceased. He was taken at Liverpool.

Bonner and Middleton's Bristol Journal
31 January 1784

Shrewsbury Jan. 31.
Last Monday was committed to this county gaol, Robert Corbett, charged upon the oath of Ann, wife of Thomas Atkins, with feloniously and violently ravishing her.

Shrewsbury Chronicle
31 January 1784

PERFUMERY GOODS

A fresh Supply of the following valuable Articles lately received by the Printer of this Paper.

For the Ladies

LADY MOLYNEUX'S ITALIAN PASTE, prepared by Mrs. GIBSON, (and by no other Person in the World) so well known to the Ladies for enamelling the Hands, Neck, and Face, of a lovely white; it renders the most rough or brown Skin, smooth and soft as Velvet; nor will the most severe frost crack the skin. May be had of Mrs. GIBSON, at No. 22, in Lower Charles-street, Hatton-Garden, in Pots at 6s. and 3s. each. With printed Directions with each Pot for using it. Mrs. GIBSON also prepares LADY MOLYNEUX'S LIQUID BLOOM, which in a Moment gives to Pale Cheeks the Rose of Nature, and which the most nice Eye cannot possibly suspect for Art, nor will it come off the Cheek be the Face ever so hot. Each Bottle is 10s. 6d. or 5s. 3d. with printed Directions sealed up with each Bottle for using it.—Likewise Mrs. GIBSON'S curious COMPOUND which will in Half a Minute take out hair by the Roots, which grows too large or irregular; also takes off Hair that grows on Ladies Cheeks, on the Chin, and round the Mouth, which is a very great Blemish to the Fair Sex.—Mrs. Gibson sells this useful Compound at Five Shillings an Ounce, with printed Directions sealed up for using it.—Her LIQUID, which changes red or grey Hair to a beautiful Brown ꝋr Jet Black: is as harmless as Oil or Water, nor will the Colour ever wear off. Each Bottle is 1 l. 2s. or 10s. 6d. with printed Directions sealed up with it for its use.—Also her PREPARATION, which fastens hair that is loose on the head, keeps it from combing off, causes it to grow thick, and makes it grow again on any part after it is worn off by any illness. In Pots at Half-a-Guinea each.

N.B. Mrs. Gibson has, for the Convenience of Ladies who reside in, and near the undermentioned Places, authorized the following Persons to vend the Articles she prepares: either of which may be had in Shrewsbury, only, of Mr. Wood, Printer; also of Mr. Crutwell, Printer in Bath; Messrs. Pearton and Rollason, Printers in Birmingham; Mr. Chase, Printer in Norwich; Mr. Collins, Printer in Salisbury; Miss Williamson, at the Royal Exchange, in Liverpool; but (as yet) no other person in England.

Shrewsbury Chronicle
31 January 1784

FEBRUARY

Saturday two men who went to shoot wild ducks on the river in a boat, got so completely wedged between the ice near Ranelagh, that they were obliged to wait upwards of seven hours before the water rose high enough to float them off. Had the wind blown equal to what it had done two days back, they must have perished, as they could get no assistance from land.

Yesterday afternoon as a party, who had amused themselves with skating, were refreshing their stomachs with cold ham and wine, at the side of the Serpentine-river, the ice suddenly gave way, and the bench, table, and company, had an upset; but by the situation the gentlemen were not above knee-deep in water; and the confusion for the moment, made the scene of distress more laughable than alarming.

London Chronicle
31 January–3 February 1784

Wednesday a machine, nearly upon the plan of that constructed by Mr. Moore a few years back, was exhibited upon the Serpentine river. The inventor called it an Ice Balloon, and it travelled with amazing celerity, having a sort of keel made of iron, and being impelled forward by a spring giving motion to a wheel at the front of the carriage. The novelty of the invention induced several people of fashion to ride in the above machine, and several of them handsomely complimented the proprietor for his ingenuity; but the price demanded was but the moderate sum of one penny from each passenger. A hog was roasted whole upon the ice the same day, and afforded an extempore meal to a great number of people.

Whitehall Evening Post
5–7 February 1784

Gainsborough (Lincolnshire), Jan. 24.

A few days since the following melancholy accident happened on the river Trent; the river being froze over, a great number of people assembled on it, when a dispute happened between two men, upon some slight difference, they went to blows, which drew the people to one spot, and the ice gave way, upwards of 90 fell into the water, and notwithstanding every method was taken for their preservation, only four of the number were saved. The untimely fate of so many has cast a gloom upon the inhabitants, there being scarcely a family who has not some of their kindred to lament.

Bath Chronicle
5 February 1784

The following joke has lately been played at Islington: A brewer's servant having married, and fixed himself and wife in a little shop, which she was to manage the business of while he was employed in the brewhouse in London, in order to prove the sincerity of his wife's attention, planned the following scheme: He went with some of his convivial friends a few miles into the country, where they continued about a week; in the interim it was industriously reported, that while he was sitting on the edge of the copper in the brewhouse, he fell into it, where he was found boiled to pieces. This shocking news was carried to his wife, who received it like a good wife, and has been in a state of distraction ever since. A day or two afterwards her husband having been informed how she received the news, and assuring himself of the sincerity of her affection, condescended to return home and make her happy, when he found her in a state of mind the most deplorable; and it is out of the power of her friends to satisfy her that he is really alive, she declaring that the ghost of her husband is continually haunting her. This is inserted to shew the wickedness and folly of such jocularity.

London Chronicle
5–7 February 1784

It is with the utmost pleasure we inform the Public at large, from the best authority, that there is not the least truth whatever in the extract of a letter from Gainsborough, which asserted that 90 persons were drowned in the river Trent, by the breaking of the ice.

London Chronicle
5–7 February 1784

Last night the snow was knee deep in every street in this town.

Ipswich Journal
7 February 1784

Tuesday the noted Mrs. Hall, Mother of the still more notorious Lydia Hall, alias Jones, &ç. &c. who is supposed to have cohabited with a greater Number of Men that have suffered at Tyburn and in the Country, than any other Woman whatever, was charged before William Blackborow, Esq; with robbing John Garrat, who had hired a Bed at her House in Black-boy alley on Monday Night, of four shillings; and the Charge being substantiated, she was fully committed to New Prison.

Public Advertiser
7 February 1784

The Count de Soissons was seated at play one evening, when happening to cast an eye up at a looking-glass that was before him in the apartment, he saw a man at the back of his chair, whose physiognomy predicted nothing in its owner's favour, and gave the Count suspicion. He had reason for his mistrust; for he had not sat long before he felt the diamond loop of his hat cut away. He took no notice, but pretended a necessity to go down stairs, and desired the thief to play his cards in the mean time, which he could not refuse. The Count immediately descended into the kitchen, and got a large and sharp carving-knife; then going softly behind the fellow, dexterously took him by the ear, and cut it off: and, holding it out to him, said, "Return me my diamond-loop, Sir, and I will return you your ear."

Gazeteer and New Daily Advertiser
7 February 1784

One morning this week a duel was fought upon Mousehold-heath between two officers of Elliot's light horse. A brace of pistols were discharged by each, without doing any further execution than grazing the feather of one of their hats: when the seconds interfered, and the affair was amicably adjusted.

Norfolk Chronicle or Norwich Gazette
7 February 1784

Yesterday morning a man walked across the river on the ice, at low water, from Redriffe to Wapping New-stairs, with very little inconvenience. The Thames is now very nearly frozen over.

Norfolk Chronicle or Norwich Gazette
7 February 1784

The present Emperor of Morocco's favourite concubine is an English woman, and her history is remarkable: her name is Seagood; her husband was a linen manufacturer in Devonshire, who, failing, determined to go to America. He endeavoured, by every persuasion, to get his wife to remain in England, while he went and established himself, promising then to return and bring her. She insisted on going with him, and actually did so. Off the coast of Spain the ship was taken by a Sallee rover. On carrying her in Mrs. Seagood's charms (for she was but five and twenty, and one of the finest women ever seen) made such a

35

general imperession, that she was at once declared the Emperor's property, and sent accordingly to Mequinez. She captivated his heart, and has been his favourite now five years, having three children living by her. The husband was sold, and, by orders from Court, removed into the interior country, and not heard of since. By the beauty of his wife he has therefore probably lost his life, or, which is worse, his freedom.

Gazeteer and New Daily Advertiser
9 February 1784

[A Sallee rover was Moorish pirate-ship.]

A divorce case came on on Friday in the House of Lords, which afforded some entertainment. A Mr. N——tt was the petitioner. Mr. Bearcroft, his Counsel, called three witnesses to prove the adultery of Mrs. N——tt. The most material was the gentleman's butler who proved that having, for two or three years, observed too great a familiarity between a Captain T——y (an intimate friend of his master's) and his mistress, he watched them so closely, that, on the 6th of May last, knowing they were in bed together at his master's house, he informed a friend of his master (then in the house) of the circumstance, who told Mr. N——tt of the matter: the lovers had not the discretion even to bolt the chamber-door, so that they were detected *nudus cum nuda, et solus cum sola*: the enraged husband was, with difficulty, prevented by the bystanders from using violence.

One of the other witnesses being present at the detection, confirmed what the butler proved.

The third evidence could only say, that a suspicion of this criminal intercourse was communicated to him by the butler a long time before the detection.

Gazeteer and New Daily Advertiser
9 February 1784

Bon Mot of G. S—w—n, Esq.—Some years ago, during the sale of an eminent banker's effects, Mr. S——n, who attended there almost the whole of the first day, bought nothing but a pillow, which belonged to the Banker's bed: being the same evening rallied by some friends on the oddity of his purchase, he replied, "He was naturally accustomed to be very restless; therefore he bought it to compose him: for (added he) I'm sure it must be an excellent *soporific*, since he could sleep on it, who owed so many thousands."

Gazeteer and New Daily Advertiser
9 February 1784

[The author of the *bon mot* was perhaps George Augustus Selwyn (1718–91), MP, a noted wit.]

On Friday morning a man was found dead in the yard of Mr. Owen, in Red-Lion-street; his skull was fractured, and a great deal of blood was found upon the pavement, with bits of tiles. It is therefore supposed that he, in attempting to get over the tiling from some adjacent houses, slipped down. In his pockets were found some picklock-keys, with small instruments for opening drawers, &c.

Whitehall Evening Post
7–10 February 1784

We hear from Galloway, that upon the 23rd and 29th ult. the Supervisor and Officer of Excise there seized at the Clone and Mull of Galloway, on the Assistance of a Party of the 45th Regiment, 68 Boxes and two Bags, containing 5520 lb. of Tea and 60 Casks of Brandy; which Seizure is worth upwards of 2000 l. Sterling.

The Smuggling Trade was never carried on in such an open and daring Manner in the North Riding of this County as at present. It is almost incredible to what a Pitch it has now got, and the Persons concerned bid Defiance to all Laws.—*Would not a Troop or two of Dragoons stationed on the Coast (who might be well spared from this City (York)) tend to prevent this illicit Practice?*

York Courant
10 February 1784

The rage for Air Balloons has become universal in France; small ones are sold in the shops for the use of children; and Mons. Bourboulon, a manufacturer at Javel, near Paris, advertises to *sell inflammable air* for the purpose of filling aerostatic globes, at the moderate price of three sols, six deniers (not quite two-pence English) a cubic foot!

General Evening Post
7–10 February 1784
[The 'inflammable air' was hydrogen gas.]

The conduct of the young, beauteous, and virtuous Duchess of Devonshire is a pattern worthy of imitation; finding lately that deep play and hazard was become frequent at all fashionable routes the beginning of this winter, at her first grand route for the season had written in large characters in every chamber, "No higher play than crown whist permitted here; other games in proportion; and no dice."

The General Evening Post
7–10 February 1784
[Georgiana, Duchess of Devonshire, daughter of Earl Spencer, was described by Markham as "the most famous woman of her day".]

Sunday se'nnight, a fellow was apprehended and committed to prison in Glasgow. He for some time past has imposed upon the credulous in that city and neighbourhood, pretending to be dumb, to tell fortunes, and to cure all diseases. He calls himself James Jackson, and was accompanied by one Gordon, who personated a servant. Gordon is not yet found.

Caledonian Mercury, Edinburgh
11 February 1784

They write from Metz the following extraordinary adventure: A young girl in love with a soldier of the garrison, knowing him indisposed, and obliged to be on duty at midnight, during the late inclemency of the weather, went to see him, and finding her poor sweetheart quite benumbed with cold, pressed him to go and warm himself in her room, which was not very far. While she would remain in his place. The soldier refused for some time, but at last yielded to the tender solicitations of his Dulcinea. The moment he was gone, she wrapt herself in his great coat, and began to walk *à la militaire*, with the firelock on her shoulder. Unfortunately the round going by, the Corporal asked her the order, which not being able to answer, she was detected and taken to the guard-house, where she related her story. Her lover was immediately fetched, and being found almost dead, though before a good fire, he was revived by means of some cordial, and put in prison next morning. He is now going to be tried, and there is no doubt but he will be cast, pursuant to the strictness of military laws. It is however supposed, that he will easily obtain his pardon. The ladies are early in his interest, and some of them have already subscribed for the paraphernalia of his mistress if she chuses to marry him.

Norfolk Chronicle or Norwich Gazette
14 February 1784

This morning a numerous meeting of the inhabitants, and others, of the City of Westminster, was held in Westminster-hall, agreeable to public advertisements for some days past. The hall, or rather the hustings, had been taken possession of early in the morning by the particular friends of the contending parties, and nothing but a scene of noise and confusion ensued: It was impossible to hear any of the orators, tho' many attempted to speak; even Mr. Fox himself was obliged to cut short his address to his constituents. Instead of the *sense*, nothing but the *nonsense* and madness of the people could be collected. Many respectable characters were there, but could not obtain a hearing.

By the violence of the mob, the hustings was broken down, and it seemed not unlikely but the business of the day would be finished with breaking each others heads with the fragments of it. . . .

From another correspondent we are informed that this meeting met . . . when Mr. Fox and Lord Mahon alternately addressed the electors from the hustings. The uproar was so violent, that nothing could be heard but hisses, groans, and huzzas. About half past twelve the scaffolding fell down, and some people were much hurt. Mr. Fox's friends then carried him to the Tavern in Palace-yard, where he addressed the populace from the window, and about half past one went home in his chariot amidst the acclamations of the people. The Hall was uncommonly crouded, and all the environs to it were impassable for three hours. Both parties, as usual claimed the greatest shew of hands.

General Evening Post
12–14 February 1784

ESCAP'D from HELMSLEY, A broadset Man, (who calls himself RICHARD PYBUS) about 5 feet 9 inches high, and betwixt the Age of 25 and 30, a little pitted with the Small-pox, and straight flaxen Hair: Had on, when he went off, a slouched Hat, a dark Chocolate new silk Handkerchief round his neck, a light coloured shabby rough Great Coat with a velvet Collar, a new coarse lappelled dark-blue Waistcoat, a Pair of dirty leather Breeches, a Pair of light-coloured coarse Worsted Stockings, a Pair of old Shoes with a Cap on the Side of one, and a Pair of round Copper Buckles.—As he is supposed to be the Person who has stolen the LACE, &c. (which is now sworn to) as advertised in our last Paper, whoever will apprehend and bring him to a Justice of the Peace, shall have a sufficient Reward from the Constables of the above Place.

York Courant
17 February 1784

The bag thrown before Mr. Fox while on the Hustings, at Westminster-Hall on Saturday last, and which deprived him of his breath for several minutes, was full of a poisonous compound. It has been examined by a chymist of eminence, who has delivered an analysis of the contents, which he declares to be a mixture of *euphorbium* and *capsicum*, two of the most subtle poisons in nature, whose quality it is to blister and ulcerate whatever they touch.

General Evening Post
14–17 February 1784

On Saturday a Highwayman stopped the Carriage of Robert Watkins, Esq; in the Deptford Road, and robbed him of his Purse, in which were Five Guineas, and some Silver. The Highwayman made an Apology for stopping him, and said that nothing but Necessity could drive a Man out upon the Road in such Weather, and upon so hazardous a Piece of Business.

Public Advertiser
20 February 1784

The following is a summary account of the inquisition taken on Monday evening at the *Albemarle Arms*, in Albemarle-street on the body of Captain *Moyston* of the

Navy, who was killed on Friday last, at three o'clock in the afternoon, in a field near *Lochier's Academy, Little Chelsea*, by Captain *Clark* of the Army.

IT appeared from the evidence of Mr. Townsend, master of the New Exchange Coffee-house, and his principal waiter and bar-maid, that Captain Clark, and Captain Moyston, the deceased, had for several months occasionally lodged and dined at the New Exchange Coffee-house, but without keeping company together, or having any kind of intimacy or acquaintance; that on Friday the 6th inst. Captain Clark had turned down a plate at the large table, usually called the *long* table, in the Coffee-room; and that Captain Moyston's acquaintance were to have dined at a smaller table; but finding *that* too small for their numbers, Mrs. Townsend, the mistress of the Coffee-house, requested Capt. Clark to give up his place at the long table, and take his dinner at the square table, to accommodate Capt. Moyston, which Capt. Clark did with great complacency.—That the hour of dinner being come, the deceased seemed desirous that the company at the long table, who were chiefly his friends, should wait dinner for his brother, and sent the waiter to seek him; but the company not chusing to wait, and having ordered up dinner, Capt. Moyston withdrew from that table dissatisfied, and sat down at the square table, to which Capt. Clark had before retired to accommodate him; that shortly afterwards a gentleman of Capt. Moyston's acquaintance came in and sat down with him; and that Capt. Moyston's brother having soon after joined them, had ordered in and taken their soup. After which Capt. Clark having ordered in his dinner also, the deceased rose up, went to the bar, and damned the bar-maid for a b——h, for suffering that fellow to sit down to dinner with him; that Capt. Clark must have heard the expressions, but, though he seemed hurt, took no other notice of them than by turning a little aside, and not addressing any conversation to the company whilst they remained at the table; that on Tuesday evening last, there was some noise made in the Coffee-room by a man who offered prints to sale, and was encouraged by some of the company to stand up on a table and put his wares up for auction, when Mrs. Townsend requested, that there might be an end to the noise, as there was a gentleman sick in the house; upon which Capt. Moyston, the deceased, gave her some abusive language, declaring that those who did not pay her for four and five months together, or perhaps never paid her at all, were treated like gentlemen, whilst those who paid her like gentlemen were not treated so well; that Capt. Clark being present and knowing himself to have been in an arrear of that kind, (tho' not at the moment) took off his hat, and telling Capt. Moyston, that he supposed himself to be the person alluded to, and would be glad to explain himself on the subject which he imagined had given offence: Capt. Moyston acknowledged that he *did* allude to him, but refusing to hear any reason on the matter, called Capt. Clark Rogue, Rascal, Scoundrel, *Coward*, and other abusive names, and seizing him by the collar, would have struck him, if not prevented by the gentleman who was afterwards Capt. Moyston's second: that after Capt. Moyston had retired to bed, his brother repeated the epithets of Rascal, Scoundrel, and Coward, challenging Capt. Clark, if he dared to fight *him* or his brother; and declaring, that if he would fight his brother, he would be his brother's second; upon which Capt. Clark declared that he would fight *him* or his brother, but he must *talk* to his brother first.

It appeared further from the witness, that Capt. Clark was a most worthy, honest, and inoffensive man; and that the deceased was of a very overbearing, turbulent and quarrelsome temper; some instances of which were adduced, and one in particular, in which consequences equally serious with the present, were not unlikely to have happened. It was also observed by the waiter, that after the usage Capt. Clark had received on the Tuesday night, he appeared much agitated, and tears trickled down his cheeks.

The rest of the witnesses advanced little else but *hearsay* – except that, upon an intimation from a friend of Capt.

Clark's, that he expected an apology for the abuse he had received, Capt. Moyston and his second called on Capt. Lysaght of the African corps, who was second to Capt. Clark, about three o'clock on Friday afternoon; and that the parties in consequence thereof, met in a field near Lochier's Academy, Little Chelsea, where the seconds, having measured twelve yards, Capt. Moyston said the distance was *too great*, and the parties took their ground at ten yards; when Capt. Clark having offered the first fire to Capt. Moyston, was desired by him, to fire *first*; which he did accordingly, having only flashed in the pan, he declared *it was a fire*.—Capt. Moyston fired next, and his ball entering Capt. Clark's breeches pocket, bent a key and several pieces of money in a very extraordinary manner, and lodged in his purse, making only a very small contusion in his thigh; after which Capt. Clark fired, with that unlucky effect, which instantaneously deprived — a most worthy tho' unfortunate man of life.

The Inquest lasted from six in the evening till four in the morning, when the Jury brought in their verdict, *manslaughter*, against John Montague Clark, Esq.

Jopson's Coventry Mercury
23 February 1784

Captain Moyston was about the age of 25, served with great professional reputation in the West-Indies at the close of the war, and was made post in the Solitaire, the French ship of the line which was taken by the Ruby. At Antigua he got into 2 or 3 disagreeable contentions.

Captain Clark stood high in the corps to which he belonged, and when in Africa took an active part in having Capt. McKenzie brought to England, on a charge for the murder committed on a serjeant in his company. He was expected to have been the principal evidence against him, had not the above catastrophe taken place. Capt. Clark and the seconds are gone to the Continent.

Ipswich Journal
21 February 1784

[To be 'made post', or appointed post-captain, was to be commissioned as officer in command of a vessel of 20 guns or more.]

London, February 21.

On Thursday night a party of upwards of 30 fellows stopped almost every carriage and chair which was going to or returning from the Pantheon. The peace officers being unable to suppress the villains, a party of the Guards were sent for, and with their assistance the nobility went in some degree of safety. About three in the morning the gang dispersed, but about five of them were taken whilst they were robbing two Gentlemen in a Hackney coach.

London Chronicle
19–21 February 1784

[The Pantheon was a theatre and public promenade in Oxford Street famous for its masquerades.]

WORCESTER

LOST, on Friday last, on the Turnpike Road between this City and Hayford Bridge, a DEAL BOX, (about Three Quarters of a Yard long, and Twelve Inches deep) containing a Drab Colour Coat, with yellow Buttons, One cut Sattin Waistcoat, One Pair of black Sattin Breeches, all new; Six new Ruffled Shirts, Six good Ruffled Ditto; one Worked Ruffled Ditto, Six White Neck Handkerchiefs, Six Stocks or Neckcloths, Six Pair of Silk Stockings, Four Pair of Worsted Ditto, One Set of gilt Shoe and knee Buckles, and several other Articles, not immediately recollected; Whoever has pick'd it up, and will bring it with its Contents, to Mr. Wilkins, Hop-Pole Inn, shall receive FIVE GUINEAS Reward; or any Person giving Information in whose Custody the said Box is detained, shall receive Two Guineas for their Trouble.

N.B. The Linen and Stockings are all marked W.D.

Wanted, a Young Man, of good Character as Porter and Book-Keeper.

Berrow's Worcester Journal
February 1784

A remarkable instance of charity.—Last week a lady unknown came into the Court of Conscience, and requested to speak to Alderman Warren; when after the usual compliments, she took a gold watch from her side, and presented it to him as the last valuable article she had left in this world, desiring him to sell it, and the cash arising, to distribute it amongst the poor distressed manufacturers in the Liberty, as no gentleman could know their situation better than the Alderman; he was greatly embarrassed at the oddity of this request, and remonstrated with the lady, but in vain, she persisted in her desire, and took her leave.

Magee's Weekly Packet, Dublin
21 February 1784

Monday se'nnight a person at Derby, of the name of Pratt, in firing off a gun, it burst, and shattered his hand in such a manner that it was obliged to be amputated.—It is remarkable, that a few years since he dreamed that in firing off a gun he had lost a hand, which made such an impression on his mind, that he never touched a gun till the time of the above unfortunate accident.

Cambridge Chronicle and Journal
21 February 1784

A very extraordinary affair happened lately at Dr. Katterfelto's exhibition room, No. 24, Piccadilly, a Welch gentleman being informed that the Doctor was a very great favourite of his Majesty and the Royal Family, being the greatest philosopher in the three kingdoms, and that he had exhibited several times before the King and Royal Family, which raised the above gentleman's curiosity to see that gentleman's exhibition; and as Dr. Katterfelto began to shew some of his dexterous feats, the Welch gentleman swore that the Doctor was the Diawel, the Diawel, which is in English the Devil; so one of the gentlemen present asked the Doctor what he had done with his black cat and kittens; the Doctor to the great surprise of the whole company, conveyed immediately one of the kittens into the Welch gentleman's waistcoat pocket at six yards distance, purposely to make that gentleman believe he was the Devil; on finding the kitten in his waistcoat pocket, the above gentleman ran out of the room, and cried in the street, as well as in the exhibition room, that the Diawel, the Diawel, was in London; and we are informed that the Doctor is to shew this and to-morrow evening one of his other great wonders

Morning Herald
23 February 1784

[Gustavus Katterfelto was a quack notorious in the latter part of the eighteenth century. He appeared in London during the influenza epidemic of 1782 exhibiting "philosophical apparatus" in Spring Gardens. "Colonel" Katterfelto professed himself "sorry that many persons will have it that he and his famous Black Cat were Devils, but such suspicions only arise through his various wonderful and illustrious performances; he only purposes to be a moral and divine Philosopher, and he says that all Persons on earth live in darkness if they are able, but won't see that most enterprising, extraordinary, astonishing, wonderful, and uncommon exhibition on the Solar Microscope" (*General Advertiser*, 15 May 1783).]

On Friday evening died, after a very *sharp* illness, which he bore with the greatest *shivering* for more than *eight weeks*, THOMAS FROST sen. Esq; a Gentleman who arrived from the North on Christmas Eve; his disorder baffled all the apothecaries skill and nostrums in town, and the only temporary relief he ever experienced, was from those eminent physicians, Messrs. *Cloaths, Fire, Gin* and *Brandy*. On opening his body the faculty were unanimously of the opinion that his death was occasioned by the change of the moon.

Gazeteer and New Daily Advertiser
24 February 1784

London, Feb. 24.
On Monday morning a desperate battle was fought in the Ring, Hyde-park, between two privates in the first regiment of foot-guards. The contest lasted two hours and three-quarters, and was then adjourned for a week, the parties being so much wounded in the face, that they were not able to distinguish each other.

Ipswich Journal
28 February 1784

To the Nobility and Gentry

THE Celebrated Mrs. BERNARD and Mr. DAVY, DENTISTS from Berlin, are just arrived again at Mr. Sturdy's Glass-Shop, at the Corner of Goodramgate, YORK, and respectfully acquaint the Public, that they perform the various Operations incident to the Teeth and Gums, viz. Transplant Human Teeth, or fix artificial Teeth from one to an entire Sett, in a much easier and by a far superior Method than practised hitherto in this Kingdom.—Their Pearl Lotion is particularly recommended for restoring the Teeth to their native Whiteness and Beauty; (although ever so tarnished) without injuring the Enamel. The Efficacy of their admirable Preparations for eradicating the Scurvy, in causing the Gums to adhere close to the Teeth, in fastening such as are loose, in preserving them from future Decay, and in removing all offensive Smell from the Breath, (the natural Consequence of Disease, and Fowlness in the Teeth and Gums) has been honoured with the Approbation of all foreign Universities, and all the principal cities of these three Kingdoms.

They have also a peculiar Mode (more preferable than ever practised), of extracting Stumps, ever so difficult, with no more Pain than Bleeding; also Children's first Teeth, to cause the second Sett to grow regular and even.

** *The Tooth-Ach* cured without drawing. Mrs. BERNARD and Mr. DAVY return their grateful Acknowledgements to the Nobility, Gentry, and Public in general, in the City and County of York, for the great Encouragement they have received these two Years past, and hope for a Continuance of them, as they intend making this City their residence. If required, Ladies and Gentlemen waited on at their own homes.

York Courant
24 February 1784

Yesterday morning the number of prisoners in Newgate (including about 140 for debt) was exactly 500; a greater number than ever remembered.

General Evening Post
24–26 February 1784

A ROBBERY, IN NORTHAMPTONSHIRE

WHEREAS the House of John Wiggins, on Cockley-hill in the Parish of Greatworth, was about Nine o'Clock in the Evening of Monday the 23d of February Instant entered by four Ruffians, dressed in Smock Frocks, with their Faces blacked, who, after taking a Silver Watch and some Money out of the Pockets of John Wiggins, confined him and his Wife to the Cellar, and plundered the House of every Thing valuable in it, viz. Silver Tea Spoons, six

Pewter Plates marked J.W., some Cash, Provisions of several Kinds (particularly Bacon), and wearing Apparel, two Holland Shirts were marked J.W. in the Skirts, and a new Pair of Buck-Skin Breeches remarkably worked in the Thighs. The Watch was marked J. Wiggins, 1773, on the Outside of the outside Case; the Maker's Name, B. Chapman, London; the Number 3921.

Whoever will discover any one or more of the Offenders, shall, upon his or their Conviction, receive a Reward of TWENTY POUNDS, over and above the Reward allowed by Act of Parliament. Applications to be made to Mr. Bignell, Attorney, in Banbury, Oxfordshire.

Jackson's Oxford Journal
28 February 1784

A letter from Northampton, dated Feb. 10 says, "The Snow is so deep in this Country that in many Parts the Cottages are so covered as to be no longer discovered by the Eye. Great Apprehensions are entertained for the poor Inhabitants, who are probably starved to Death."

York Courant
24 February 1784

CONCAVE RAZORS

On philosophical principles of genuine German Steel, philosophically tempered, which require neither Setting nor Grinding, but continue to preserve a keen and smooth edge.

THE PROPRIETOR returns his most grateful thanks to the nobility, gentry, and the public in general, for the very great encouragement he has long met with in the sale of his razors, the demand for which, he humbly begs leave to assure them, is still daily increasing.

The general approbation the proprietor of the Concave Razors has been honoured with, has (as usual in these days) induced some imitators to sell a counterfeit sort, of which he thinks it a duty incumbent on him to apprize the public. The genuine Concave Razors, on philosophical principles, &c, are sold only by JOSEPH WRIGHT, at No. 16, London-house-yard, a few doors from the West end of St. Paul's. Two Razors and a Diamond Strop will serve a gentleman his whole life.

N.B.   Good allowance to Merchants and Captains of ships for exportation.

General Evening Post
21–24 February 1784

Bon Mot.—Mr. Macklin the Comedian going the other day to one of the Fire-Offices to insure some property, was asked by the clerk, how he would please to have his name entered: "Entered!" replied the veteran of the sock; "Why, I am only plain Charles Macklin, a VAGABOND by act of Parliament; but in compliment to the times, you may set me down, Charles Macklin ESQUIRE, as they are now synonymous terms!"

Bath Chronicle
26 February 1784

A discovery pro Bono Publico.—Nothing is so good for washing the hands in this cold weather as coarse brown sugar; it is infinitely preferable to all wash-hand balls, bran, cosmetic waters or powders, almond powder, and a thousand other expensive articles which are so loudly extolled, and which are only pickpocket washes in comparison to this cheap and false discovery. The others harden the skin, and make it stiff and husky; on the contrary, sugar softens the skin, and renders it silky and pliable. If ladies were to make trial of it for a week, they

51

would soon find its efficacy in whitening and softening their delicate skins.

Bath Chronicle
26 February 1784

Bath, Feb. 26.
Last Week a Shoemaker's Apprentice at Castlecomb was enticed by two young Fellows of the same Town, to steal Shoes from his Master, for which they gave him Sixpence; to elude a Discovery, they procured a Quantity of red Precipitate, and (shocking to relate!) persuaded the Boy to poison his Master and Mistress with it, for which Purpose, he put it in the Cup in which they used to warm their Beer; it soon threw them into the most violent Convulsions, but having had timely Assistance, they were happily so recovered as to be thought out of Danger.

Jackson's Oxford Journal
28 February 1784
[Red precipitate is mercuric oxide.]

Bath, Feb. 26.
Thursday Afternoon a dreadful Accident happened at Wellington by the Explosion of about 30 lb. of Gunpowder in a Druggist's Shop, which blew Mr. Rogers, his Apprentice, and a Farmer out of the Shop, and burnt them in a terrible Manner. The Violence of the Shock broke all the Windows in a Shop adjoining, as also some on the opposite side of the Street. It was a fortunate Circumstance that a covered Waggon stood just before the Door, otherwise the Pieces of Bottles (which were almost all blown out of the Shop) must have done much Hurt to the Farmers in the Market-place. The Covering of the Waggon was cut in a thousand Holes. The Spirits and other inflammable Articles burnt for some Time after, but were happily extinguished without spreading any further.

Jackson's Oxford Journal
28 February 1784

London, Feb. 26.
On Tuesday last a Duel was fought in Hyde-Park, between
Captain C. and Mr. D. an Army Surgeon, some Time
since from Gibraltar. Eight Paces being measured, Mr. D.
desired the Captain to fire: The Ball wounded Mr. D. in
the Neck; Mr. D. then fired, and slightly wounded the
Captain on the Ribs: The Captain fired his second Shot
without Effect; Mr. D. fired his second Pistol, the Ball of
which wounded the Captain considerably on the upper
Part of his Thigh, who instantly dropped, declaring he had
made Use of rash and improper Expressions, for which he
was sorry.

Jackson's Oxford Journal
28 February 1784

["The rise of this happened some time since at Lisbon, in
consequence of the Captain making use of some exceeding
unhandsome language. The parties are now both happily
out of danger" (*London Chronicle*, 21–24 February).]

A few days ago a Balloon supposed to have been let off at
Birmingham, fell at Cheadle, in Staffordshire. The farmers
took it into a two-pair-of-stairs room, and attempted to
blow it up again by a pair of bellows, during which, one of
them approaching too near with a candle, the remaining
inflammable air tore off the wainscot, broke all the
furniture, and drove out the casement to a considerable
distance, but did no damage to the Bye-standers, except
singing their hair.

Bonner and Middleton's Bristol Journal
28 February 1784

[A two-pair-of-stairs room is a second-floor room; a one-
pair-of-stairs room, a first-floor room.]

A letter from St. Edmunds Bury says, that the Post-boy
going last Thursday from thence to Farnham, missed his

path, and fell into a pit, which was covered with snow, and was found dead, with the bag of letters under his arm.

London Chronicle
24–26 February 1784

On Saturday last a Miller went on the mill wheel, at Byfleet, near Guildford, to clear the cogs of the ice, which, with some pains he accomplished. The Millers in the inside, finding the machinery free, set the mill a going, without considering the situation of the poor man, who, at that time, stood on the shafts; but being unable to extricate himself, he was broke to pieces by the going round of the mill wheel.

London Chronicle
24–26 February 1784

Yesterday morning came on at the Old Bailey the trial of that well-noted and genteel pickpocket George Barrington, for privately stealing from the person of Sir Godfrey Webster, Bart., a purse containing ten guineas and a half, and a 50 l. note, on the 31st day of January last, at the Opera House. Sir Godfrey swore, that being desirous of going into the tea-room, but not being able to get in on account of the crowd, he leant with his left hand against the door, and instantly he felt somebody pressing upon his right hand in an unpolite way, and in a manner which he thought very singular. That three seconds before, he felt his purse, and at the same time the person's hand was upon his arm, there was an unusual trembling; that looking round, he saw the prisoner, who then went away, and that in three seconds afterwards he missed his purse.—That suspecting him, he followed him from place to place, and saw him put his hand upon a little man's arm, and say, "Is my carriage ready?" but though he watched him attentively, he saw nothing pass from one to the other; that Barrington mixed with a great number of Ladies, at last stepped hastily out of the Opera House; but continuing his pursuit, he stopped him at the bottom of the Hay Market, took him back to the Opera House, and from thence, by a file of soldiers, he was conducted to St. James's Watch-house, where he was searched, but nothing found. Sir Godfrey was then relating a message from the prisoner's Attorney, and an offer of restitution but the Court would not hear it, as it was not evidence. Barrington was called on his defence, which rested solely on the point of pre-judging his case, on account of his former character, and nothing being found on him.—Baron Perryn, in his summing up, reminded the Jury of their duty, to wave all prejudices, and to determine their verdict by the evidence; observing, that although the case was very suspicious, yet there did not seem such evidence to arise out of it, where life was in the case, as was sufficient to convict. On this hint, the Jury grounded their verdict of — Not Guilty.

London Chronicle
26–28 February 1784

[Sir Godfrey Webster was the 4th baronet (1748–1800), and MP for Seaford, 1786.]

Monday evening an air balloon was let off from the Prospect, at Ross, in Gloucestershire. It took up in it the noted Old English Jew Barber of that place, and ascended to the height of 116 yards, then descended gradually, and brought the old Jew down unhurt to the astonishment of more than 1,000 spectators.

Mr. Sadler's air balloon, which was let off at Oxford on Monday the 9th instant, at half past one, fell about four o'clock in the evening of the same day, at Stansted, in Kent, upwards of 79 miles distance from Oxford.—Mr. Sadler, we understand, is constructing another balloon, which, when compleated, will measure 54 feet in circumference, and contain 22,842 gallons.—It is to be filled with air extracted from burnt wood, a method entirely new, and which has hitherto been unattempted in this Kingdom.

Cambridge Chronicle and Journal
28 February 1784

[On 28 February Pitt received the Freedom of the City of London at Grocers' Hall.]

The ceremony being over, a very sumptuous dinner being provided by the grocer's company Mr. Pitt accompanied by his brother Lord Chatham, Lords Sidney, Camelford, Mahon, &c. dined with the company at Grocer's-Hall.

The dinner consisted of every dainty that could be procured, among the rest were 4 quarts of green peas, at 5 guineas per quart; 12 plates of strawberries at one guinea and a half per plate; and 200 cherries, at one shilling each.—The whole expence of this entertainment, was upwards of a thousand pounds.

Lord Chatham was robbed of his gold watch, on Saturday night last, on his return from Grocer's-Hall, where he dined with his brother Mr. Pitt.

Shrewsbury Chronicle
6 March 1784

Near twelve o'clock at night, Mr. Pitt set out on his return home from Grocer's-hall, his carriage being drawn by the populace, and some of this mob behaved riotously, breaking the windows of several houses which were not illuminated; among the rest, they broke the windows of a certain house in St. James's street; a number of men sallied out with bludgeons in their hands, and attacked those who were drawing Mr. Pitt's carriage, &c. They then assaulted the carriage, and broke it, and also broke the windows of several houses. Mr. Pitt was obliged to quit his carriage and retire to White's for protection. His coach was much injured, and the mob that followed him went and broke Mr. Fox's windows in revenge.

No other mischief, we hear, was done. In about ten minutes a guard arrived, but before this time all was order and peace; the mob was dispersed, and the candles extinguished. This was exactly the sort of conclusion which might be expected to such a fray. It was wrong of the friends of Mr. Pitt to inflame men by making them light up their houses against their consent. But it was on the other hand as wrong for the friends of Mr. Fox to take umbrage at the absurdity and nonsense of the scene. It was altogether a piece of boyish folly, but these men ought to know, that by such boyish folly the lives of his Majesty's innocent subjects may be lost.

London Chronicle
28 February–2 March 1784

It is surprising, says a correspondent, that the present enlightened age should be entirely devoted to trifling amusements, whilst the more important articles of life are totally overlooked; above all, scarce one thinks it worth his while to patronize that most essential and greatest blessing to mankind in general, namely, the invention which restores health, strength, vigour, decayed, wasted, contracted, and crippled limbs; banishing the Gout, Rheumatism, Palsy, &c. *without medicine.* Our correspondent adds, that he is aged 63, and in the last 30 years has taken a waggon load of medicines to no purpose; subject to the gout 45 years, and pronounced incurable by the Faculty; yet, by applying at last where he should have applied years ago, he now enjoys perfect health: he avers, that he has been witness to 36 surprising cures, the most part performed on Members of Parliament, Bishops, Clergy, and Gentry; and solemnly declares, that every one was thankful and perfectly satisfied with his treatment. Our correspondent is sorry to add, that though miraculous cures are thus daily performed, yet the honest doctor takes care to answer no questions, his rule being implicit obedience and no enquiries; all speculative questions are therefore gravely answered with, "Sir, your cure is warranted, as for the means I am no schoolmaster;" which induces me to fear that Buzaglo intends his secret to die with him; for the universal good of mankind our correspondent sincerely wishes, that some noble Lord, or Member of the Lower House, having the welfare of his fellow creatures at heart, would propose something, that would induce Buzaglo to disclose faithfully those inventions and discoveries, which do so much honour to himself, and would so greatly benefit mankind; no doubt such a proposal would be warmly seconded in either House, and be finally confirmed by the Legislature at large.

General Evening Post
26–28 February 1784

MARCH

London, March 2.
Friday night last two postmen (one going from Bury to London, and the other coming from thence), were both bewildered in the snow on this side Newmarket. They each in their distress had recourse to their horns, the sound of which excited their mutual surprize. They were heard and relieved by Mr. Parson's family of Snailwell-hall, near which place they were lost. One of them was so much frozen, that he was obliged to have his boots cut off his legs.

London Chronicle
28 February–2 March 1784

Vienna, February 4.
During the Emperor's Voyage in Italy, one of the wheels of his Coach broke down on the Road. With much Difficulty he reached a poor Village. On his Arrival his Majesty got out at the Door of a Blacksmith and desired him to repair the damaged Wheel without Delay. That I would be very willing, replied the Smith, but it being Holiday all my Men are at Church: My very Apprentice, who blows the Bellows, is not at Home.—An excellent Method then presents of warming one's-self, replied the Emperor, still preserving the Incognito; and the great Joseph set about blowing the Bellows, while the Blacksmith forged the Iron. The Wheel being repaired, six Sols were demanded for the Job; but the Emperor, instead of them, put into his hands six Ducats. The Blacksmith, on seeing them, returned them to the Traveller, saying, Sir, you have undoubtedly made a Mistake, owing to the Darkness; instead of six Sols, you have given me six pieces of Gold, which nobody in this Village can change. Change them where you can, replied the Emperor; the Overplus is

59

for the Pleasure of blowing the Bellows. His Majesty then continued his Voyage without waiting an answer.

Adams's Weekly Courant, Chester
2 March 1784
[The emperor was Joseph II of Austria (1741–90), Holy Roman Emperor (1765–90).]

London, March 3.
It is with infinite concern we inform our readers that the business of Mr. Pitt's visit into the city on Saturday, had a conclusion most disgraceful, and perhaps unequalled in the annals of infamy.—On Mr. Pitt's carriage arriving, in St. James's street, opposite Brookes's, about half past twelve, whither the populace had joyously drawn it along, about 2 or 300 ruffians, evidently hired for the purpose, armed with bludgeons, and other offensive weapons, sallied forth and attacked him in a most violent manner, beating and abusing the defenceless multitude, who had drawn him along, and totally destroying his carriage. Mr. Pitt, however, we are happy to hear, escaped into a tavern without having received any injury. Such an assassin-like attack on a gentleman of such distinguished virtues and abilities, demands more than indignant reprobation.

Cambridge Chronicle and Journal
6 March 1784
[The blame for the incident fell upon Fox, for having arranged for the chair-men to attack Pitt. Fox claimed that he was nowhere near Brookes's on that night, having been in bed at the time with Mrs Armistead, who, he said, was ready to substantiate the fact on oath.]

On Monday the Earl of D—— met Lord S—— in the street; and after the common salutation of the day, the Earl asked the noble Lord how he could sit in his carriage, and quietly see the windows of the Prince of Wales broken by the rabble? Lord S—— said, that no such thing had happened; and when the Earl assured him that he had heard it asserted on the best authority, the noble Lord replied, "I will put an end to the discourse in a single word; your Lordship may tell your authority that it is a direct falsehood, and that I desired you to tell him so." "My Lord," replies the Earl of D——, "it was the P—— of W—— that told me so."

General Evening Post
2–4 March 1784

Bristol, March 6.
Monday last two fellows came to a young man who had a horse to sell in our fair, and after enquiring the price, desired that one of them might try him; on which he got up and rode off the horse, while the other was keeping the man in conversation till he likewise had an opportunity of escaping, under pretence of seeking for his companion.

Bath Chronicle
11 March 1784

On Wednesday se'nnight the clerk of Thornton church, in Lancashire, had his 28th child baptised, which occasioned no little addition to the pastime of Shrovetide in that village!

Cambridge Chronicle and Journal
6 March 1784

The three brothers lately committed to Chelmsford gaol for highway robberies occupied a genteel house on Epping Forest, near the residence of the celebrated Turpin. As a cloke to their real profession, they hired a piece of ground of 36 1. a year rent, which they cropped and farmed:— though they were never without women at the house, they regularly slept together on a large straw bed, in the middle of which they concealed their changes of apparel and various accoutrements. Mr. Benyon's gamekeeper was the first person who suspected them to be the highwaymen that had committed so many daring robberies between Ingatestone and Brentwood: – he therefore, with three other men, armed and watched them out one morning, apprehended them as they were returning home with a load of wood from the forest and conveyed them to Rumford. Since their commitment, several persons who were robbed have sworn to their identity; their horses found in a private stable, are remarkable for their spirit and speed; they shod them always themselves, and having complete sets of all kinds of tools, did all their own work, such as shoemaking, tayloring and even making their own candles. They are three of eight extraordinary brothers; some of whom occasionally reside at Fulbroke in Oxfordshire.

Ipswich Journal
6 March 1784

[The Dunsden brothers appear under various spellings in different papers. The capture of John and Henry was reported by the *Cambridge Chronicle* of 12 June. A brace of pistols, pincers for casting leaden bullets, a blunderbuss, and 106 pick-lock keys were found in the house (*Bonner and Middleton's Bristol Journal*, 28 February 1784).]

Last week a poor woman, named Banks, wife of a labouring man in Eastgate-street, Bury, was delivered of three boys, who were christened by the names of Abraham, Isaac, and Jacob, they all died the day following.

Last week was married Mr. Sippings, a considerable farmer at Southacre, to Miss Sally Martin, eldest daughter of Mr. Matthew Martin, of Castleacre Newton; a young lady in every respect qualified to render the married state compleatly happy.

Norfolk Chronicle or Norwich Gazette
6 March 1784

At half past seven o'clock yesterday morning the unhappy criminals ascended the scaffold, attended by Mr. Sheriff Skinner . . . and passed about half an hour in devotion, wherein they all joined with great fervency. Lee was very genteelly dressed in black, with his hair powdered . . . [he] made a request that he himself might give the signal to the executioner when to draw the lever which let the floor drop from under them; which, after a short time he did, by dropping his handkerchief, and they all in an instant paid their debt to justice.

Mr. Lee was born and educated a Gentleman: he possessed a strong understanding and polished manners. When very young, he entered the army an Ensign, and by force of merit and address obtained a company. His companions were of the first rank, which led him into expence, and obliged him to sell his commission. He attached himself to Miss J——, the actress, and went upon the stage, where, notwithstanding his accomplishments, he cut but an indifferent figure. While they were, as a part of the Edinburgh company, playing at the theatre of Aberdeen, they were encouraged to open an academy for the teaching of the English language. Mrs. Lee was much patronized, and had the daughters of the principal gentry at her house. Capt. Lee was too fond of gambling long to preserve his character in a place where, though they are less rigid than in other parts of Scotland, they yet pay attention to the morals of those who are invested with public duties; and on the death of Mrs. Lee, Lee was again suffered, without regret, to go abroad into the world. He renewed his acquaintance with the stage, and played at Portsmouth and other theatres. A few days previous to the commission of the crime for which he suffered, he arrived in London without a farthing, and being literally starving, and ashamed to beg, urged by the calls of nature, he went to the Rose-tavern, in Bridges-street, where he had often spent large sums, and having dined, borrowed from the proprietor of the house a guinea and a half, giving him as security a paper purporting to be Lord Townshend's draft on the Ordnance office; the draft, being offered for payment, was stopped, and Mr. Lee being soon after apprehended, was tried, and convicted. His friends did every thing that friendship could dictate to save his life, but in vain.

The execution of Mr. Lee may be considered as an example which must cut off from hope of mercy, every person convicted of a similar crime. The money obtained by the forgery he committed was but one guinea and a half, and he was urged to the unfortunate act by hunger, not having eaten for two days before. Exertions of the first interests in his favour proved ineffectual, and it is to be hoped his death will have the effect intended.

The mother of Capt. Lee, who has for some years lived upon a small pension at a retired village near Weymouth, was so affected upon hearing her son was ordered for execution, that she was seized with convulsions, and died in a few hours.

London Chronicle
4–6 March 1784

A few days ago a person in a man's habit, who has for several years begged in the streets of Edinburgh, being intoxicated, was run over by a cart, and had one of his legs broke. This person being taken to the Infirmary, where a number of students were present, positively refused to be undressed: however, as this ceremony was necessary, it was performed by force; when, to the astonishment of all present, the patient proved to be a woman. She is about fifty, and says her name is C——; that a love affair in the early part of her life occasioned her leaving her family, which is a genteel one, that she inlisted in the army, and was in several campaigns in the same regiment in which her beloved was an officer, who was killed by her side; and that after her discharge, she chose to continue the disguise, in order to conceal herself from her relations.

General Evening Post
6–9 March 1784

For the Whitehall Evening-Post.
THE
FUNERAL PROCESSION
OF THE
H—— of C——
"A short Pause! A single Day! Twenty-four Hours to
mourn over the Funeral of the House of Commons."

Mr. Powys's Speech.

———

Twenty-four Irish Chairmen with Bludgeons,
to keep the Peace, and clear the Way.
Twelve Butchers in crape Shirts; with Marrow bones
and Cleavers muffled.
SAM HOUSE in his Night-cap and Slippers; beating the
"*dead March in Saul*", on a Kettle-drum.
A Jack-Ass in Body-cloaths of Sable, carrying the
Resolutions of the Majority.
A News-Hawker, with Mr. Fox's Speeches in Black letter.
The Two Addresses lately presented to his Majesty, in a
Wheelbarrow hung with Black.
The Door-Keeper of the House of Commons,
with a Key pendent on his buttonhole.
THE MACE in a Mourning Coach.
THE SPEAKER in Character of a Mute.
THE CHAPLAIN;
with a small Volume of occasional Sermons in his Head.

with the following Inscription on the Plate:
"I have said to Corruption, Thou art my Father."

Job, chap xvii, verse 14.

65

The Pall supported by Twelve Gentlemen of the St. Albans.
Mr. Powys, chief Mourner, in Weepers.
Mr. Fox in brazen Armour;
with this Motto on his Helmet:
"Aut Caesar aut Nullus".
Lord North, in a Sackcloth Surtout.
A Chimney Sweeper carrying a Crucifix.
Mr. Burke reading the Office of Vespers.
Mr. Rigby, *solus*.
The Commissioners of Accounts, Two and Two.
Armstrong, the Sheriff's Officer,
with several Writs of Extent in his Hand.
Mr. Brinsley Sheridan.
The Treasurer of the Opera House, with an empty Box.
Italian Performers, in deep Mournings.
Thomas Levi Simon, and Nadab William Ishmael;
two responsible Christian Bail.
A Licenser of the Press carrying an empty Purse.
The Opposition Writers, Two and Two.
AN ANTHEM, the Words,
"And now, Lord, what is our hope! Truly our hope
is not in Thee."
General *Conway*,
His Servant with a Rusty Firelock.
General Burgoyne.
A Trumpet sounding a Retreat.
Mr. *Sawbridge*, in Jack-Boots, and an
Alderman's Gown.
George Byng, dressed like a Jockey.
Lord John Cavendish,
with the amended Receipt-Tax bound in Calf.
Opposition Ballad Singers, Two and Two.
The Waiters at *Brookes's*, carrying a Faro Table
on a new Construction.
The Procession closed by
Mr. *Keys*, the *Messenger of the People*,
in Character of MERCURY.

Whitehall Evening Post
6–9 March 1784

It is not true, as has been reported, that Sir Harbord Harbord is dead: it is with great pleasure we inform the public that he is much better.

General Evening Post
9–11 March 1784
[Sir Harbord Harbord, 2nd baronet (1734–1810) was MP for Norwich 1756–86 and created Baron Suffield in 1786.]

It was observed a few Evenings since in a Coffee house, that the greatest *Baker* in England was dead. "Who was he?" says a Bystander: "Why (answered the Person who made the Remark) the Master of the *Rolls* to be sure!"

Public Advertiser
12 March 1784

Thursday died Mr. Dawson, of Barton-street, Westminster; whose death was in consequence of the bite of his own dog, which he was accustomed to play with.

General Evening Post
11–13 March 1784

Yesterday a balloon was sent off from St. George's Fields: it took an Easterly direction, and was soon out of sight. The spectators amounted to many thousands, of all ranks, degrees, kindred, nations, and tongues. The following seemed to be the principal species:

Dukes *in their carriages.*
Lords *in ditto.*
Ladies of Quality *in ditto.*
Ladies of *a certain quality on foot.*

Ladies *of all qualities*.
Merchants *gaping*.
Tradesmen *staring*.
Boys *sinking in the mud*.
Footmen in the shape of Gentlemen.
Maid servants in all shapes.
Tag, rag and *bob tail*, in parties.

As the balloon went up, several handkerchiefs *disappeared*,
and took a direction towards *Field-lane*.

General Evening Post
11–13 March 1784

London, March 13.
Yesterday Sir Watkin Williams Wynn had his pocket
picked of his gold watch, as he stood to see the air-balloon
go off in St. George's Fields. Lord Gallway also lost his
purse.

Shrewsbury Chronicle
20 March 1784

London, March 13.
Wednesday one of the gang who belonged to David Hart,
who was committed to the new gaol, Southwark, for a
burglary in the house of a hosier in Lambeth, surrendered
himself to justice Swabey and impeached 31 more of the
gang; and the same day they went to the house of Hart's
father in Lambeth-walk, and found buried in the garden,
under the gooseberry trees, plate to a very considerable
value, which they took away in a cart.

Ipswich Journal
20 March 1784

Oxford, March 13.
Monday last Daniel Cato, a sweep-chimney, convicted at our last assizes for the wilful murder of Tho. Rosser, his apprentice, was executed pursuant to his sentence, and his body was afterwards delivered up at the Anatomy school at Christ-Church for dissection, pursuant to the statute. At the place of execution he appeared to be much agitated, and exceedingly reluctant to meet his fate; persisting however to the last in a declaration, that he had no design of murdering the boy; at the same time desiring that both young and old would take warning of him, and avoid passion, and begging the prayers of the multitude, as he said he was not able to pray for himself.

Bath Chronicle
18 March 1784

The rage for the aerostatic globe is not so great here as might have been imagined. In France every subscription for experiments has been filled. The manly philosophy of England perceives that nothing useful can be derived from this sort of aerial navigation – it would cost more money to fit out and dispatch a balloon capable of lifting only two persons, than to equip a vessel of 200 tons burthen.

General Evening Post
13–16 March 1784

London, Thursday March 18.
The town was yesterday thrown into a very great ferment by one of the most extraordinary incidents that ever happened in the annals of history—Some robbers having got out of the fields, over the garden-wall of the Lord Chancellor's house, in Great Ormond-street, from thence found means to get into the area, where they forced two bars of the kitchen window, and proceeding through it up stairs, made their way into a room adjoining to his

Lordship's study. Here they broke open several drawers, and at last coming to that in which the Great Seal of England is deposited, they took it out of the bag in which it was kept, and carried it off, together with two silver-hilted swords, and about 100 guineas in money.

The two swords appeared to have been drawn, on their getting possession of them, probably in order to secure their retreat, and the scabbards left behind. The instrument also, by which these daring robbers forced their entrance, was left behind, which is said to be a plain, but extremely well-tempered tool, at once calculated for defence, or breaking open locks. It is remarkable that the robbery was effected with so little noise, that not one of his Lordship's servants heard them, either during their stay, or in wrenching off the bars.

The Great Seal consists of two parts, about the size of a small plate, one folding over the other, and the impression made by it, is on both sides of the wax. The matter of which the Seal is composed, is chiefly silver, in value about 30 l. but the workmanship amounts to a vast deal more.

No small confusion ensued yesterday in the cabinet on the discovery of this very mal-a propos robbery, which was the more unlucky on account of the very pressing demand for new writs, consequent to the expected dissolution.

As soon as the Chancellor was apprised of the robbery, information was instantly sent to Bow-street; from whence, as well as from every justice-shop in other parts of the town, the runners were dispatched on all sides, but hitherto without effect. Two watchmen, however, who had stands near, were taken into Custody.

The publick remain full of expectation on the subject; and both yesterday and this day, the conversation of the town is more engrossed about the above robbery, than either about the Prorogation or Dissolution of Parliament.

One would imagine, from the robbing of the Chancellor's house being the sole topic of conversation amongst all ranks of people, that the Great Seal had never been lost before; but a correspondent informs us, (and a very remarkable circumstance it is) that a similar accident happened in the unfortunate reigns of John, Charles the First, and James the Second.

Norfolk Chronicle or Norwich Gazette
27 March 1784

Paris, March 19.
The Severity of the Weather has driven the Wolves in many Places even into the Villages, where they have devoured several Persons. Many foreign Aquatick Birds have also been driven into some of our Provinces; among the Rest we have Accounts from Rheims, that Numbers of a Bird, called the Saw-Bill, have frequented the Marsh of Champigny this Winter.

St. James's Chronicle or British Evening-Post
March 1784

Saturday last, as a young boy of five years of age, son to James Stevenson, collier at Bannockburn Muir, was diverting himself with a small quantity of peas, one of them unfortunately stuck in his throat, and notwithstanding immediate assistance being called for, he expired, before any experiment could be tried.

Caledonian Mercury, Edinburgh
20 March 1784

London. Thursday evening a beautiful young lady, the daughter of a Peer, and the son of a Scotch Lord, set off in a post-chaise and four for Scotland. They had not proceeded far before they were pursued by the young Lady's brother, an officer in the Guards: The route was, as the brother thought, plainly before him, and he soon gave up. The happy pair was masked; begged they might not be exposed, but permitted to return in the same disguise. The request was granted, But lo! when they arrived at papa's

71

house, and took off their vizards, they appeared to be the gentleman's valet and lady's maid. The happy master and mistress had taken another road, and laid this plan to delay and to deceive the pursuers. Master Brush and Miss Fringe were taken before a Magistrate, but his Worship, to his honour be it spoken, said he could not commit either, as there was no charge of guilt against the law of the land on which he could make out a warrant against them.

Bonner and Middleton's Bristol Journal
20 March 1784

John Angel, Esq; who died on Friday last, aged eighty-four years, at Stockwell, is said to have died possessed of one hundred and thirty thousands pounds in specie. It is said he has left his property to the next of kin, without specifying the name, which it is imagined will create much emolument to the gentlemen of the long robe.

London Chronicle
20–23 March 1784

On Friday evening last a labouring Man was stopped in the Middle of Upper Moorfields by two Footpads, who took from him Twopence Halfpenny, which was all that he had, and damn'd him for having no more Money.

Public Advertiser
23 March 1784

Saturday last a man and boy (the first of whom had apparently lost his right arm, and the latter the use of the same limb, it being bound with a handkerchief) were both apprehended, and taken before the sitting justices of Chester; when, upon examination, they were soon found to be impostors, the man's arm being very curiously fastened to his body, and secreted under the waistcoat, in such a manner as to escape the nicest eye; the boy's arm was also proved to be perfectly sound. After the use of their limbs had been thus, humanely restored to them, and the man had feelingly received the efficacy of the officer's right arm, in a salutary flagellation, they were both dismissed; and 'tis hoped, the discernment of the public will not suffer them, in future, to profit by so shameful and impious a prostitution of their limbs.

Bath Chronicle
25 March 1784

The Country People, on observing the Air Balloon descend, which was let off from the Observatory of Marischal College, Aberdeen, were greatly alarmed, some taking it for an Evil Spirit, and others for an Angel coming to sound the Last Trumpet. When it came very near the Earth, it was carried parallel to it for some Time; and at the same Time, some who followed it would have shot at it, but for Fear of the Consequences; at last a Mason more bold than the Rest said, "under the Fear of the Lord he would venture to approach and see what it was," and accordingly went to it and took it in his Possession.

Public Advertiser
25 March 1784

On Tuesday night the most uncommon enormity since the stealing of the Crown by BLOOD, was committed by some abandoned desperadoes. The Lord H. Chancellor's house in Great Ormond-street was broke open, and the GREAT SEAL of ENGLAND stolen from the office in which it was deposited. The peculiar circumstances of the affair shew clearly that it could not have been perpetrated by any common robber. On Thursday it is universally expected that the Parliament will be dissolved: This, it is well known, can be done only by proclamation; and to this proclamation, it is necessary that the Great Seal be affixed.—When we consider, that this robbery happened

73

on the eve of a dissolution,—that a dissolution must be fatal to the hopes of certain gentlemen, who have united themselves into a party, as it should seem, for the express purpose of impeding public business: that the seal itself could afford no temptation to robbers intent on booty alone, and, above all, that without some particular object, that office could not have been particularly destined to plunder, we cannot hesitate to impute it to agents of the party alluded to. Their design, however, has proved abortive, a new seal having been ordered to be made, which, it is expected, will be ready by tomorrow.

Morning Post
25 March 1784

[Lord Thurlow (1730–1806) was Lord Chancellor, 1778–92.]

On Friday night between the hours of six and seven as two gentlemen (foreigners) were passing through Little Russel-street, they were attacked by thirty or forty villains, who rushed from a court opposite the box-door of Drury-lane theatre, surrounding them and crying, "a pickpocket, a pickpocket" when they pushed them backwards, till finding an opportunity for their infernal purposes, they robbed them of everything they had in their pockets turning them inside outward. In the scuffle one of the gentlemen lost his hat and one of his shoes, with a silver buckle; having his gold watch fast in his hands, the villains cut and bruised him in a shocking manner, in hopes he would drop it; two of the soldiers on guard at the theatre at last came to their assistance, and rescued them: one of them lost 25 guineas that he had just received, but saved his watch at the expense of his hand

On Saturday last a young countryman, having a portmanteau full of cloaths and linen, coming from an inn at Bishopgate-street, pitched it in St. Paul's churchyard, to rest himself, when a man genteelly dressed, desired him to step to a shop at the upper end of Cheapside with a note, and he would give him sixpence, and stand by his things till he returned; accordingly he complied with the man's desire; but when he returned, the portmanteau was gone: the poor fellow is almost delirious at the loss.

Norfolk Chronicle or Norwich Gazette
27 March 1784

A member of the Nine Muses club at Willis's a few nights since, amidst a political colloquy, being called upon for a toast, gave *Messrs. Pitt and Fox.* On the President demanding his reason for giving such heterogeneous characters, he replied it was a convivial one, as they had afforded more conversation and mirth to the good people of England than any two gentlemen he had heard of!

General Evening Post
25–27 March 1784

This afternoon, about half past three o'clock, a person, apparently a genteel person, for we cannot call him a gentleman, came into a public-house, in Wych-street, Drury lane, along with a drummer of the Guards, and enquired for a private room, which being refused, then took the opportunity of making overtures, or rather the preliminaries of an amour, in the tap-room, which being observed by the landlord, who acquainted a gentleman in the house with it, the latter, after having secretly watched them in their amorous *rencontre*, suddenly jumped between them, and with a very large cane played an overture on the head, shoulders, back and arms of the genteel man, from Wych-street up Little Stanhope-street, into Clare-market, where the Butchers joined in the serenade with their marrow-bones and cleavers, till humanity got the better of resentment, and he at last walked off with all the colours of the rainbow. The drummer made his escape.

Middlesex Journal or London Evening Post
27–30 March 1784

APRIL

At last Worcester assizes a farmer, being a parish officer, was convicted of hanging up a pauper by his hands in a stable, (where in all probability he would have perished had he not gnawed the rope in two) and sentenced to pay a fine of 50 l. and to be imprisoned 3 months.

Bath Chronicle
1 April 1784

Mr. Samuel House, the patriotic citizen of Westminster, has maintained for upwards of forty years, in the neighbourhood where he at present resides, the character of an HONEST ENGLISHMAN.— In the year 1763, at which time he was much more corpulent than he is at present, he undertook for a trifling wager, to jump off Westminster Bridge; this extraordinary feat he performed, and wore for several years after a plush-coat, with large silver buttons, the produce of the bett.—It was remarkable that he pledged himself to jump from the bridge at a time when he was *intoxicated*. His friends afterwards endeavoured to dissuade him from the undertaking, by observing he was *drunk* when he made the proposal; "then, says Sam, it the more becomes me to *keep my word* now I am *sober.*"

Gazeteer and New Daily Advertiser
2 April 1784

This morning at Seven o'Clock the Convicts under Sentence of Transportation were escorted from Newgate by a proper Guard, and put on Board a Lighter at Blackfriars, from whence they fell down the River, in order to embark on board a Transport Vessel bound for Nova Scotia.

The above Offenders were near 90 in Number; upwards of 20 of whom were Women and Girls: Among the latter, that atrocious Criminal, the Pawnbroker's Apprentice, aged about 14, who a short Time since set Fire to her Master's House—Two little Boys were also among these unhappy Wretches, who did not appear above twelve Years old.

Jackson's Oxford Journal
3 April 1784

London, April 2.
Last week was committed to Ilchester Gaol, Tho. Rabbitts of Frome Selwood, charged on the Coroner's Inquest, of the wilful Murder of Jane Long his Mother-in-Law, by Poison. His Intention seems to have been the Destruction of the whole Family, having mixed Arsenic with some Flour with which a Pudding was made; by eating which, his Wife and Child were also violently affected; but timely Assistance being given, they happily recovered. His Trial for the same is respited until the next Assizes.

Jackson's Oxford Journal
3 April 1784

London, April 3.
A gentleman of Wiltshire, lately deceased, ever remarkable for his pecularities, closed the scene of his life with the following singular bequest, which was specified in his will:

"Whereas the poor of the parish of E—— are grievously afflicted with coughs and colds at the winter season of the year, *Item*, I give for the use of the poor of the said parish the sum of 5 l. to be laid out in Spanish liquorice."

Ipswich Journal
10 April 1784

Ran away, and left his Family chargeable to the Parish of Holm Hale, JOHN WEBB. He is a middle aged Man, blind of one Eye, and follows the Business of Sieve mending. Whoever will apprehend him, and convey him to the Overseers of the Parish aforesaid shall receive ONE GUINEA Reward, and all reasonable Charges, by me, GEORGE WATTS.

Norfolk Chronicle or Norwich Gazette
3 April 1784

DR. GRAHAM having now left his house in Pall-Mall, by particular desire, previous to his departure for Edinburgh, he will deliver a Lecture this evening, and every evening this week, at the King's Head Tavern, in the Poultry, three doors from the Mansion-house, on the simplest and most certain means of preserving bodily health, and mental serenity and happiness to extreme old age, or in other words, in a long pathetic, and valedictory Lecture, he will point out the means by which persons of tolerably good constitutions will live healthfully, honourably, and usefully, till about an hundred and fifty years of age.

N.B. Although this curious, most useful, and most eccentric Lecture, is immediately calculated for the Meridian of Black-hole, Guttle-down, and Port-soaking Wards, yet Dr. Graham pledges his honour that the language and sentiments will be so perfectly delicate and chaste, as not to give even the smallest offence to the most virtuous female ear in the world.

To begin precisely at half past seven o'clock.—Admission only One Shilling, and as the room, though large, and elegant, is expected to be much crouded, the Ladies are requested to come very early, that they may be agreeably accommodated with seats.

The Gazeteer and New Daily Advertiser
5 April 1784

[James Graham, quack doctor and owner of the Temple of Health and the Hymeneal Temple, claimed to cure

78

infertility by means of magnetism and electricity. At the Temple of Health his assistant was Emma Lyon, later Lady Hamilton, Nelson's mistress. His treatment does not appear to have worked. He was obliged to return to Edinburgh where he was sent to gaol as a lunatic.]

There is nothing talked of anywhere but the Election . . . The play-houses are but thinly attended owing to the Election. The opera-house is deserted owing to the Election. Trade is neglected owing to the Election. Sobriety and Peace are banished owing to the Election. Friends quarrel owing to the Election. In short, every thing is neglected that ought to be attended to, and the whole people in their hearts murmur at a certain person for all those misfortunes which are owing to the Election.

Gazeteer and New Daily Advertiser
6 April 1784

Mess. Staveleys, Carvers in this City have been favoured with the following Letter from a Gentleman of Character at Horncastle in Lincolnshire, dated Saturday March 13, 1784:

"In Consequence of the Intimation fixed on your Aerial Balloon, I inform you it fell in our Neighbourhood on Thursday the 11th Inst. about 20 Minutes past Three in the Afternoon, as near as can be computed. The Person who first discovered it is a Servant belonging to one Todd, a Farmer, who lives at an odd House in the Parish of Thimbleby, about half a Mile from Horncastle, in Lincolnshire. The young Man was just coming out of a Barn from feeding some Horses he had been at Plough with, when he perceived it pitch on the Ground. The odd Appearance it made not only affrighted the Sheep that were depasturing in the Field, but alarmed him greatly, insomuch that at first he durst not go to it. Being a little recovered from his Surprise, he pursued it. It ran, or rather bounded, after its first touching the Ground, about 600 Yards over Hedge and Ditch, and would have evaded his Pursuit, had not a very high Quickset Hedge, in which it got entangled, prevented it from proceeding further; sending forth now and then great Cracks and Hissings, occasioned as I suppose, from the inflammable Air making its Escape from the Balloon. Just as the Boy was taking it on his Back, it made a very large Report, which affrighted him amazingly, and made him throw it down again crying out, "He was sure the Devil was in it." At its first alighting, the young Man says it was very little damaged; and when I saw the Remains of it at Horncastle the Crown was not in the least impaired, and the Conveyance for the inflammable Air into the Balloon at the Bottom quite secure and close tied. Some of the inflammable Air continued in it till Yesterday Morning, and held it out much in the Shape of a Petticoat. The distance from Horncastle to Caistor is 27 Miles; from Caistor to Barton 18; from Barton to Hull 5; from Hull to Beverley 9; and from Beverley to York 28: In all 87 Miles. I am &c."

The York Courant
6 April 1784

[A quickset hedge is one formed of live plants, especially hawthorn.]

London, April 6.
Bon Mots.—Mr. Fox, on his late Canvas, having accosted a blunt Tradesman, whom he solicited for his Vote; the Man answered, "I cannot give you my Support; I admire your Abilities, but d——n your Principles."

Mr. Fox smartly replied, "My Friend, I applaud you for your Sincerity – but d——n your Manners."

Mr. Fox having applied to a Shopkeeper in Westminster for his Vote and Interest, the Man produced a *Halter* with which he said he was ready to oblige him. Mr. Fox replied, "I return you Thanks, my Friend, for your intended Present; but I should be sorry to deprive you of it, as I presume it must be a *Family Piece*."

Jackson's Oxford Journal
10 April 1784

APRIL-FOOL

The papers have told us of the extraordinary number of April-fools which the present season has produced; the following is an instance in which a very happy use was made of this practice: Francis, Duke of Lorrain, and his Duchess, being kept prisoners at Nancy, and contriving to make their escape, they chose the *first day of April* for affecting it. Under the disguise of peasants they passed the guards at day-break, and got out of Nancy. They owed their escape to the nonsense of the day; for an old woman observing them, run to a soldier upon guard, and told him, that the Duke and Duchess were making their escape; "Poh, poh, says he, you wish to make me an April fool;" the woman run to the officer, but he was equally afraid of receiving le poisson d'Avril; and the noble prisoners had time to make their escape to a castle at the distance of twenty Leagues; and from thence they passed to Florence. It was this marriage that continued the House of Lorrain, and to which the German Empire at this day, owes its illustrious Sovereign, and France its Queen.

The Gazeteer and New Daily Advertiser
10 April 1784

Some account of Mr. THOMAS CLARGES, the noted Miser of Shropshire

This person inherited a very good estate, which he run through in every species of extravagance in a space of time surprisingly short, but was struck with so much remorse at his conduct, and the near appearance of a gaol, that his disposition took a sudden turn, and he became, in the management of the shattered remnant of his fortune, the veriest miser that ever existed; he retired to a cottage on a hill that overlooked the estate he had sold, and laid down a resolution unalterably, never to rest until he had regained it. He lived upon nothing but refuse; wore second-hand clothes, old liveries, or any thing he could get cheap, lent money all through the country in small sums, at enormous interest. Travelling on foot night and day to find out farmers in distress to buy their cattle which he drove to market himself – jobbed – traded – turned every penny, and spent nothing – by degrees money was collected, he dealt in mortgages; and found out young heirs to supply at extravagant interest. After this he became an attorney, and fleeced all that came into his hands; lent money on his former estate, and then cried out, My business is done! and so he contrived that it should, for he cheated the gentleman of above 1000 l. and regained the estate at the same time; added to it, almost every year ruined hundreds by his machinations and practices. It was remarked that nobody borrowed money of him; that did not rue it in a series of misery, and yet he lent with such facility, that numbers were every day tempted. He set up claims, by distant relations, against half the estates in his neighbour-hood; and after throwing their property into confusion, and involving it in law, bought it cheap himself. In a word, by a series of transactions, incredible to those who did not know him, he amassed above 200,000 l. and when in possession of that immense fortune, spent no more in all sorts of personal and house expences than 62 l. a year.

Ipswich Journal
10 April 1784

Yesterday another Tumult happened in Covent-Garden, between the Sailors and a Body of Chairmen, in which many were hurt, and two of the former are said to be dead of their Wounds, and four so desperately bruised, that they cannot recover. In Friday's Tumult a Gentleman had his Arm shattered to Pieces; and on Saturday three Fingers of a Boy were cut off.

Jackson's Oxford Journal
10 April 1784

Gone into foreign parts for the recovery of her health, *Public Virtue*; the lady has long been in a decline.

Postponed to the day of judgment, the payment of the national debt.

In full bloom, notwithstanding the severity of the weather, the Duchess of Devonshire.

Missing, the honour and conscience of several electors who call themselves independent men.

Wanted, integrity in politics, moderation in religion, judgment in physic, and good-breeding at the Bar.

Aimed at by all the world, qualities that do not belong to them.

The Whitehall Evening Post
8–10 April 1784

The following adventure lately happened at Paris. A young gentleman in a milk-white pair of silk stockings was waiting under a gateway till a storm, which was then at its height, should give over. At the same time a man, meanly dressed, but wearing a rusty sword by his side, came running alone, and in his haste was so unfortunate as to splash the young man all over; this put the offended petit-maitre out of all patience; with uplifted cane, he makes towards the culprit, but the latter was too much for him, whilst with one hand he stayed his impetuosity, he with the other reached out of his pocket a sixpenny piece, telling the enraged beau: Here my pretty youth, be more cool, take this trifle, I can afford to pay for the washing of your stockings, but I am not master of so much money as I should want to make my escape, if I should run you through the body.

Jopson's Coventry Mercury
12 April 1784

Last week Henfrey and Rider were executed at Nottingham, pursuant to their sentence at the last assizes for a highway robbery.— The executioner fixing the rope too far back in Henfrey's neck, he said aloud, Put the noose forward, my boy: but still not fixing it to his mind, he bid him stand away, and fixed it himself. The caps provided being too little, Rider tore his behind, and Henfrey tied his handkerchief over his face. A Methodist Preacher gave out a hymn, and it was remarked that Rider was louder than any other person; when the Preacher was leaving the cart, Henfrey said, O! Mr. Fox, I am happy, I never was so happy in my life. The cart beginning to move, Henfrey called upon Rider to make a spring, doing so himself at the same instant, by which he broke his neck, and never moved afterwards. They were both dressed in their shrouds; and Rider, when he was going to be turned off, asked a gentleman for his watch, to look at what o'clock it was.

Jopson's Coventry Mercury
12 April 1784

If JOHN GILBERT, who absented himself from his Wife about 29 Years ago, and who about Ten Years since was employed as an Under Gardener at Lord MONTAGUE's at MIDHURST, be still living, and will apply to ANN GILBERT, near BUTCHER'S CROSS, in MAYFIELD, he may hear of something greatly to his advantage; or any Person giving a proper Account of the Death of the said John Gilbert, to Ann Gilbert, as above, shall be satisfied for their trouble.

He is about six feet high, of a black complexion, a thinnish Man, and turned 60 Years of Age.

Sussex Weekly Advertiser or Lewes Journal
12 April 1784

Soon after the theft of the Great Seal the story goes, with what truth we know not, of a basket being sent to Ormond-street, the contents of which, were found to be a thumping boy, wrapped in swaddling clothes.

Whitehall Evening Post
10–13 April 1784

It was observed of the Duchess of D—— and Lady P——, while they were soliciting votes in favour of Mr. Fox, on Saturday last, that they were the most *lovely portraits* that ever appeared upon a *canvass*!

The General Evening Post
10–13 April 1784
[The initials stand for Devonshire and Portland.]

An over-drove ox ran into Covent-garden yesterday noon, and occasioned the utmost confusion among the populace; he threw great numbers down, and tossed a butcher's boy, by which his thigh was fractured.

General Evening Post
10–13 April 1784

EASTER MONDAY

How vain are human hopes, and how uncertain human pleasures! Not an unsuccessful candidate after the loss of an election could possibly be more disappointed, than were the smart lads and lasses by the gloominess of the weather yesterday. They had dressed themselves in their best attire, and anticipated the joys of a trip on the Thames, a ride in the coach, and a pleasant walk to the inviting town and hill of Greenwich. But all these fond expectations were frustrated, and those who formed them confined to London. The inn-keepers and publicans, in the various towns and villages contiguous to the metropolis, shared in the general regret. The luscious viands, and the inspiring draughts which they had procured for their expected customers, were prepared in vain, and left an expensive burthen upon their hands. But the old adage says, "It is an ill wind that blows nobody any good." What was lost in the country was gained in town. The former failing to invite the humble votaries of pleasure, they turned their thoughts to the amusements of the latter.

Whitehall Evening Post
10–13 April 1784

Derby, April 15.
Early yesterday morning this town was alarmed by an account of a most daring robbery having been committed at three o'clock.—The house of Mrs. Roe, the upper end of St. Peter's Parish, had been entered by three villains, who forced open the back door, notwithstanding its being secured by several iron bolts. Their faces were blacked, and two of them were disguised in smock frocks; the other had on a blue coat. One of the ladies in the house, being alarmed, got up, and was met on the stairs by two of the villains, who held pistols to her head, and with dreadful imprecations and threats demanded what money there was in the house; and upon her telling them there was very little, they d——n'd her, and said, "how could they live without money", or words to that effect; and if she did not shew them where the plate was, they would blow her brains out. One of them encouraged his partner to blow her eyes out, if she was not silent, and did not direct them

where the money and other valuables were: She was therefore obliged to comply, and the robbers plundered the house of upwards of thirty-eight pounds in cash, together with a silver watch, tankard, coffee-pot, pint mug, half pint, &c. &c. and to such lengths were they proceeding that if the neighbourhood had not been alarmed, it is thought they would have entirely stripped the House.—It was near day-light when they left the place, and their departure was so abrupt, that one of the men who carried the plate fell down before he had ran sixty yards, and was observed by a boy, who says he can swear to his person. A quantity of snow having fallen, their footsteps were traced, and they were soon secured.

Whitehall Evening Post
20–22 April 1784

TO THE LADIES

OLYMPIAN DEW, or GRECIAN LOOM WATER, is recommended, being the only thing discovered that will effectually clear the skin of freckles, pimples, tan, and every deformity; it instantly makes wrinkles disappear, and gives a loveliness to the countenance too charming to be described. This elegant article is not only used all over Europe as a Cosmetic by the Ladies, (and by Gentlemen after shaving) but is universally used as a Perfume for the Handkerchief. No Perfume so sweet, so refreshing, so delicate, as Olympian Dew, says the QUEEN of FRANCE; she not only uses it herself, but has commanded all her attendant Nobility to do the same. Sharp's curious Chinese gloves and Cyprian Wash-Balls are held in the highest esteem for softening and whitening the hands, prevents their chapping, and cures them when chapped even in the coldest weather. His warranted Tooth-Brushes, the Prince of Wales's Tooth-Powder, and Royal Tincture of Peach Kernels for the Teeth and Gums, are held in the greatest esteem, being the most pleasant and efficacious of any thing of their kind. Sold, wholesale and retail, by Charles Sharp, perfumer, No. 131 Fleet-street, London, and, by appointment, by Mr Mulcaster, of Hull; Mrs. Robinson, of York; Mrs. Carr, Newcastle on Tyne; Mr. Sykes, of Manchester; Mr. Murphy, of Chester; Messrs. Evans and Barnett, of Salop; Andrass, of Bristol; Burges, of Beverley; Davis, of Leeds; Mawdsley, of Wakefield; Nailor, of Sheffield; and Sleaford, of Doncaster.

General Evening Post
15 April 1784

EASTER MONDAY
Hunt at Epping Forest

There were collected about two thousand horsemen, mostly on hired hacks from the metropolis, bebooted, besticked, bewhipped, and behatted. There were but two black caps and two scarlet coats in the field. The city bucks, notwithstanding the badness of the day, treated their *blowings* to a buggy, a post-chaise, a chaise cart, or a seven-and-sixpenny hack, just as the pocket could afford; and a motley figure they made. Sheltered from the shower under the branches of a pollard were collected in different situations the beau, the buck, the sloven, the lady of easy virtue, the lady of no virtue, and the lady of all virtue. The heavens rained hail-stones upon them in plenty, and many a new riding-habit was spoiled. A painted doll in a green habit, on a miserable horse, her face painted like a mercer's sign, paraded about very much. She was attended by a wretched substitute of manhood on a grey horse, whose bones towered above his flesh. This hunter, instead of a whip wore an umbrella, with which every now and then he laboured his slow-paced Rosinante. The butcher's journeymen, apprentices, and a considerable cargo of the mop-squeezing sisterhood were mounted in carts, and the Pedestrian gentry were not a few. At near twelve o'clock the poor innocent unhappy victim of the day's sport was

88

conveyed by shouting attendants, in a wooden cage drawn by four horses to the place of execution, just on the summit of a rising ground which commands a beautiful prospect of the country. The blood hounds followed with the club of gentlemen to whom they belong. The terrified trembling being was uncaged, and self-preservation, in spite of the croud, directed him to seek the friendly shelter of the forest to the south, instead of trusting to the swiftness of his limbs across the open country on the north. The multitude opened like a pack of hounds, and preceeded the dogs above a mile through the wood, when the four-footed beasts took the lead of their two-legged brethren, and sung a deep toned stave to their flying game. One of those events, from what cause we know not, put it into the head of the stag to make a double to the south-east point, which the keenness of the scent of his pursuers oversmelt, and their eagerness for blood made them not recollect time enough to turn so as to come upon the foot again. The consequence was, that the stag baffled his pursuers, made his escape, and slept that night in safety. Such of the horsemen as were thrown out (and that made exactly nine hundred and ninety nine out of the thousand that pursued for the first three miles, not a man but the huntsman being even within hearing of the dogs at the end of the fourth mile) were extremely happy at this, for as they could not have the pleasure of being in, it was a satisfaction that the creature was not killed. There was a general gloom when the escape and the impossibility of recovering was made known, which clouded this satisfaction not a little. It seems that on those sportive days the ears, stern and skin of the stag is usually disposed of to the London huntsmen at one shilling per inch, to stick in their hats as they ride home; but there being no death, it was improper to wear the tokens of accessories to murder. Many a booted beau from Whitechapel, the Minories, and as far as Temple-bar, had bought from the woman at Mile-end an inch of trophy to put in his bonnet. The woman always sells as much deer skin and ears and stern on Easter Monday at Mile-end turnpike for six-pence, as can be bought from the huntsman on the forest for a shilling. Trade and city oeconomy, therefore taught them to save cent per cent. by a purchase at the cheapest shop, and therefore most of the hunting trophies were brought from London to the forest.

The huntsman however, who is a keen fellow, saw that his death-shilling must be lost if there was no killing. He therefore, a long time after the dogs were drawn off, sent his whipper-in to a neighbouring cottage, where was deposited for cure, a lame buck, and this lame buck was brought out and put behind a little copse, his throat cut, and a bag of anniseed dragged through a part of the deepest ground of the forest for two miles to where the hounds were. Hounds will run any thing. The huntsman said he would throw off the dogs, and try if he could get the stag, as a countryman informed his whipper-in that he was seen passing that way.—The dogs took to the anniseed, and soon came up with the murdered deer, whom they immediately tore to pieces.—The shillings were collected, and the hunters, such as were not smothered in the mire, or had their brains dashed out against stumps of trees, returned highly pleased with this anniseed gallop.

The Bald Faced Stag Tavern was a scene of uproar about three o'clock, with shouting and singing, and blowing of horns, and quarrelling for four female trollops, who had arrived there on speculation with the tyre woman from a bagnio in Charles-street, Covent-garden, as ugly as the foulest fiend below. The nymphs got drunk and sung, and the men were lost in love. Some genteel people were at the Forest, but they all went to the Green Man, where it is but justice to say, every good accommodation was to be had from an excellent larder; and in the Bar was a fine prospect of filial beauty, virtue, and domestic loveliness.

There were not many limbs amputated, nor a very great number of necks broke, as the hunt was so very short.

Greenwich

The weather untenanted the Hill of its annual rollers, and the Easter cloaths are laid up for the Whitsun-holidays.

Whitehall Evening Post
13–15 April 1784

On board a French Merchant Ship lost the beginning of March on the Coast of America, laden with rich Flanders Lace, there were Twenty Thousand Umbrellas. It is somewhat singular that the Captain of her, who was in Part Owner, had been cast away twice before in the Course of three Years. He died of Grief, and was buried in Connecticut.

Public Advertiser
17 April 1784

Letters from Quimper, in Brittany, mention, that on Sunday the 21st of last month, while the greater part of the inhabitants were at church, they were alarmed by dreadful noises from the sea-side. On going to the place whence the noises proceeded, they found that thirty-two whales had been thrown by the storm of the preceding night into a kind of creek, whence they were not able to disengage themselves; they were taken, and the produce of their sale amounted to 200,000 livres. These fish were from thirty-six to forty feet in length; and among them one of the enormous length of eighty-two feet.

Gazeteer and New Daily Advertiser
17 April 1784

His Royal Highness the Prince of Wales came to town yesterday from Windsor, where, since her Majesty's indisposition, he has attended with the most laudable duty and affection.

The Prince of Wales was on the Beacon course at Newmarket when news arrived to him of the Queen being indisposed; he instantly left his company, got into his chaise, and set off for Windsor, where he arrived in a few hours. This particular mark of his Royal Highness's affection to his mother has diffused such a joy as is indescribable.

General Evening Post
15–17 April 1784
[Queen Charlotte was suffering from a "bilious colic".]

Saturday night a man, known by the name of Black Harry, was taken at Hyde-park-corner, on the roof of the Worcester coach, and conducted to Tothill-fields Bridewell. He is one of the Convicts that escaped from the transport vessel at Falmouth a few days since, and one of the prisoners who broke out of Bridewell a few months ago.

Gazeteer and New Daily Advertiser
20 April 1784

On Tuesday at Noon a Gentlewoman, rather young, and genteelly dressed in a white Polonese, was unfortunately killed near Hyde Park Corner. The Accident was occasioned by a Horse which the Rider could not manage, by which Means her Head was dashed to pieces against the Park Wall.

Public Advertiser
23 April 1784
[A polonaise was a dress consisting of a bodice, with a skirt open from the waist downwards.]

NEWMARKET, April 23, 1784
THIS is to acquaint L. H. S. DUROURE, that if he does not take his CHESTNUT HORSE, called BANK, and a

BROWN MARE, from Thomas Perrins, Stable-Keeper, in Newmarket, Cambridgeshire, before Wednesday the 5th day of May, 1784, they will be Sold by Auction by Thomas Foreman, at the Coffee-House in Newmarket, to pay for the Purchase and the Expense of Keep, &c.

General Evening Post
23 April 1784

Oxford, April 24.
At the General Quarter Sessions for this City, held on Thursday last, William, alias Bumper Smith, and John Hawkins, were tried for burglariously entering the Dwelling-house of Mr. Isaac Lawrence, Grocer, and stealing from thence about Thirty-seven Pounds in Money, a Pair of Ear-rings, a few Bottles of Port Wine, some Cheese, and other Things, in company with Edward Lads, who was admitted Evidence, for which they were capitally convicted, and received Sentence of Death.

Public Advertiser
24 April 1784

William Vandeput was on Monday committed to the New Gaol, where he is now double ironed, on a charge of a burglary in the house of the Lord Chancellor, and stealing thereout the Great Seal. A Jew in Petticoat-lane, was on Monday apprehended on an information against him for having purchased and melted the Great Seal into an ingot; but while he was conducting to the Rotation-office in Southwark, for examination, he was rescued from the peace officers by eight ruffians. The Jew melted the Seal, while the robbers remained in his house.

Cambridge Chronicle and Journal
24 April 1784

Yesterday was executed, at Boughton, near this City, pursuant to her sentence, Elizabeth Wood, for the wilful murder of James Simister, late of Bradbury, in this county, by poison.—This unfortunate woman procured a suspension of her execution for upwards of six months by a pretended pregnancy. It is therefore to be hoped that she cultivated the length of time allotted her in such a manner as to secure to her that remission in *another* state, which the enormity of her crime rendered impossible in *this*.— She appeared to be about 42 years of age, and met her melancholy end with the utmost resignation.

Whitehall Evening Post
24–27 April 1784

A season so backward as the present, has never been known. Vegetables of all kinds are dearer than in the middle of winter. Asparagus has not yet made its appearance. A few trees are yet in blow. On Saturday morning the hills around Gloucester were covered with snow. The letters from Holland and Germany represent the severity of the weather such as to render their situation even worse than ours.

Whitehall Evening Post
24–27 April 1784

Extract of a letter from Bath, April 27
"Last night our Members gave a very elegant ball and supper at the Town Hall, and being desirous of confining it to the most respectable of the inhabitants, avoided giving tickets themselves, but sent a particular number to each gentleman of the corporation, that they might distribute them to their relations and neighbours; by seven o'clock about five hundred were collected in the neatest and best proportioned ball room in England, when the minuets commenced, and were chiefly danced by ladies and gentlemen of Bath, in a stile that did infinite credit to the

94

two ladies by whom they were instructed in that pleasing and elegant accomplishment. Mr. Moysey and Mr. Pratt, by their very polite and particular attention to every one throughout the evening, obliged, pleased, and gained the esteem of all present.

"The ball and card rooms were splendidly illuminated; the ladies were better dressed, and a more beautiful group than I ever saw assembled before; country dances began at nine, when tea, orgeat, negus, cake, and other refreshments were plentifully handed about; at eleven the supper-rooms were opened; it is impossible for me to describe the taste and elegance displayed in fitting up the rooms for this occasion, or the vast variety of delicate viands with which the tables were covered; one room in which were six tables had a quantity of light pillars, each of which were surrounded spirally with brilliant lamps, and from the top of one pillar to the other hung large festoons or wreaths of myrtle and roses; the ornaments of the tables, such as temples, triumphal arches, pagodas, &c, were superb; and the profusion and variety of sweet things astonishing; in short, Mr. Phillott, who had the entire providing and management on this occasion, made such a display of his taste and abilities as gave universal satisfaction."

Whitehall Evening Post
29 April–1 May 1784

[Orgeat is a cooling drink made from barley or almonds and orange-flower water. Negus is hot sweetened wine and water.]

Extract of a letter from Bath, April 24

"Do not think, my friend, that I delight in tales of horror, or search for subjects of melancholy to relate to you. I never experienced greater anguish than I do when I acquaint you that Dr. Staker put a period to his existence this morning, at his house in Queen-square, with a pistol. The cause of this rash action can only be attributed to a sudden phrenzy, to which poor human nature, however blessed with reason and genius, or perfected by learning and assiduity, is liable. He was most elegant in his person and address, polite without affectation, humane and liberal, a scholar of acknowledged erudition; and as a physician, he had a most extensive practice. Scarce four-and-twenty hours are past since the pulse that trembles whilst it indites this, felt the pressure of that hand which is now so prematurely cold. The Jury are now surveying the corpse: I am conscious there is not a heart amongst them, but sorely laments the loss of so worthy a benefactor, nor an eye but trickles at the horrid scene."

Whitehall Evening Post
27–29 April 1784

MAY

Thursday morning one of the Constables in Covent-garden observed a fellow put a cord about the neck of a remarkably large and handsome Newfoundland dog, and lead him out of the crowd, upon which he took the man into custody, and conducted him to the Public Office in Bow-street. In his pockets were found several cords, and a knife of a peculiar form, it being very sharp at the point, and made with two edges, like those for killing and flaying sheep and calves. The man was committed to Tothill-fields Bridewell. From an inscription on the collar, the dog appeared to be the property of General Dalrymple.

Whitehall Evening Post
29 April–1 May 1784

Thursday a Constable on duty before the Hustings in Covent garden, perceived among the croud a man named James Bigsby, who stands accused of stealing out of the Slaughter-house of Mr. Godson, carcass-butcher, in Cow-cross, a quantity of fat and two bullocks hides. He was taken to Clerkenwell Bridewell.

The Hustings at Covent Garden now resembles the Stand at Newmarket; "an even bett that he comes in second!" and "five to four on this day's poll!" being the language hourly vociferated from every part of the building.

The *Faro Table* which was last winter kept at Brookes's, by the confederates of a Right Honourable Candidate, should be opened at the Hustings at Covent Garden, and the scene would then be quite compleat—An *Hazard Table* in *the Vestry* would be still more in character.

Whitehall Evening Post
29 April–1 May 1784

The ladies of fashion, in the interest of Mr. Fox's election, are distinguished by wearing a feather in exact imitation of a fox's brush, which is so near a copy, that it cannot, at the smallest distance, be discovered from the real. This feather was invented by Mr. Carberry, Plumassier to his Royal Highness the Prince of Wales, at No. 34, Conduit-street, near Bond-street.

Morning Herald and Daily Advertiser
1 May 1784

THE THIRD CHAPTER OF THE TIMES

1. And it came to pass that there were great dissensions in the West, amongst the *rulers* of the nation.

2. And the *Counsellors* of the *Back stairs* said, let us take advantage, and yoke the people even as oxen, and rule them with a rod of iron.

3. And let us break up the *assembly* of *privileges*, and get a new one of *prerogatives*, and let us hire false prophets to deceive the people; and they did so.

4. Then Judas Iscariot went amongst the citizens, saying, "Choose me one of your elders, and I will tax your *innocent damsels*, and I will take the bread from the *helpless*, and the *lame*, and the *blind*.

5. And with the scrip which will arise, we will eat, drink, and be merry." Then he brought forth a roll of sheep-skin, and came in unto the gin-shops, cellars, and bye-places, and said, "Sign your names;" and many made marks thereunto!

6. Now it came to pass that the time being come when the People should choose their Elders, that they assembled together at the *Hustings*, nigh unto the Place of Cabbages.

7. And Judas lifted up his Prerogative Phiz, and said, "Choose me, choose me!" but the People said, Satan avaunt — O! thou wicked Judas, Woe unto thee! hast thou

not deceived thy *best Friend*? Would'st thou deceive us also? Get thee behind us, thou unclean spirit!

8. We will have the man, who ever has and will support our cause and maintain our rights, who stands forth for us, and who never will be guided by secret influence.

9. And moreover, after they had spoken these words, the People shouted, and cried with an exceeding loud voice, saying — Fox is the Man!

10. Then they caused the Trumpets to be sounded as at the feast of the full Moon, and sang — Long live Fox! May our Champion live for Ever! Amen.

Morning Herald and Daily Advertiser
1 May 1784

By a private letter from French Flanders, we have the following singular, yet true circumstance: In a monastery near Ailworth, a monk, being tired of his confinement, endeavoured to get released, but finding he could not, was exasperated to such a degree as to threaten to burn that place down, of which the Prior being informed, confined him in a cell, which was so small that he could scarce lie down or turn himself round, where he was fed on bread and water for the space of 36 years; and when he grew weak and sick, they took him out and administered nourishment and cordials until he was recovered, when he was sent back again to his former habitation. A lady who lived near, happened to hear the groans of some human being, upon which she sent to the monastery, and enquired into the reason, and was told the above: then she interceded for his releasement, but the relentless father would not comply; upon which she sent to the parliament at Paris, represented his case, who sent an order for his being released. When he was almost gone, on being asked how long he had been confined, he replied, an hundred years; they showed him an almanack, and asked him, if he could explain it? which he did; by which, and several questions asked him, it was calculated he had been

confined in that dark dungeon as long as the aforementioned time.

Ipswich Journal
1 May 1784

RIOT AT COVENT GARDEN

That spirit of riot and disorder, which disturbed the peace
of Westminster in the beginning of the Election, broke out
on Saturday evening with fresh violence, and with those
marks of desperation which generally accompany an
expiring interest.

Some persons with Fox ribbands in their hats passing by
Wood's Hotel about eight o'clock, were assaulted by a
party of sailors without the slightest provocation, and
several were severely wounded with cutlasses, spits,
pokers, and bottles dashed from the windows indiscriminately upon the multitude.

Intelligence of this gross outrage having reached the
friends of the assaulted party, some of them came to their
assistance, and the mercenaries of the Court Candidates
were forced to make a retreat as disgraceful as their attack
was unmanly and savage. Several shots were fired from
Wood's house, but providentially the ruffians who fired
them failed in their barbarous attempts, for no life was
lost, though many persons were shockingly mangled.

The worthy conductors of this assassinating scheme,
finding that the courage of their enemies could not be
overpowered, even by this vile and cowardly mode of
attack, had recourse to the arm of authority to give effect
to their projects, and by misrepresenting the cause and
progress of the affray, had the address to prevail upon Sir
Sampson Wright to take up a few poor men who were
found in an adjacent public house, and who were carried,
by the help of a party of troops from the Savoy, to Covent-
Garden watch-house.

These men were brought up to the Public Office, in

Bow-street, yesterday morning, where, upon a full investigation of all circumstances, they were discharged without bail. The Magistrate, with every laudable indignation, reprobated the conduct of the gang that rushed from Wood's upon innocent and unoffending passengers, and in very pointed terms reprimanded Mr. Wood himself, for the indecent behaviour of those who frequented his house, and who in so wanton and audacious a manner violated the peace of the public, and the tranquillity of a neighbourhood but too long disturbed and disarranged by similar practices.

Parker's General Advertiser
3 May 1784

MAY

THIS long wished for, inspiring, cheerful, merry, piping, dancing, promising month is now arrived. The commencement of it was rather cloudy, but we are happy in the reflection, that we live under the direction of Providence who will not fail to bless us with as much sunshine as is equal to our necessities and adequate to our deserts. We ought therefore to banish the despondency of despair for the brilliancy of hope, and to picture the season in those propitious colours with which it has been usually described. We may now anticipate all the pleasures of Summer, and luxuries of Autumn, that we may hereafter expect to *enjoy*. Now blooms the garland, now swells the tabor, and now sports the dance; the ruddy milk-maids with rustic gaiety trip in the mazy round, while healthful swains join in the happy throng. Even the sable knights of the sooty order now

"Flaunt in rags, and flutter in a gilt parade."

The flowers now begin to put on their brightest hues and tints, the trees begin to bud apace, and the meadows daily assume superior verdure. May is the mother of love, the

101

herald of hope, the nurse of poetry, and the cherisher of mirth. In this month the amorous are pleased, the afflicted revived, the fanciful inspired, and the gay delighted. Nature now speaks her annual prologue to her most splendid and beautiful exhibitions: Let us then take a lesson from the feathered choristers, adopt their harmony, and cultivate their happiness. Let the trifling feuds of party give way to the consideration of general peace, and a disposition to enjoy the social blessings of approaching Summer universally prevail. So shall the rural walk be replete with satisfaction, the pleasing cyder alleviate our thirst in the day, and the brisk ale enliven our spirits and promote our gentle sleep in the evening.

Whitehall Evening Post
1–4 May 1784

London, May 4.
Friday night an alarming riot happened at a house of ill-fame in White-Hart-Yard, Drury-lane. The circumstances which gave rise to it are as follow: Some few weeks since, a girl of creditable parents in Westminster, about 12 or 13 years of age, having eloped from her friends, was unsuccessfully advertised in several of the public prints. Her uncle coming through the piazza that night, was accosted by his niece in a manner that too plainly shewed her early initiation into vice and infamy. He secured her, and insisted on her informing him where she lived, when taking him to the above house, he reprobated the conduct of the old *gouvernante*, then shewed his indignation by destroying glasses, china, &c. some of which he threw into the street. A mob gathered, and being informed of the particulars, proceeded to demolish the house; the windows and casements were entirely broken, and the street-door forced open and also destroyed, as likewise a part of the furniture; nor was it till an intimation that the guards were coming they could be prevailed on to desist. The *mother*

abbess and her *nuns* escaped by a back door from the fury of the enraged populace.

Ipswich Journal
8 May 1784

A letter from Montgomery says, that one Evan Evans, a little Farmer, who lived within a Mile of that Town, being suddenly seized with a Fit of Lunacy, killed his Wife and two Children, and immediately threw himself into a Pond and was drowned. He had another Son, who was at work in the Fields, by which he saved his Life.

Adams's Weekly Courant, Chester
4 May 1784

Saturday night as Mr. Carpenter was conducting a man committed by Peter Greene, Esq. for an assault, from Radcliff, the prisoner became extremely outrageous; and by an amazing exertion of strength, twisted the handcuffs he had on in such a manner as the oldest gaol-keeper had never been witness to. When he came to New Prison, he fought desperately with the turnkeys; but being at length overpowered, he was heavily fettered, and confined in the black hole.

Public Advertiser
4 May 1784

Extract of a letter from Ayton (Berwickshire), April 26
"On Thursday the 15th inst. there was found a balloon upon the farm of Paul Darling, Esq. about two miles from this place. It was perceived by two country-boys floating in the air, who, upon its coming to the ground, ventured to approach it; and foolishly conceiving it to be a whale's bladder, they got it upon their cart, to bring it home. A

woman whom they met, perceiving it to be made of silk, and supposing it might be cleaned by boiling, persuaded them to give it to her, and enjoined them secrecy; but, within these two or three days, the matter has been discovered. Had it fallen into the hands of any sensible person, they might perhaps have made a discovery from whence it came, and the time it had taken to perform its voyage."

Whitehall Evening Post
1–4 May 1784

Mr. Mesmer, who some time ago thought to cure all disorders by magnetism, has got a hundred scholars, or a hundred initié's as he calls them, at one hundred guineas each, to whom he is to reveal his stupendous secrets.

Morning Chronicle and London Advertiser
5 May 1784

A letter from Tiverton says, that twelve or fourteen of the convicts that escaped from on board the Grand Duke of Tuscany, have been seen about those parts, and plundered several houses in the villages of provisions and money; they are a desperate set of thieves, and have terrified the country people wherever they go.

Bath Chronicle
6 May 1784

On Friday last an air-balloon, with a painted fox suspended at the end of it, was launched into the atmosphere from the garden of John Milnes, Esq. of Wakefield. It continued in sight twenty-five-minutes, and at first took a south-east direction, but altering its course, fell two miles south of Melton Mowbray, in the county of Leicester, and eight miles north of Oakham, in the county of Rutland. The balloon was launched at six minutes after twelve o'clock, and was taken up at forty-five minutes after two.

Whitehall Evening Post
4–6 May 1784

A foreigner (not the Duc de Chartres) asked an Englishman, with great concern, "How do you avoid ruin, when your Ministers are so often changed, and men of seeming experience succeeded by those who can have none?" The Englishman answered, "Mr. Pelham has often regretted to me the *great* incomes enjoyed by *great* officers; for that the business of the nation was done by clerks in office, with salaries of fifty or a hundred a year; as the business of the church is done, not by Bishops and Deans, who have thousands, but by curates, with twenty or thirty pounds per annum."

General Evening Post
4–6 May 1784

Extract of a letter from Deal, May 1
"A desperate contest took place on Friday evening last, between Capt. Bray, of one of his Majesty's cutters stationed here to watch the smugglers, and the noted Brown, who committed so many depredations during the late war, and had been outlawed. He being a native of Deal, there was not one who would be bold enough to attempt to apprehend him. Since the war he had carried on the practice of smuggling, and on Friday morning last he sailed out of Dunkirk with a cargo of contraband goods. Captain Bray had watched him very narrowly, and about ten o'clock on Friday evening a terrible firing was heard in the Downs, which was occasioned by an attack made by Capt. Bray in a row-boat on Brown, who was also in a row-boat. Captain Bray boarded him; and though Brown presented a blunderbuss, both of them not being half a

yard distance from each other, the Captain was not daunted. One of his men seeing his brave master in this situation, with a cutlass cut Brown's cheek clean off. Bray seconded the stroke, and with his cutlass nearly severed his head from his body, and put a period to this pirate's life. Bray lost one man, and had one wounded. Brown had, with himself, three killed, two wounded, and two taken prisoners. Too much praise cannot be given to Captain Bray for his spirited behaviour, not only in this but every other occasion in his Majesty's service; and, were another cutter or two stationed in the Downs, commanded by officers as spirited as himself, there is no doubt but the swarm of smugglers at Deal would be soon extirpated. It is a national reflection, that the inhabitants of Deal, instead of preventing this illicit practice, give every encouragement to it. Another party of dragoons would effectually stop it."

Whitehall Evening Post
4–6 May 1784

The Rev. Dr. Wilson has left eighteen thousand pounds to eighteen young women; a most noble bequest, and highly worthy of the great and generous character who made it.

An elderly and wealthy widow lady, an acquaintance of the Doctor's, who knew of his intention respecting the above legacy, took occasion when on a visit to the Doctor, to observe that he might as well make his number *twenty*, and include her two nieces; upon which the Reverend old Gentleman replied, "I do not intend to leave any thing to young women who *have rich aunts*."

Gazeteer and New Daily Advertiser
8 May 1784

[Thomas Wilson DD (d. 1784) was Prebendary of Westminster and Rector of St Margaret's. His body was brought from Bath to London "in grand funeral procession. There were near 200 flambeaux in the cavalcade, a long train of mourning and other carriages. The ornaments were remarkably elegant and striking" (*Gentleman's Magazine*, vol. 1, 1784, p. 379).

On the 23rd ult. was found dead in his house at Froome, William Thatcher, an old man, who for many years past subsisted on the charitable benefactions of his neighbours.—His success in the begging trade has been considerable, as may be perceived by the following inventory of property found in his house at his death: 22 l. in silver, 2 guineas in gold, 5 l. in copper, 12 old hats, 14 pair of shoes, 14 pair of stockings, 35 cakes, two bushels of morsels of bread, cheese, flesh, &c. &c.—The above has not been long accumulating; for about two years since his house was robbed of the valuables it then contained, which were much more considerable than the above.

Norfolk Chronicle or Norwich Gazette
8 May 1784

A late celebrated Lecturer is now confined in Newgate for Debt; where he is putting in Practice, either from Choice or Necessity, that Plan of simple Diet, by which, according to his own Hypothesis, he is to live to extreme Age.

Public Advertiser
10 May 1784

London. May 11. After the close of the Poll Yesterday for Westminster, an Affray happened at Covent Garden.—It seems there had been summoned an extraordinary Number of Constables, to keep the Peace. At Three o'Clock all was quiet; but in half an Hour afterwards, when the Business of the Day was finished, a violent Conflict took Place between the Constables and the Mob; the former of which were driven out of the Garden down King-street. At Four o'Clock Justice Wilmot brought up a

Detachment of the Guards, who, after twice or thrice parading from Wood's Hotel to the Corner of Henrietta-street (headed by a few Constables) seized on the Butchers who attended with Marrow-bones and Cleavers, &c. and conducted them to Hood and Wray's Committee Room. Several of the Peace Officers, and many of the Populace, were much bruised and wounded. The Guards were attending late last Night.

Covent Garden, King-street, James-street, and all that Neighbourhood, Yesterday from Three in the Afternoon to Nine at Night, exhibited a Scene of Riot, shocking to describe, totally in Defiance of all Law and the Police of a great City. The Inhabitants, since the Commencement of the Poll, have been deprived of pursuing Occupations, being daily obliged to shut up their Shops, on Account of the desperate Gangs of Sailors, Chairmen, &c. who are constantly committing Outrages in that Quarter.

Last Night at Half past Ten, fifteen of the Covent-Garden Rioters were carried to Newgate, under a strong Detachment of the Guards.

We hear 1500 l. in Bail was offered for one of the above Persons, but refused by the Magistrates.

Jackson's Oxford Journal
15 May 1784

Saturday afternoon as the two sons of Mr. Lawley, maltster at Edmonton, were fishing in the New River, near Bowers' Farm, they were joined by two men, who, after some conversation, with horrid imprecations demanded their money, upon which the younger ran away, but they seized his brother (who is about 13 years old) and robbed him of his hat, silver shoe-buckles, a shilling and some halfpence.

General Evening Post
8–11 May 1784

AFRICAN CUCUMBER

J. RATCHFORD, Gardener, in MANCHESTER, respectfully acquaints his friends, and the public in general, that
he has collected from Africa, a quantity of African
Cucumber-seed, of the best and earliest kind ever seen in
this kingdom. This Cucumber is much pickled; of a fine
green colour, covered with a white powder, has a long
stalk to the fruit, bears much earlier and more plentifully
than any other sort whatever.

To be had of Messrs. Hewett and Smith, Nursery and
Seedsmen, at Brompton, near London; of Adam Robson,
No. 39 Holborn-hill; of Messrs. Grimwood and Hudson,
Seedsmen, the corner of Aslington-street, Piccadilly,
London; of Mr. Collier, Seedsman, at Liverpool; of
Messrs. McNivens, Nursery and Seedsmen, at Manchester;
of J. Ratchford, Manchester; and no where else, in papers
of five shillings each, containing 25 seeds.

N.B. To prevent mistakes, each paper will be sealed
with the cypher of J.R. and named Ratchfords Superb
Royal Cucumber.

General Evening Post
8–11 May 1784

The Paragraph that appeared in our Paper on Monday last,
of a certain Lecturer being confined in Newgate for Debt,
is erroneous and without Foundation.

Public Advertiser
14 May 1784

The King and Queen, on their entrance into Covent-
garden Theatre last night, received from the people the
same unbounded acclamations which have particularly
accompanied him since he complied with the late earnest

wishes of the community, and annihilated that monster of iniquity, the Coalition.

Whitehall Evening Post
13–15 May 1784
[George III had been forced to accept Fox and North as his ministers. The ministry had been called "The Unnatural Coalition" because Fox and North had been bitter opponents. The alliance shocked public opinion and the King was thus able to take the first opportunity that offered to dismiss them.]

Mrs. Siddons' engagement at the Dublin theatre is on the most prodigious terms perhaps ever granted to any Player: a thousand guineas for twenty-two nights. This Daly the manager has actually advertised, and we think from the extreme liberality of his adventure, he deserves all possible encouragement.

Besides this Mrs. Siddons takes Edinburgh in her way to Ireland. At Edinburgh she is to play eleven nights, and the twelfth for her own benefit. Her terms there were to have been twenty guineas the night, and the charges of the house, which are thirty-five pounds, being remitted, and distributed on the rest of her engagement made her remuneration on average 24 l. per night. These terms are, however changed, and she now is engaged to divide half and half of the profits with Mr. Jackson the manager, after deducting forty pounds for the nightly charges.

London Chronicle
13–15 May 1784

Thursday afternoon a flock of fine sheep took fright in St. John's street Road, and crossing the field between that and the road from Goswell-street, leaped almost at the same moment over the wall into the New River, but in about an hour they were taken, though with much trouble and difficulty, safe out of the water. Their fleeces being filled with red oker, the stream quite to Sadler's Wells was coloured a deep red, as well as a great part of the reservoir below; a circumstance that greatly excited the surprize of the passengers, some of whom, without enquiring into the cause, went away under a firm persuasion, that the sanguinary aspect of the water was a phaenomenon portending some great calamity to the country.

Morning Chronicle and London Advertiser
15 May 1784

Last Week many of the Inhabitants of Bristol were thrown into the greatest Consternation, by a Fellow's preaching the general Dissolution of the World, and all worldly Things, on a certain Day, now past.—The Magistrates committed him to Bridewell.

Adams's Weekly Courant, Chester
17 May 1784

Nicholas Casson, who was killed last Monday in Covent-Garden was for many years one of those persons called crimps, whose business it is to decoy men and procure soldiers for the East-Indies, in which employment he had amassed enough to retire upon. His wife deals in smuggled gin.

Gazeteer and New Daily Advertiser
17 May 1784

The burial of the *crimp* was really farcical; and it was perhaps the first time that a pantomime was made of a murther. When the cavalcade returned from the church they stopped at Wood's Hotel; and the mourners drank brandy, wine, and gin, until they were intoxicated to beastliness.

18 May 1784
[Casson is elsewhere described as a peace officer.]

111

Maxims: Men fear to die, and so do Children to go to-bed; they are both afraid of the Dark.

Adams's Weekly Courant, Chester
18 May 1784

Thursday afternoon, as a man was passing through Half Moon Passage, in Aldersgate-street, the sewing of a sack that he was carrying on his shoulders gave way, and out fell several pieces of copper, which evidently appeared to be part of the skeleton-sheets from which the blanks for counterfeit halfpence had been cut. A woman collared the fellow, and a number of people assembled; but while they were disputing, as to whether they should be justifiable in detaining him, he took the opportunity of making off, unobserved, with the copper.

London Chronicle
15–18 May 1784

WANTED, a Gardener's Place, a Person who has served more in the Fruit, Flower, Framing, and Kitchen Garden Way than in Botany and Exotic Way, never delighted in that, would be glad to serve a good-natured, civil Family, as he always endeavours to behave himself, and always retained the Character of a sober, honest Servant, and a good Gardener; and can have a good Character from his last Place, where he lived upwards of six Years.

Any Lady or Gentleman this may suit will be pleased to direct to A.B. at Mr. William Jackson's, at Brompton, near London, Middlesex. No one need apply that don't employ at least two or three Men or more, besides the gardener; matters not what Part of the Country or Kingdom.

Public Advertiser
18 May 1784

London May 17. This day at three o'clock the poll for Westminster was finally closed, when the numbers were,

For Lord Hood   6692
Mr. Fox   6233
Sir Cecil Wray 5998

Majority for Mr. Fox over Sir Cecil Wray 235.

Whereupon Lord Hood and Mr. Fox were declared duly elected; and the successful candidates were chaired with the usual forms.

At a quarter past four Mr. Fox was carried through Russell-street, down Catherine-street, and along the Strand, through the principal streets of the city and liberties of Westminster, attended by an immense concourse of people on horseback and afoot, carrying wands in their hands, and wearing laurel in their hats, and followed by a vast crowd. The throng was so great that the shops in the front streets were shut.

Shrewsbury Chronicle
22 May 1784

Mr. Fox was chaired, preceded by about 100 gentlemen on horseback, dressed in blue and buff, a band of music, and the marrow-bones and cleavers, and followed by the Duchesses of Devonshire and Portland, in their carriages, who were attended by a number of gentlemen on horseback, and a great number of servants.

Whitehall Evening Post
15–18 May 1784

Two gentlemen walking towards Islington on Monday evening, upon seeing a vast crowd of carriages and people, [one] asked the other where all those folks were going? going! to the devil and dogs as fast as they can.

Morning Chronicle and London Advertiser
19 May 1784

113

A short account of the Public Breakfast given by the Prince of Wales, in the Gardens of Carleton House last Tuesday.

About six hundred of the most distinguished persons in the kingdom assembled in his beautiful gardens about two o'clock. The preparations on the occasion were full of taste and magnificence. Covers were laid under nine extensive marquees for 250 persons, and the entertainment consisted of the finest fruits of the season, confectionaries, ices, creams, and emblematical designs, ornamented with mottos and other devices in honour of the triumph which they were to celebrate. Four bands of instruments were placed at different parts of the garden, and the company were entertained with various novelties of a comic kind.

After they had taken refreshments they rose to dance. A beautiful level in the umbrage of a groupe of trees was the spot which his Royal Highness selected for their ball, and he led down the country dances, first with the Duchess of Devonshire, and afterwards with one of the Lady Waldegraves. The company frequently changed their partners, and at times grouped off into cotillons. The Duchess of Portland danced with Mr. Greville, Lady Jersey with Lord Carlisle, Lady Ann Pawlett with Lord Berner, Lady Duncannon with Sir Peter Burrel, Miss Keppel with Mr. St. John, Lady Beauchamp with Lord Berkely, Mrs. Anderson with Mr. Fitzroy, Mrs. Meynell with Mr. Wyndham, Miss Ingram with Sir Harry Featherstonhaugh. Miss Townshend, Lady Augusta Campbell, Lady Derby, the Miss Keppels, the Miss Norths, Mrs. Crewe, Mrs. Sheridan, and many other ladies danced; and we do not believe that a more superb exhibition of beauty was ever seen. The gentlemen were in blue and buff. The ladies in morning dresses, fancied in all the varieties of cultivated taste. The Duchess of Devonshire was in slight mourning; Lady Beauchamp in an elegant white crape, spangled with silver; Mrs Anderson in a Venetian habit; the elder Mrs. Meynell was most elegantly dressed in a white fancy habit.

The political party, Lord North, Mr. Fox, Col. North, Col. Fitzpatrick, Mr. Byng, and others, retired under

114

another groupe of trees to talk of the politics of the day; and the dowager ladies and gentlemen occupied themselves in the admiration of the graces which the scene afforded. During the height of the Fete his Majesty passed the garden in procession to the House of Peers to open the new Parliament, and the band of violins was for the time accompanied by the state trumpets.

The breakfast ended about six in the evening, when the Ladies retired to dress, only for a renewal of their pleasure at the Select Ball, which Mrs. Crewe gave last night in honour of the same event. But the whole of this *al fresco* festival was so delightfully conducted, the spectacle on the green was so grand and beautiful, and the entertainment so truly novel and rich, and the company were so uncommonly gratified, that his Royal Highness, with his usual magnificence, invited them to a repetition of the *déjeune* on Tuesday next. A select party of thirty gentlemen afterwards dined with the Prince.

Whitehall Evening Post
18–20 May 1784

MRS. CREWE'S BALL

Mrs. Crewe's ball on Tuesday night, in honour of Mr. Fox's victory, was the most pleaant and jovial ever given in the circle of high life, and united all the charms of elegant ease and conviviality. The company was select though numerous, and assembled about ten o'clock in blue and buff uniforms; the dancing began about eleven, and at half after the Prince's quadrille arrived, consisting of his Royal Highness, the Duchess of Devonshire, Lady Duncannon, Lady Bamfield, Miss Keppel, Mr. Stepney, Mr. Greville, &c, who, all dressed in uniforms, sashes and feathers, danced the most elegant figure dance that could be formed; the Prince then danced minuets with the Duchess of Devonshire, Lady Bamfield, &c. and then followed country dances, led by the Prince and the Duchess, till half after two, when the company descended to a truly elegant and comfortable supper, which was soon dispatched, when, at the unanimous request of the Ladies, Capt. Morris was placed in the chair, and a general call ensued for the Baby and Nurse; he sung it in his very best stile, and the fair circle chorused with the most heart-felt spirit. The Ladies then drank his health, and cheered him three times with true festive glee; upon which Capt. M. after thanking the fair company for the honour of their charming approbation, gave as a toast, *Buff and Blue, and Mrs. Crewe*, which Mrs. Crewe very smartly returned in a glass, with *Buff and Blue, and all of you*. The toasts being drank, a party in another supper-room, consisting of Lord North, the Duchess of Portland, Lady Jersey, and others, sent a deputation to Capt. M. requesting him to come into their room; upon which he went and gave that company the *Baby and the Nurse*; he then came back to the great room in a crash of applause from the Ladies fair hands, and resumed the chair; the company from the other room soon followed, and he entertained them with a continual succession of the wittiest and finest compositions that ever were penned, and sung them with a spirit that made every fair eye in the room dance with delight. Never was an evening spent with so much true pleasure and comfort, and every tongue in the room was unanimous in their expressions of satisfaction and admiration.—At four the company returned to dance, and a wit in the room said, Capt. Morris had set the Ladies spirits into such a motion, that he supposed they would be *Morris-dancing* till dinner time. There were present, among others, the Prince of Wales, Duke of Devonshire, Earl Fitzwilliam, Earl of Jersey, Earl of Carlisle, Earl Cholmondely, Earl of Derby, Lord North, Lord Euston, Lord Beauchamp, Lord Melbourne, &c. &c.

Whitehall Evening Post
18–20 May 1784
[Buff and blue, Fox's colours, were the colours of Washington's uniform. Fox had defiantly worn them in the House of Commons throughout the American war.]

Extract of a letter from Derby, May 20

"The moment Mr. Fox's victory was announced (about 8 o'clock yesterday morning) the principal inhabitants of this town assembled at Mr. Symond's, the Greyhound, in the Market Place, by repeated huzzas; the bells in the five churches were immediately ordered to be rung, and have continued ringing ever since without the least intermission. In the evening an elegant supper was given at the same house, to a select party of gentlemen, and this day a grand dinner was given at the George Inn, at which almost all the principal inhabitants were present. Mr. Fox's health was drank with two hundred and thirty-six cheers, (his majority upon the poll;) and the evening concluded with every possible demonstration of joy, illumination, bonfires, fireworks, &c. &c. &c."

Morning Herald and Daily Advertiser
26 May 1784

Yesternight, between nine and ten o'clock, as Mr. Scantlebury of Coleman-street was returning to town on horseback, he was stopped at Bull's Pond by two footpads, who with horrid imprecations demanded his money; but while Mr. Scantlebury had his hand in his pocket, some drovers with sheep for Smithfield came within hearing, upon which the villains made off.

Public Advertiser
22 May 1784

EPSOM RACES

The multitude which attended the course on Thursday, poured in literally after the manner of the Jewish calculation, by thousands and tens of thousands.

The Olympic games of Greece, nor the sports of the Roman Emperors, could not boast greater numbers.

If we may judge of the wealth of the country from the

117

appearance of the people, however they may cry out in private, they are still able to contribute liberally towards the necessities of the state.

The number of carriages and horsemen were astonishing; of the former there was every denomination, from the elevated phaeton to the humble buggy.

It is remarkable that no serious accidents occurred; a few *hair-breadth 'scapes* there certainly were, owing to some *gigs* that run against each other, and overturned the *drivers*.

Among the lesser casualties were the following:

> Several lost their senses – by drinking.
> Several lost their money – by play.
> Several lost their hearts – by ogling.
> And several lost themselves – in various ways.

Whitehall Evening Post
20–22 May 1784

Wednesday a Son of Mr. William Dalton, Grocer, at St. Edmund's Bury, who had just come from Boarding-school, took up a Fowling-piece, and in Play pointed it at his elder Brother, not knowing it to be loaded, when it unfortunately went off, and killed him on the Spot. The Youth who by this unlucky Accident lost his Life, was about 18, and was in a few Weeks to have gone to College, being intended for the Church.

Public Advertiser
24 May 1784

London.
A well-dressed man yesterday had the insolence to snatch at a diamond pin that a lady, who was looking at the procession in Cockspur-street, wore in her hair; but failing in his intent, was seized by some gentlemen's servants, who found two watches and 13 handkerchiefs upon him, which were delivered to a Peace Officer. The mob carried

off the culprit to the horse-pond in the King's Mews, where he was severely ducked and suffered to escape.

Jopson's Coventry Mercury
24 May 1784

On Monday last a well-dressed woman came to a mantua-maker's in Great Warner-street Cold-Bath-fields, in order for her to make her a gown, which she wished to have done on the Wednesday following; – she accordingly came on the day appointed, but the gown not being then finished, she promised to call for it next day, and begged to leave a bundle, tied up in a handkerchief, till her return, which was granted; – in the stranger's absence, curiosity led the mantua-maker to open the bundle, where she found six pair of white sattin women's shoes, worked in gold, with the names of different ladies on the inside, which were defaced by scraping a pen over them; – when the woman returned, the mantua-maker sent for a constable, and carried her before Justice Blackborough, where she confessed they were stolen at the late fire in Holborn, and belonged to Mr. Davis, where the fire began: she was committed to gaol for trial.

London Chronicle
22–25 May 1784
[A mantua was a woman's loose outer gown.]

Saturday a great cricket-match was played near Whiteconduit-house, by the Cricket club of Noblemen and Gentlemen at Willis's. The Prince of Wales and a great number of Nobility and foreigners of distinction were present. Lord Winchelsea the best bat, Col. Tarleton the best bowler.

General Evening Post
22–25 May 1784

Thursday an Officer belonging to the Culloden Man of War, passing by Hanging Wood, near Woolwich, observed a Fellow dressed in the Artillery Uniform, and suspecting him to have done some bad Design, asked him, what he did there? The Fellow giving a sulky Answer, a Scuffle ensued between them, which continued for some Time; at last the Officer being undermost, another Fellow in the same Dress came out of the Wood, and, holding a Cutlass to his Throat, bid him stir again at his Peril; but the first Fellow saying, "D——n him, don't hurt him; he's a good Fellow;" they robbed him of 30 Guineas, and made off.

Public Advertiser
26 May 1784

Last Sunday one of the Western-stages, in going out of town, was attacked by a single highwayman near Gunnersbury-lane, who after breaking the windows of the coach, demanded the passengers money. The guard at that time was asleep, but being awoke gently by the coachman, he asked the highwayman what he wanted, who replied nothing; d——n you, then, said the guard, but you shall have something, and immediately discharged his blunderbuss at him, the contents of which entered his body, and killed him on the spot. He was conveyed to Bow-street, for the Coroner's inquest to sit over him, who brought in their verdict *self-defence*; the guard was acquitted.

Morning Chronicle and London Advertiser
26 May 1784

London, May 27.
The thunder and lightning on Tuesday night were truly awful: so many astonishing loud claps of thunder in so short a space of time have not been frequent in this climate, nor have such broad sheets of fire been often here seen to descend from the elements in such rapid succession. Thunder and lightning have a wonderful effect

120

in clearing fruit-trees, and indeed all kinds of vegetables, from the insects fatal to them at this season.

Two cows belonging to Mr. Parker, milkman, in St. John's square, were killed by lightning yesterday morning, in the Spa-field, Clerkenwell. The entrails of one of these animals were spread in innumerable fragments over a space of perhaps not less than 500 yards in circumference.

Jopson's Coventry Mercury
31 May 1784

JUBILEE

Yesterday morning about nine o'clock, the carriages began to move towards the east, the west, the north and the south doors of Westminster Abbey, and before one o'clock, by the puffs and paragraphs, the novelty of the entertainment, and the private workings of the directors, near FIVE THOUSAND pleasure hunting people of all descriptions, and from all parts of the kingdom were assembled, some dressed, some undressed, some noble, some ignoble, some vulgar, some fashionable, some unfashionable, a small number that understood music, and a great number that could not even distinguish between a quick and a slow movement, and to whose ears the sacred songs of the blind fiddling chaunter in St. Paul's church yard would have been equally delightful, as the full band and chorus in the Abbey.

On so hot a day, and at such a season of the year, no persons who regarded the health of their fellow creatures would have planned so palpably destructive a scheme to the lives of individuals; and the truth of this observation will be verified in the event of yesterday. Above one hundred persons overcome by the *calcuttean* heat which naturally arose from the effluvia of so many close packed bodies, fainted away, and were with the greatest difficulty and the most imminent danger carried out. Some recovered by being brought into the air, and others were taken home with very little hopes of recovery. The idea of the *black hole* in India can only convey to the public what the visitors to this lucrative jubilee, suffered.

By the time that the place was nearly full, the rosy cheeks of many a beautiful woman displayed a channel on the natural skin, down which the warm moisture run in such plenteous streams as caused visible distinction between the real and artificial colour of the face. The roots of the hair became from the same cause unpowdered, nor could even the strong perfume of Olympian dew or Lavender water, prevent the vapour from overcoming every delicate constitution in the Abbey. Even the gentlemen in the Orchestra felt it, and one of them was so much affected, (Mr. *Claget*) that he was taken out, and carried home quite senseless. Two young ladies from Buckinghamshire, who came to town on purpose to be present at this Jubilee, and who were hitherto accustomed to the sweet air of the country, are likely to forfeit their lives. One of them in particular has totally lost her senses, and the other is in a most dangerous fever. There certainly has never been in this country a meeting from which so much injury to the health has and will arise, and which in future must bring down so many curses on its authors from parents for the loss of children, and from children for the loss of parents. It seems to be a too great fondness for the immediate profits that induced the Directors not to defer this entertainment to winter, when it might have been performed without endangering the lives of so many people. We may therefore with the more justice state this matter in the manner we have done to the public, and warn them how they croud to such places at so very hot a season as this is.

Westminster Abbey, from the nature of its situation in a hollow, from the numerous bodies that are interred both within the aisle, and round the building, and from its continued damp beneath, must cause the most unwholesome air that can be breathed. Many hitherto have been the fatal colds caught by only sauntering there to view the tombs. What then must be the effects arising to an assemblage suffocating there for want of air during six or seven hours. Our duty to the public, however highly we may respect the performance, obliges us to speak the truth, and in doing so to be of as much service as we can on such an occasion to the community. Indeed we speak the sense of almost every person present; for the general expression when the concert ended, was: "I would not undergo such another purgatory to hear even Handel himself – and I am sure I feel myself, but ill, very ill paid for what I have suffered."

Parker's General Advertiser and Morning Intelligencer
27 May 1784
[The occasion marked the 25th anniversary of Handel's death.]

Mr. Martin on Tuesday, during the Debate on the Bedfordshire Petition, addressed Lord North by the Title of *the Noble Lord with the Fox at the Head of his Stick*, upon which he was called to Order, when he declared he knew not in what better Manner he could point out the Noble Lord he meant to address, since there were in this Parliament three other Noble Lords with Blue Ribbands, alluding to the Lords Courtown, Mornington, and Ilchester, who wear Sky-blue Ribbands, as Knights of St. Patrick. Lord North, with his wonted good Humour, smiled at this new Instance of Mr. Martin's Familiarity, and assured the Hon. Gentleman, the Figure of the Animal carved at the head of his Stick, was meant to represent a *Pig*.

Whitehall Evening Post
25–27 May 1784

Mr. Fox having had the honour of being elected by the men of Kirkwall, Wick, &c. none of whom probably ever saw him, perhaps never heard of him, till he was nominated a candidate for their suffrages, may now with propriety wear a highland plaid, the livery of his new masters, in grateful return for the honour they have done him; at least while he continues in their service. If a sidewind should unfortunately blow him off their friendly though ragged coast, he can but return to his former practice of abusing the Scots with all his might, and thereby re-ingratiate himself with furious Southern Patriots, who have shamefully driven him upon a lee shore, and compel him to take shelter with the people whom his soul abhorred.

Whitehall Evening Post
27–29 May 1784

[Fox was not allowed to take his seat as MP for Westminster: a scrutiny or re-examination of the *bona fides* of the voters was ordered.]

Friday se'nnight the paymaster of one of the regiments on Dublin duty, received a thousand pounds in bank notes, from the agent, for the use of the regiment; on his return to the barracks at night, he was induced by a female he met on Essex Bridge to retire to her lodgings at the rear of Fleet-street, where he went to bed; but before morning his companion robbed him of all the notes, thirty guineas in cash, and his gold watch, with which she and her confederates escaped; and when the gentleman awoke there was not another human being in the house. This loss had such an effect on him, that it totally deprived him of his reason, and he lies in a very melancholy situation.

Norfolk Chronicle or Norwich Gazette
29 May 1784

Shrewsbury, May 29, 1784.
WHEREAS on Sunday Evening the 16th or Monday Morning the 17th instant some wicked malicious Person did Poison Mr. Ravenhill's DOG, whereby the poor Animal languished Six Days in great Pain, Whoever will

give Information to Mr. Ravenhill of the Person that has been Guilty of this barbarous Act, so that he may be dealt with accordingly to the Law, shall receive a Guinea Reward of him.—A DOG, will upon a just Consideration, be found to be the greatest Emblem of Heroic Virtue, being eminent for these three noble Qualities, Fidelity, Gratitude, and Courage.—There is no Allurement, Blandishment, or Sufferance whatsoever, which can make him Desert his Master, no not Hunger itself, which is the greatest Pain this Creature can suffer, as being by Nature of an Appetite most craving and insatiable. He fawns and expresses all Joy upon the Approach of his Master, he takes all Correction at his Hands with Patience and Submission, he will Accompany him wheresoever he goes, he will Defend him with the Peril of his own Life, and will venture upon any Thing though never so difficult and dangerous, when he is encouraged by one who can protect and reward him. Such then is the Force and Power of Nature, and such too is sufficient to instruct those who are not under the Customs of a vicious Education, and to convince Human kind that Nothing will justify them in committing such Acts of Cruelty, as to torture and kill by Poison, so faithful an Animal as a Dog.

Shrewsbury Chronicle
29 May 1784

Wednesday Edward Maclew, who lives in Sutton-street, Clerkenwell, committed the following act of barbarity: having conceived some displeasure against the woman with whom he cohabits, he seized her by the right arm, which he snapped across his knee in two places. The woman was taken to St. Bartholomew's Hospital, where amputation was at first deemed necessary, but at length a reduction of the fracture was attempted, and with difficulty effected.

Norfolk Chronicle or Norwich Gazette
29 May 1784

On Tuesday morning the following melancholy accident happened at Mr. Grosvenor's at Walthamstow: The greenhouse of the above gentleman having been repeatedly broken open, and a variety of plants stolen thereout; it was determined, in order to find out the offenders, to place a spring gun therein; but, unluckily, an assistant to the gardener, having occasion to go into the green-house, trod upon the wire which communicated with the gun, and was killed upon the spot.

Morning Herald and Daily Advertiser
31 May 1784

A correspondent has communicated the following directions for the recovery of persons seemingly drowned.—In the first place strip them of all their wet cloaths; rub them and lay them in hot blankets before the fire: blow with your breath strongly, or with a pair of bellows into the mouth of the person, holding the nostrils at the same time: afterwards introduce the small end of a lighted tobacco-pipe into the fundament, putting a paper pricked full of holes near the bowl of it, through which you must blow into the bowels. Rub all the body, particularly the backbone, hands and feet, with flannels dipped in warm brandy, mixed with sal ammoniac or spirit of hartshorn: strew the flannel as you use it with a little salt. Bleed, if possible, in the jugular vein: give fourteen or fifteen drops of sal ammoniac in water, as soon as it can be swallowed; afterwards, upon recovery, give a cordial of brandy and water warm. Bathe the temples, and rub the nose with any volatile spirit, such as hartshorn or sal volatile: give a clyster of an infusion of tobacco with salt and oil.

Do not easily be persuaded to give over rubbing, or using means for the recovery of the person: many having been recovered, who have shewn little or no signs of life for a great while, and who have lain under water for a considerable time. Apply stone bottles of hot water to the soles of the feet.

126

When all other things have failed, persons have been recovered who have lain several hours under water, by being lain upon a bed of pot-ashes (or dry salt, if that is not to be had) three inches deep; sprinkle upon the person some more pot-ashes about two inches deep: put a cap upon the head containing a good quantity of the same; fill a stocking likewise, with the pot-ashes, and put it round the throat: lay the blankets of the bed over all, but so contrived as not to hinder the person from breathing. When the person begins to recover give a cordial.

The relief from this last application will be from the urinary passages. The person must lay in the pot-ashes seven or eight hours after recovery. Do not roll the body upon a tub; it can do no good, and may do much harm. Let the head be reclined with the face downwards, to let the water come out of the mouth.

Jopson's Coventry Mercury
31 May 1784

A SINGULAR IMPOSTURE

A portly well-dressed man, lately walking along the Strand, London, suddenly dropped down in an apopleptic fit: and though no less a man than Sir J——n E——t was coming by at the time, and was willing to give every assistance the Materia Medica could afford, it was all in vain; the body was dead beyond the reach of any physician. A corpse in the Strand unmourned, soon drew a crowd; among them came a well-dressed, good looking young gentleman, who was curious to see the dead man. He had no sooner made his way through the mob, so as to get a full view of the corpse, than he was struck with amazement; he remained fixed, his countenance changed – Oh God my poor Uncle! Is he gone? Is he? – "Well" said he with a deep sigh, "so perish all my hopes! I am happy, however, that I luckily passed at this awful moment, to rescue his poor remains, and see them decently interred."

127

Accordingly the sorrowful youth called a coach; and the charitable mob, who pitied the disconsolate nephew, assisted to put the corpse in the coach; where the pious young man soon stripped the body, and desiring to be set down at a famous surgeon's, very conscientiously sold his pretended uncle for two guineas.

Scots Magazine
May 1784

JUNE

Two or three people were drinking one day the last week at the Angel Inn at Spalding in Lincolnshire, when one of the company for a trifling bet offered to carry a red hot poker in his teeth as far as the obelisk in the market-place there and back again. The bet being agreed to, the man took the poker between his teeth and performed it.—The consequence was, the poor man was so affected, that his teeth dropt out, his mouth and his throat were so scorched that he languished till the next day, and expired in great agonies.

Leeds Intelligencer
1 June 1784

At Hurley, in Berkshire is the following curious inscription over the door of the Parish Clerk of that place:—"John Briggs Clerk, Draws all Sorts of Teeth in Human plays the Violin, Shaves and Cuts Hair, Grinds Razors Scissors Penknives, Takes any thing out of Eyes, Measures Land, and cures the Itch out of hand, And many other Articles to Teadious to mention—N.B. Likewise Makes Womens Shoes & Boots & High Shoes & Mens Shoes and Translater 1783."

Leeds Intelligencer
1 June 1784

JEU de MOT.— A certain *Sage of the Law*, whose celebrity arises not from his "tempering the judgment seat with *mercy*," condemned for execution at the last summer assizes on the Western circuit, eighteen out of twenty malefactors whom he tried at one place. On leaving the town next morning, a fine young coach-horse, that he was about to purchase, dropped down dead in his carriage —

129

"Strange accident, indeed," exclaims the Judge pettishly: "Not at all, my Lord," replied the Coachman sulkily: "for I thought how it would befal the poor beast, when I was told that you had *taken him upon TRIAL!*"

Morning Herald and Daily Advertiser
1 June 1784

Such a change in the weather was never before experienced in this country as last week, when from Tuesday night to Thursday, the liquor in the thermometer fell near 20 degrees, or from 77½ to 58.

Morning Chronicle
2 June 1784

It was yesterday reported that C. F. Sheridan, Esq; Secretary for War, lay without hopes of recovery. On Sunday, on his way to the Park for an airing, he happened to be delayed for some little time on the road by a few cars. The person who drove them not making a passage immediately, and giving some reply that was not quite agreeable, provoked Mr. Sheridan so much, as to strike him with his whip, which the carman resented, by throwing a stone that unfortunately fractured Mr. S's skull. This accident is attended with consequences that threaten to be so fatal to the life of a gentleman, not less distinguished for his abilities, than amiable good nature.

Gazeteer and New Daily Advertiser
2 June 1784

[Charles Francis Sheridan (b. 1750) was the brother of Richard Brinsley, statesman and dramatist. In fact he survived until 1806.]

130

Monday a Man, indifferently well dressed, went into the Horseshoe and Magpye in Fetter-lane, and seeing the Mistress, Mrs. Pritchard, reading in the Bar, asked her, if she was fond of Books? Being answered in the Affirmative, he said he had just pawned a large Volume of Josephus for Eighteen pence, and though he did not mind Books himself, it was a Pity it should be lost for such a Trifle, and therefore if she thought it worth redeeming, he would fetch it out for her. The Landlady agreeing to this Proposal, gave him the Money, with three Halfpence, which he said the Interest would come to; but has heard nothing since of Man, Money, or Book.

Public Advertiser
3 June 1784

[Josephus was the author of *The Jewish War* and *Antiquities of the Jews*.]

On the 23rd ult. about half past five in the afternoon, at Spalding, in Lincolnshire, there was the most violent hailstorm known in the memory of man, attended with a continual thunder and lightning, which lasted till past six. The hailstones were large solid pieces of ice of an angular form; great numbers of them were taken up, which weighed half an ounce each, and measured from two to three inches in circumference. Several windows were broke, and the garden glasses were entirely destroyed. Though the day had been excessive hot, the hailstones covered the market-place almost an hour after the storm was over. The storm extended to James Deeping and Lutterworth-Drove, where the stones that fell measured six inches in circumference.

Norfolk Chronicle or Norwich Gazette
2 June 1784

The person who is employed by Mr. Moore in watering the Streets, was on Friday by backing his horse and cart

131

into the Serpentine River, carried too far by the current, and unfortunately drowned.

Gazeteer and New Daily Advertiser
7 June 1784

Dublin, May 27.
The Gang of Robbers, in the County of Kildare, took a very extraordinary Method to drive the Shepherds from the Roads which cross the Currah, that they might with more Ease plunder and ill-treat Travellers.—One of the banditti was dressed up in a most frightful Manner, painted black, dressed with Skins and Stags Horns, to represent the Devil; this had the intended Effect upon all but one, who, in a fearless and undaunted Manner, ventured to approach the mock Satan, when a Dialogue ensued, the Purport of which was, to command the Shepherd to desist from coming on that Road; he, without the least Fear, bid him Defiance, saying, he would walk there; that he cared not for the Devil, nor had the Devil any thing to do with him; the Robber finding threatening in vain, drew out a Pistol and shot the Shepherd's Dog, saying, that he was Satan's Servant, and as he served the Dog he would serve the Master. The Shepherd then, for Self-preservation, made the best of his Way off, and left the Coast clear to the inhuman Gang, no one of the Country daring to come within two Miles of the Place.

Public Advertiser
7 June 1784

So prevalent is the unnatural and disgusting Custom of Painting become among Women, that in polite Circles, after the Exercise of Dancing, *Rouge* is handed about the Room, and the Ladies lay on false Complexions publicly. Such Impostors should be punished like Pirates who fight under false Colours.

Whitehall Evening Post
5–8 June 1784

A few Days since as Mr. Philips, of Reading, was fishing in the Thames, he felt something in his Net unusually heavy, and upon drawing it out, found the Body of a Drummer who had been missing for several Days.

Public Advertiser
9 June 1784

Friday morning a melancholy accident happened to Mr. Vigor, glass-maker, of Bristol, who being on an excursion into the country, stopped at a pond at Twickenham in this county, to water his horse, the beast stumbled going into the pond, threw Mr. Vigor, and falling on him, deprived him of life, tho' immediate assistance was given.

Bath Chronicle
10 June 1784

Such was the amazing practice of the late Dr. Barter, of Market-Lavington, that he for many years consumed after the rate of a quire of paper every day in prescriptions only; his fee was never more than one shilling per time, and to the real poor he charged nothing. Convinced of the great virtue of many public medicines, he rarely failed recommending one or more of them in every prescription he wrote.

Bath Chronicle
10 June 1784

Extract of a letter from Edinburgh, June 4

"Such is the rage for seeing Mrs. Siddons, that hundreds of ladies and gentlemen are waiting at the gallery doors from one o'clock (though the play does not begin till half an hour after six) and the moment the doors are opened (three o'clock) both galleries are filled with ladies and gentlemen. The loss of hats, cloaks, canes, wigs, &c. are reckoned very trivial misfortunes. In short, the public seem to be perfectly *Siddonized*."

General Evening Post
8–10 June 1784

About a couple of months ago, the death of Nehemiah Donnellan, Esq. constable of Carrickfergus, was, through mistake, announced in the Dublin papers, and generally believed. On which Secretary Orde wrote a polite letter to the Earl of Granard, acquainting his Lordship that the death of Mr. Donnellan had given the Duke of Rutland an opportunity to provide for his Lordship's friend Major Doyle, by appointing him constable of Carrickfergus. The Major attended the next levee to return thanks, was congratulated on the occasion by all his friends, and strenuously supported Administration for the remainder of the session with his vote in the House of Commons; but alas, how transitory and fleeting is all sublunary bliss! The constableship, like Juno, was to be possessed in idea only, and a cloud was to fill the Major's arms; for oh! lamentable and sad to tell! One morning last week Nehemiah Donnellan, Esq. in *propria persona*, alive and well, drove into the Castle-yard, to pay his respects to Secretary Orde. "The Devil welcome the stranger," cries the Secretary to his cook, on seeing Donnellan alight.

Parker's General Advertiser and Morning Intelligencer
11 June 1784

London, June 3.
On Sunday se'nnight John and Henry Dunsden, two villains who have long infested the neighbourhood of Burford, and are part of a gang some time since discovered to inhabit a cave in Epping-forest, went to Capp's Lodge, a publick house on the edge of Whichwood-forest, where they sat drinking till four o'clock next morning. Their conversation and behaviour created a suspicion what sort

134

of guests they were, and that they had accomplices lurking about the house. Henry going out, William Harding (the waiter) followed him upon which, with an oath, Henry asked him what he wanted, pulled out a pistol, and bid him keep off. Harding still advancing, the villain fired, and the ball broke his arm. Harding, nevertheless, attempted to seize him, when he fired another pistol, and two balls entered his breast; at that instant one Perkins, who was in the house, came out and kicked up Dunsden's heels, who fell under Harding, and taking up the discharged pistol which Henry had thrown away, he turned upon John Dunsden (who at that moment was presenting a pistol at him) struck him with it on the forehead and he dropped. The landlord then coming up, Hen. Dunsden (who lay upon the ground) drew a third pistol, and discharged it at him: But the landlord having a quantity of Halfpence in the pocket of his apron, it turned the ball, and most likely preserved his life. The villains were then secured; and on Monday committed to Gloucester gaol. Harding is not yet dead but lies dangerously ill of his wounds at Burford. It is supposed the intention of these Dunsdens was to murder the landlord, and rob the house; but it being Holiday time, the company fortunately staid too late for them to put their design into execution.

Cambridge Chronicle and Journal
12 June 1784

Wednesday last, about noon, the side of a house in Water-lane, St. Martin's at Oak, suddenly fell to the ground, by which accident James Lilly, a weaver, who was at work in his loom in a garret, up three pair of stairs, was much bruised, but providentially escaped with life.—His wife and three children who were in the room, received no hurt. There was another loom in the same garret with that which Lilly was at work, which also fell into the street. The man was taken out of the ruins, and though he escaped with his life is so much bruised as to be incapable of doing any business at present; he has been relieved by some well-disposed neighbours, whose favours he has a very grateful sense of.—Further donations will be thankfully received.

Norfolk Chronicle or Norwich Gazette
12 June 1784

On Saturday afternoon the body of a young woman was taken out of the New River, close by Sadler's Wells. A lad had dropped his fishing cane, and getting a rake to draw it up, hitched it in the woman's clothes, and by that means discovered her. The body had apparently lain in the river some days.

Gazeteer and New Daily Advertiser
14 June 1784

Canterbury, June 14.
Yesterday Mr. Charles Mason of Wingham, undertook for a wager of fifty guineas, to walk 48 miles in twelve hours, which he performed with ease in eleven hours and thirty-four minutes.

Parker's General Advertiser and Morning Intelligencer
27 June 1784

Londonderry, June 1.
Some time ago, a gentleman handed to us the following for insertion; we now give it without alteration:—"About ten days ago some thing very remarkable occurred in this city. An eminent Philadelphia Quaker, who had been for some time in Ireland, passed through most of the streets, covered with a habit of sack-cloth, and repeatedly called on the inhabitants, to repent and turn to God. What makes it extraordinary that those who have conversed with the Quaker, have found him a remarkably intelligent person,

of extensive information, and entirely remote from every sympton of insanity. He declares he came from America on purpose to admonish the inhabitants of Londonderry. It is not unworthy of note, that some time before the memorable siege of this city, an eminent Quaker of that day called William Edmundson, visited the town, and passed through the streets nearly in the same manner."

Morning Chronicle
15 June 1784

Friday a youth of nineteen was brought before the Aldermen Halifax, Plomer, Picket, and Pugh, at Guild-hall, and charged with the forgery of an indorsement to a bill of exchange for 23 l. which he paid to Mr. Jacobson in the Poultry for some Irish cloth, and received the change. After an examination of two hours, he was committed for trial. He was also detained for a similar forgery. The genteel appearance of this stripling made a very affecting impression on the minds of the Magistrates, who very much to the credit of their feelings, said, it was a painful task for them to perform; but a crime which struck at the root and heart of trade, required more their duty to the public than any private consideration whatever.

Whitehall Evening Post
12–15 June 1784

On Wednesday a footman to a gentleman in King-street, Cheapside, hanged himself behind the door in the Chamber where he lay, and yesterday the Coroner's Inquest sat on the body, and brought in their verdict Lunacy.

Whitehall Evening Post
12–15 June 1784

A Lesson for Duellists.— Two friends happening to quarrel at a tavern, one of them, a man of a hasty disposition, insisted on the other fighting him the next morning. The challenge was accepted, on condition that they should breakfast together, previous to their going to the field, at the house of the challenged. When the challenger arrived next morning, according to appointment, he found every preparation made for breakfast, and his friend, his wife, and children, all ready to receive him. Their repast being over, and the family withdrawn, without any hint of their fatal purpose having transpired, the challenger asked the other if he was ready to attend? "No, Sir," replied he; "not till we are more upon a par; that amiable woman, and those six innocent children, who just now breakfasted with us, depend solely upon my life for their subsistence; and till you can stake something equal, in my estimation, to the welfare of seven persons, dearer to me than the apple of my eye, I cannot think we are equally matched."—"We are not indeed!" replied the other, giving him his hand, and they became firmer friends than ever.

General Evening Post
12–15 June 1784

ANECDOTES OF MR. PITT

As nothing which relates to this great man can be indifferent to the public, we are happy in laying before our readers the following particulars, the truth of which may be depended on:

Mr. *Pitt* rises about nine, when the weather is clear, but if it should rain, Dr. *Prettyman* advises him to lie in about an hour longer. The first thing he *does* is to eat *no* breakfast, that he may have a better appetite for his dinner. About ten he generally blows his nose and cuts his toe nails, and while he takes the exercise of his *Bidet*, Dr. Prettyman reads to him the different petitions and memorials that have been presented to him. About eleven his valet brings in Mr. *Atkinson* and a *warm shirt*, and they talk over *new scrip*, and other matters of finance. Mr. *Atkinson* has said to his confidental friends round change, that Mr. *Pitt* always speaks to him with great *affability*. At twelve Mr. *Pitt* retires to the water closet, adjoining to which is a small cabinet from whence Mr. J——n confers with him on the *secret instructions* from Buckingham House. After this Mr. *Pitt* takes a long lesson of dancing, and Mr. Gallini says, that if he did not turn in his toes, and hold down his head, he would be a very good dancer. At two Mr. *Wilberforce* comes in, and they both play with Mr. *Pitt's black dog*, whom they are very fond of, because he is like Lord M——e in the face, and barks out of time to the organs that pass in the street. After this Mr. *Pitt* rides. We are credibly informed that he often pats his horse and indeed he is remarkably fond of all *dumb creatures*, both in and out of parliament. At four he goes to sleep.

Mr. Pitt eats very heartily, drinks one bottle of Port, and two when he *speaks*; so that we may hope that Great Britain will long be blest by the superintendence of this virtuous and able young Minister.

Morning Herald and Daily Advertiser
18 June 1784
[Sir George Pretyman (1750–1827), later Bishop of Winchester, Pitt's former tutor at Cambridge, was until 1787 his Private Secretary.]

The following curious advertisement was last week stuck up at Lorton, near Cockermouth.— "To all my loving frins As my wife has for some time past been rather Cowdy and like to get the upper hand of me I am at last firmly rasolved to pock her of some way or other therefore if any of my loving frins want to borrow or buy a Wife they shall be supplied upon the most reasonable teroms — N.B.

They must apply soon or she will be disposed of. ———
———."

Cambridge Chronicle and Journal
19 June 1784

On Monday evening last, as Grime Drane, a lad about eleven years of age, was riding in the road at Wellborn, near Mattishall, his horse took fright at a wagon passing by, and ran furiously against a hedge, which occasioned the lad to fall off, and one of the wheels of the wagon went over him, by which misfortune he had an arm and a thigh broke; he was carried to the Norfolk and Norwich Hospital the next day, and is now in a fair way of recovery.

Norfolk Chronicle or Norwich Gazette
19 June 1784

Monday a well-dressed man took water at Pepper-alley-stairs, and when the boat was near the middle of the river, started up suddenly, and threw himself overboard. The Waterman, with much difficulty got him into the boat again, and endeavoured to row to shore, which the man prevented his doing, by seizing hold of his oar; and, after a struggle of some minutes, flung himself again into the Thames. Two other boats having put off from the stairs, he was, by their assistance, again taken out of the water, and brought by force to land; but could by no arguments be persuaded to own who he was, or to assign any reason for having attempted so rash an action; and seemed, from his behaviour to be still resolved to complete his horrid purpose hereafter.

London Chronicle
17–19 June 1784

A laughable circumstance occurred at the French Ambassador's ball on Monday night.—*Lord Mountmorres* had in vain canvassed the room for a partner. Not one lady of fortune was disengaged. He begged Miss *Vernon* to interfere, and procure him the honor of a lady's hand for the country dance. Miss Vernon said she would exert her interest; and in a few minutes she introduced him to a very elegant young lady, with whom the noble Lord danced for a considerable time; when at one of the side-boards a gentleman came up to him, and said, "Pray, my Lord, do you know the *lady* with whom you are dancing?" "No, (says he) pray who is she?" "Coalitions", replies the gentleman, "will never end; why it is Miss Fox, the niece of Charles, and the sister of Lord Holland." The noble Lord was thunderstruck. If Pitt should see him he was undone. He run up to Miss Vernon, and exclaimed, "In the name of Heaven how could you introduce me to Miss Fox?" The lady drew him aside, and with a significant *hist*, whispered in his ear, "that it was true she was Mr. Fox's niece, but she could not think she had acted improperly in introducing his Lordship to her, for she had *twenty thousand pounds to her fortune!*"

Morning Herald and Daily Advertiser
19 June 1784

The curiosity of the public was yesterday much excited by the exposal of the heads of two lascars at Stepney. It seems that two of those personages, vulgarly called *resurrection men*, were detected by the watchman with them in a sack, and (soon after they were stopped) found means to make their escape. It is presumed, that as the bodies were not taken with them, they were stolen merely with a view to the profits arising from the sale of their beautiful long black hair, which is particularly valuable.

Gazeteer and New Daily Advertiser
21 June 1784

Monday evening about nine o'clock, the Coroner and Jury who sat on the body of William Rowlls, Esq; of Kingston, finished their enquiry into the cause of his death, at the White Hart, at Cranford Bridge, and brought in their verdict *wilful murder* against Richard England. Thus by this fatal catastrophe a worthy young gentleman has been hurried into eternity, to the great and almost insurmountable affliction of his widow and relations; to the county of Surrey the loss of a humane and upright magistrate; to the corporation of Kingston a kind and affectionate member, and to all the world universal good will and esteem.

Gazeteer and New Daily Advertiser
23 June 1784

Saturday se'nnight, Mr. Clarke, of Newcastle, let off an Air-Balloon at Carlisle, in the presence of a great number of spectators, who expressed the highest approbation at the exhibition. It was set up a little before six in the evening, continued fifteen minutes in sight, and was found the same evening at Scaleby, about six miles from Carlisle, and was returned to Mr. Clarke next morning.

A ludicrous circumstance attended the descent of the above balloon: A man and two women, who were at work in a peat moss near the place, a quarrel having happened between the two females, a violent war of words ensued, during which they had repeatedly, mutually, and with all imaginable sincerity, wished that the DEVIL might take each other. In the instant while these ejaculations were still vibrating on the *delicate* ears of these two heroines, the man (who was a neutral power) observed a huge, and to him very uncouth figure cutting the air, and seemingly in full speed towards them. "Yonder he comes!" cried the poor fellow, struck with the most frightful astonishment. The contending females snatched a glance at the approaching prodigy; and forgetting what they had been taught in their early years, that Belzeebub's habitation is below, the whole three made as precipitate a retreat as they were able.

Their story sounded wonderfully in the village; but some of the inhabitants having different conceptions of his *Tartarean* Majesty, went in search of this terrific intruder, and found it to be the balloon above-mentioned.

Parker's General Advertiser and Morning Intelligencer
23 June 1784

Tuesday last arrived at his house in Newent, from Bombay, after an absence of 20 years, Samuel Richardson, esq.

Bath Chronicle
24 June 1784

A duel was fought near Cranfield-bridge between Captain England, and Mr. Rose, the son of the brewer, in which the latter gentleman was unfortunately killed. The duel arose from an old quarrel. Mr. England had won 200 l. from Mr. Rose at play—Mr. Rose suspected that the dice were loaded, and refused to pay. The public must remember the story, for it came into the courts of law. Mr. England still demanded the money whenever he met Mr. Rose, and using severe epithets, they agreed at Ascot races to meet. After discharging a brace of pistols without effect, the seconds interfered, but in vain, and the fourth shot took place in Mr. Rose's side, and he fell. He is since dead.

Cambridge Chronicle and Journal
26 June 1784

Tuesday the men stopped in the possession of two human heads, evidently taken off fresh from the bodies of two lascars, were finally examined before Sir William Plomer and Mr. Alderman Hart, at Guildhall. The subject matter of this hearing is generally important to society. Several gentlemen of the first reputation in the medical line appeared on the part of the prisoners, and avowed the fact to be that of decapitation for the purposes of anatomical practice, but particularly for the fine teeth of the lascars. Odious as it might seem they would not be ashamed to declare that the mode of supplying anatomical lectures were so beneficial to the public at large, that until the Legislature furnished the further means of application, beyond those convicted of murder, it was ridiculous to expect that the faculty would refrain from temptation to needy men, amongst whom were parish clerks and venal sextons. The Magistrates declared their abhorrence to such reasoning – the charge was a shock to decency and good manners, and they insisted on a prosecution; but lo! no person appeared to enter into recognizance, and the prisoners were about to be discharged, when the Deputy of a certain ward declared to be bound over to bring the offenders to justice. Two surgeons then demanded to give bail, which was taken.—The Aldermen said, they should otherwise have committed the prisoners. . . . The Magistrates sat to administer the law as it stood, not to alter or amend it.

Gazeteer and New Daily Advertiser
25 June 1784

After the fatal catastrophe at Cranford Bridge, Mr. England came post to the Golden Cross, and told some of his friends there, "That, by *Jasus*, he had killed a man, and was under the necessity of making *himself scarce*." After which he went to his banker's, and then set off for Dover.

Morning Post
26 June 1784
[The Golden Cross was at Charing Cross, London.]

The unfortunate Mr. Rolle, who fell in a duel on Saturday

144

last, after the death of his mother would have succeeded to an estate of near 7000 l. per ann.

General Evening Post
24–26 June 1784

POINTER

LOST the 7th instant, a Flea-bitten Pointer Dog, with liver-coloured head and ears; has something of the appearance of the original Spanish breed; his ears are rounded part off, and answers to the name of Rumbo.

Whoever will bring him to Mr. Smith, Buffalo's Head, Oxford-street, shall receive Two Guineas; or any person giving information as above, where the said dog is harboured or detained, after three days from this advertisement, shall (on conviction of the parties) receive a reward of Ten Guineas.

General Evening Post
24–26 June 1784

A visitation of locusts has always been dreaded, as they devour the fruits of the earth and endanger famine. When any thing of the kind impends us, it behoves every individual, to communicate what he knows adviseable to be done to destroy the formation of such animalculae, which may, when acquired a proper growth, be hurtful to the vegetable kingdom. At this present time, Queen's-square and its environs are pestered with an insect of the beetle kind, these seem to be of three sorts. One like the field black beetle without wings, another sort with wings, having legs like a chafer and a head like a locust, armed with a perforator and a sucker; which enable them to pierce almost any thing. They bite very sharp, leaving a smarting pain behind and causes the part to swell; there is another sort quite white. Some of these beetles measure an inch and a half in length; when crushed they are found to contain a large quantity of herbaceous matter, or full of black mud, which communicates a strong disagreeable smell. They pester kitchens mostly, though even the tops of the houses swarm with them, at night they sally forth by thousands and smell so exceeding offensive, that I am dubious whether a contagion might not be propagated by them, when the season is very hot; if this is not to be expected, still the detriment they do to the buildings, and the loss the inhabitants sustain by their devouring and spoiling every thing, calls upon every man who knows by what means they are to be destroyed, to communicate it in a public manner. Our correspondent would be glad to be informed whether these beetles are engendered in the earth, or whether the soil about Queen's-square nourishes them by any peculiar quality. Incredible as it may be thought our correspondent asserts that it is true, if a hand-bason full is caught every night in a house, besides the quantity a hedge hog, an insectivorous beast devours, their number seems rather to encrease than decrease.

Morning Chronicle
29 June 1784

Dublin, June 16.
Tuesday night, after the play, at the Theatre-Royal, Smock-alley, as Mr. Ogleby was handing a lady to her sedan chair, he found some person endeavouring to pick his pocket, and on Mr. Ogleby's attempting to seize his hand, he immediately perceived a genteel dressed man making away, whom he and other gentlemen quickly pursued down the play-house alley; the offender, with unusual agility ran along Essex-quay, and returning a second time into lower Exchange-street, was apprehended, after which he underwent a long examination, and turns out to be the noted identical Barrington, of whom so much has been said in the English and Irish newspapers. There were found upon him a gold watch, forty-one guineas, a small silver patch-box, with a Queen Anne's six-pence in

146

its lid. Yesterday he was brought before the Magistrates of the city, who remanded him to Newgate.

Morning Herald and Daily Advertiser
30 June 1784

Dublin, June 20.
It is impossible to imagine the *moving* effects of Mrs. Siddons's acting: on Saturday night last after the play, the following noblemen and gentlemen had their pockets picked coming out of Smock-alley Theatre: Lord Allen of 16 guineas and a half; General Luttrell of 26 guineas and a half; Sir Annesley Steward 14 guineas; and Robert Dillon Esq, a purse containing 12 guineas and a pocket-book with a Bank note of Finlay and Co. for 20 guineas.

Morning Herald and Daily Advertiser
30 June 1784

Barrington the pick-pocket, is taken up in Ireland. His real name is Waldron. He was educated in the blue coat school in Dublin, and his first essay in taking that which was not his own property, was on the pocket of Mr. Tisdale, the then Attorney General's wife, in that kingdom. He was detected, but from want of evidence, was discharged. Mrs. Siddons' overflow there was his object, and the first night it answered. . . . He defied the Magistrates, was quite easy, and put on both the man of fashion, and the lawyer. He desired the Magistrates to commit him at their peril, and hoped that he should be treated like a gentleman.

Parker's General Advertiser and Morning Intelligencer
30 June 1784

Dublin, June 24.
[Barrington] would answer no questions: but said, if any crime could be proved against him, he was ready to abide

147

its issue. No magistrate being at hand to make a legal commitment, a person went off to one of the high sheriffs, informing him of the circumstance, and begging that he would order him into custody; intimating at the same time, that some of the first nobility and gentry in the kingdom were waiting in the Theatre to have the pick-pocket committed, and that they wished for Mr. Sheriff's attendance; but he declined to come. The High Constable having at length arrived, he took Barrington into custody, and lodged him in New Prison. He yesterday underwent a long examination at Guildhall before a Magistrate; but though many people of fashion attended, some from *doubt*, and some from motives of *delicacy*, declined swearing against so *genteel-looking* a robber, and one who had conducted himself in his profession with such wonderful dexterity. He was remanded to Newgate for further examination. This extraordinary offender is about thirty-five years of age, of a very genteel address, and appears to be entirely free from fear or apprehension of his situation. Some years ago he found means to insinuate himself into the first line of company in London and for some time remained undiscovered, until at length his ill stars presented to his eye a remarkable fine snuff-box, of immense value, belonging to Prince Orlov, the then Ambassador from Russia; he was prosecuted for this theft; and for which and other similar offences he received sentence of death, but was afterwards pardoned on condition of serving on board the Justitia hulk at hard labour for three years; from this confinement he made his escape, and returned to the practice of his old trade of plunder with an uncommon degree of success.

The noted Barrington, who was taken on Tuesday night near Smock-alley theatre, and who has long been famed in England for his uncommon dexterity and *slight of hand*, it is said, was at Edinburgh during Mrs. Siddons's performing in that city, where his success in the purlious of the theatre had been very splendid. Encouraged by this circumstance he is said to have followed this celebrated actress, shortly after she set out for Dublin, where he began his career. The *tricks* he has played for these three or four nights past, are said to have been executed in his *best manner*; – few of the gentlemen robbed, having discovered their loss till some hours after.

Morning Post
30 June 1784

Monday morning, about one o'clock, the waiter at the Temple Coffee-house pressing a person to go home, who had stayed after the rest of the company, and insisted on having more liquor, the latter drew a pistol and fired at him, which fortunately missing him, the ball stuck in the wainscot: on seizing him, and searching him, another pistol, loaded with ball, was found upon him.

Morning Herald and Daily Advertiser
30 June 1784

A very imperfect account of a remarkable repartee of Dr. Brown, who was Chaplain to the Bishop of Hereford, having appeared in one of the morning papers, we think it but justice to corrrect, and give it in its genuine state to the public.—
Dr. Brown had long paid his address to a young lady without effect, whose health he always gave; but one day after dinner, being asked for a toast, he gave a Miss Lloyd. The Bishop said "What, Doctor, is become of your favourite, whose health you have so long given?" Ah, my Lord, replied the Doctor, I have been *toasting* her for eight years, without being able to make her *Brown*, and therefore I have given up the point.

Parker's General Advertiser and Morning Intelligencer
30 June 1784

JULY

Some account of George Philipson, Esq. who died lately at Paris

—This person, whose life was strangely checquered with contradictory events, was originally a footman at Northampton, when he got 10,000 l. in the lottery, with which he bought a small estate near that town, and married a woman of tolerable family and great beauty. Philipson was a good-natured easy character; and his wife, who was exceedingly volatile and sprightly, connected herself with some gentlemen in the neighbourhood, and spent so much money, that the new-made gentleman was presently in the high road to ruin. He was advised to sell his estate, and retire somewhere else; which he did; and finding that he had 5000 l. left he allowed his wife 50 l. a-year, and departed himself for France, to reside there some time, to give polish to his manners. At Paris, he was taken in by an Opera-girl, and some sharpers; and in one twelvemonth, fleeced of every shilling. He learned, however, arts of the same kind, enough to come over to England and turn gambler; which he did, with such success, that he was once worth 13,000 l. His wife, now proving a very great burthen to him, from her extravagance and profligate conduct, he retired again to France, to get rid of her, and carried with him 7,000 guineas, with which he purchased a Government annuity for his life; and after that he lived happily and creditably, and let off play entirely. That [he] had peculiar talents, appears from his making himself, in this part of his life, a very great mechanic; he sought deeply into the mathematics, theory, and into the practice part of mechanics; and actually invented several machines, which have a considerable degree of merit.

Morning Herald and Daily Advertiser
1 July 1784

There is no one who is so constant a *follower* of Mrs. Siddons as the noted Mr. *Barrington*. He attended her as closely as Sir Charles Thompson in London—he pursued her to Edinburgh—and he is now with her in Dublin. They always *act* upon the same *theatre*, and they seem like other *strollers* to *play* upon *shares*. She *entertains* the company, and he *takes* the *money* at the door.

> *Morning Herald and Daily Advertiser*
> *1 July 1784*

Yesterday died in Newgate, William Ray, who in April session was convicted of picking the pocket of George Onslow, Esq; of a handkerchief, and sentenced to be transported.

> *London Chronicle*
> *1–3 July 1784*

There seems to be something, in this free country, particularly hard in the case of Capt. McKenzie, who stands charged with the murder of a soldier in Africa. He was taken up, as we are informed, upon hear say information; his private property, consisting of near 17,000 l. in gold dust, seized upon; and he has now suffered a confinement of more than ten months in Newgate, without being brought to trial.

> *General Evening Post*
> *1–3 July 1784*

Thursday evening, about nine o'clock, a gentleman was robbed, in the field behind Montague-house, Bloomsbury, of sixteen guineas and his watch, by a single footpad, who being immediately pursued, in endeavouring to jump over a ditch, pitched in the middle, when he was taken and properly secured.

London Chronicle
1–3 July 1784

[Montague House was on the site of the present British Museum building.]

The celebrated M. Lavater, who has written upon Physiognomy, and pretends to discover every moral qualification from the features, and that vice and virtue are imprinted in legible characters on the human countenance, which require only time and experience to decypher, has lately met with a disagreeable contradiction to his hypothesis, from a beautiful young lady, with whom he was on the brink of marriage, eloping with a young Student at Geneva.

General Evening Post
1–3 July 1784

[Johann Kaspar Lavater (1741–1801), a Swiss divine and poet, is remembered chiefly as the inventor of the so-called science of phrenology.]

On Thursday last was married, at Ormsby, Anthony Floyer, Esq; of Revisby near Lincoln, to Miss Brabins, of Ketsby; a lady possessing those accomplishments that are unavoidably productive of mutual happiness.

Cambridge Chronicle and Journal
3 July 1784

PUBLIC-OFFICE, BOW-STREET, TUESDAY, JUNE 29.
A REWARD

WHEREAS RICHARD ENGLAND stands charged by the Coroner's Inquest with the Wilful Murder of

WILLIAM ROWLLS, Esq; near Cranford-bridge in the county of Middlesex, on Friday the 18th instant. Whoever will apprehend the said Richard England, or give such information to Sir Sampson Wright, at the above office, as shall be the means of apprehending him, shall receive ONE HUNDRED POUNDS reward on his commitment. N.B. The said Richard England is near 50 years old, five feet eight or nine inches high, oval faced, grey eyes, rather small, and sunk in his head, crooked nose, high cheek bones, his teeth black and rotten, except two or three in his upper jaw, supposed to be false teeth; a hole under his jaw-bone by the evil, freckled and pale-faced, stout about the shoulders, falls in in the back, badly made about the knees, large clumsy legs, rather splaw footed, and turns out his toes, brown hair clubbed or queued, lately wore a drab-coloured coat, round hat and boots, is sometimes dressed in blue and black; is by birth an Irishman, which may easily be discovered when he speaks; kept a house in St. Alban's street; lately rode a grey mare about 15 hands high, and is well known on the Turf.

General Evening Post
1–3 July 1784

London, July 3.
Wednesday last as the Prince of Wales was going on a visit on horseback, a few miles from this town, two carriages passing the road together, he rode his horse in between them, by which he was much bruised and narrowly escaped with his life. Yesterday morning his Highness was something better than he had been the preceding day, but toward the evening he went much worse; the pains occasioned by the bruise on his side attacking him very severely. His Highness has been let blood twice.

Gloucester Journal
5 July 1784

The Prince of Wales is declared by his physicians out of danger;—his fever abated on Friday evening, since which time his Royal Highness has been hourly recovering:—his indisposition was occasioned by riding to town from Windsor in clothes which were wet through by a heavy shower of rain.

Morning Herald and Daily Advertiser
5 July 1784

Copy of a curious hand-bill lately picked up at Peterborough—
Advertisement, Wanted, for a sober family, a man of light weight, who fears the Lord, and can drive a pair of horses: He must occasionally wait at table, join in household prayer, look after the horses, and read a chapter in the Bible. He must, God willing, rise at seven in the morning, obey his master and mistress in all lawful commands. If he can dress hair, sing psalms and play at cribbage, the more agreeable.
N.B. He must not be too familiar with the maid servants of the house, lest the flesh should rebel against the spirit, and he should be induced to walk in the thorny paths of the wicked.—Wages, fifteen guineas a year.

Leeds Intelligencer
6 July 1784

The Prince of Wales is considered recovered. His Royal Highness after being much heated with a ride, went into an iced bath, which struck in the heat, and threw it on his bowels; but by the care of his Physicians, he is considered better; he had a very good night on Saturday, and was much better yesterday.

Whitehall Evening Post
3–6 July 1784

Northampton, July 5.
On Whit-Sunday the congregation in the church of Northill in Bedfordshire were troubled with an offensive smell, and supposed it to arise from a corpse interred near to the pulpit; on searching into the real cause, the body of a child was found underneath the pulpit lying on some basses, and the flesh so much devoured by maggots, that the sex was scarcely distinguishable. On Monday the Coroner from Bedford took an inquisition on the body, and the Jury gave in a verdict that the child was murdered and concealed in the church by a person or persons unknown.

Whitehall Evening Post
3–6 July 1784

[Basses are mats or hassocks.]

The celebrated Dr. Benjamin Franklin is in London, and looks remarkably well for one of the age of 85; and appears to be in high spirits.

Bath Chronicle
7 July 1784

Yesterday afternoon two young women, one of them a servant to Mr. Weeks, of the Custom-house, were stopped near Ball's Pond, by a fellow who demanded their money, and actually took off the cloak of one of them; but their cries bringing to their assistance two haymakers, they seized the villain, but, after compelling him to restore the cloak, suffered him to escape, simply thinking that, no constable being present, they should not be justifiable in detaining him.

Whitehall Evening Post
6–8 July 1784

Yesterday at the Old Bailey, the trial of Robert Moote came on, for robbing Mrs. Jefferies of Dover-street, Piccadilly of a diamond pin of the value of 500 l. The circumstances of the robbery were these:– Mrs. Jefferies was going from the ball at St. James's on the evening of the King's birth-day, between twelve and one, escorted by Baron Dillon to her coach. Lord Townshend met her, and had a short conversation, when the prisoner passed between her and her coach, and used several exclamations of "how beautiful! how elegant!" Having parted with Lord Townshend, the Lady was just entering her coach, handed by the Count, when the prisoner made a snatch at the pin, which being well fixed did not easily give way, and though within ten yards of St. James's gate, and surrounded by guards and a vast concourse of the nobility and their servants, the prisoner had the audacity to keep his hold till the hair and every impediment gave way, when he ran off with the jewel, pursued by the Count, who soon secured him, but not till he had dispossessed himself of the booty; an accomplice standing near, who held a handkerchief, into which the prisoner put his hand; and though every attempt was made by a centinel to secure that fellow, he escaped under a coach. After the most fair and favourable evidence had been given on the part of the Crown, the Jury found him guilty.

It being a capital offence, Mrs. Jefferies, with great humanity, in a short but very pathetic speech, addressed the Judges to recommend the prisoner to his Majesty's mercy, and at her request the Jury joined in the recommendation, which the Judges gave the Lady assurance should be properly laid before the King.

There were four or five fellows in company, who attempted to rescue the prisoner out of the hands of the Count, after whom some of Sir Sampson Wright's men are now in pursuit. If such an use can be made of this man now, as to discover his accomplices, so as to put an end to the gang who had adopted this new species of robbery, which was begun in Hanover-square; his life with good

156

policy may be saved, and the Lady's humanity would turn to the benefit of her country.

General Evening Post
6–8 July 1784

Dr. Fisher, some time since a musical appendage to Covent Garden theatre, and whom news-paper report has so often wedded to a Russian Countess of vast property, has more modestly contented himself with the hand of Miss Storache the singer, daughter of the late double bass at the opera, whom he has accompanied to Vienna, where she has a very profitable engagement!

London Chronicle
8–10 July 1784

On Friday last, a convict made his escape from out of Wymondham Bridewell, with his irons on. He was taken in a corn-field, about two miles from the prison, and safely conducted back.

Norfolk Chronicle or Norwich Gazette
10 July 1784

Thursday morning early Mr. Linton, one of the musicians belonging to Covent-Garden and the Haymarket theatres, was attacked somewhere about St. Martin's-lane. A woman, accidentally looking out of a window about one o'clock, saw a gentleman pursuing three fellows up Bedfordsbury, into New-Street, St. Martin's-lane, where Mr. Linton was soon after found, with a wound in his belly, supposed to have been given with a knife. He was bled, and every endeavour used to recover him, notwithstanding which he soon after expired. A piece of watch chain was found in Mr. Linton's hand; from which circumstance it is probable that his watch was taken from him by force, and that his not parting with it easily was the cause of the villains stabbing him. Two persons are already in custody on suspicion of being concerned in this murder.

Cambridge Chronicle and Journal
10 July 1784

[Linton was leader of the second fiddles at Covent Garden.]

Salisbury, July 10.
Tuesday night Joseph Angell, for burglary, James Green for stealing a sheep, and Cornelius Robbins under sentence of transportation, prisoners in the cells of Fisherton gaol, effected their escape; but were, in a few hours after retaken in a field of wheat, at Ford, near Salisbury. It appears that James Green undermined the door of his cell, by working out the bricks with a small nail; and that having released himself, he then undermined a large iron-grated door, and effected a passage into the lobby of the cells, where he found a large fetter called a leg-bolt, with which he wrenched the lock from the staple of Angell's cell, and having released him, they went to work, and made a way through a thick brick wall into the garden of the prison; they now called upon Robbins, and finding he was willing to accompany them, opened his cell, and all three escaped by the hole in the lobby wall through the river into the road. By order of the Justices, Angell and Green were not fettered, but Robbins was; and the clink of his irons, and their being dressed in the gaol uniforms, gave alarm to some people who met them near Stratford, and thereby led to their being retaken.

Bath Chronicle
22 July 1784

Salisbury, July 12.
On Wednesday evening, about eight o'clock, in a dreadful storm of thunder and lightening, a ball of fire fell from a

dark cloud, in a surpentine line, on a wheat rick and a
bean rick belonging to Mr. Hooper, of Pewsey, which set
the straw on fire in an instant: it burnt with great fury, but
by the timely assistance of an engine and a number of
hands, it was prevented from firing the ricks. About ten
o'clock the same evening, another heavy storm arose in a
different quarter, attended with thunder, lightening, rain,
and hail; the hail stones were of an uncommon size, some
as large as eggs, others like large pieces of ice, which broke
the melon and cucumber glasses and sky lights.

Gloucester Journal
19 July 1784

A recent horrid and unprovoked Murder makes it
absolutely necessary (there being no sufficient Police) to go
properly prepared for those infernal Villains who infest
every Street of this Metropolis. As they are easily known
by their lounging beastly Appearance, every Man should
be on his Guard, and not suffer any Fellow at a late Hour
to approach him on any Pretence whatever; and if he does,
(after being spoke to, and desired to walk off) shoot him
dead on the Spot without farther Hesitation. It is but
common Prudence to keep in the high or open Streets
(though it may be about) rather than run the Risk of a
Surprize, and be taken at an Advantage in the narrow
Turnings of obscure Lanes, Alleys, &c. &c.

Public Advertiser
13 July 1784

The following circumstance may serve to show the folly of
sporting with certain danger, especially when it can answer
no other purpose but that of gratifying false emulation.—
A person at Hull, who used to catch adders, and boast of
his power of taking away their poison, on the 18th ult.
caught one, and the next day, being in a public house, he

curled up the adder, put the greatest part of it into his mouth, and took it out again unhurt; After this he put its head into his mouth, when it bit him, and his neck immediately swelled to an amazing thickness, his tongue hanging out of his mouth, a shocking spectacle. He lived only two hours, and in the greatest agonies.

Leeds Intelligencer
13 July 1784

Fahrenheit's Thermometer in the open air, in the shade fronting the north, at Highgate, Saturday, July 10, at noon, 69. Sunday, 11, 71.

Whitehall Evening Post
10–13 July 1784

Extract of a letter from Portsmouth, July 10

An artist lately arrived here from London with his sloop, and has since employed himself in visiting the Royal George. His vessel lays constantly along-side the wreck; he has four assistants, and being preserved from the effect of the water by a contrivance of leather with flexible tubes annexed, he often spends many hours on board the unfortunate ship without injury. By one of these tubes he is supplied with fresh air, and by the other he gives orders to the people in his sloop, on board which is an iron machine of great purchase, whereby he is enabled to hoist up the guns and other valuables, and occasionally to rip up the decks, &c. The ingenuity and enterprize of this man are astonishingly great; and whatever is recovered becomes his sole property.

Whitehall Evening Post
10–13 July 1784

Saturday last two gentlemen, lately arrived from India, came in two coaches, with several trunks in them, to a gentleman's house in Fenchurch-street; but he not being at home, they left the trunks, and went to his mother's, in Marlborough-street, Oxford-road. Two men, dressed like porters, went to the above house, in Fenchurch-street, in about two hours afterwards, there being only the coachman and maid in the house, and said they came from the gentlemen and were to have the two smallest trunks, which the coachman agreed to, and gave them to the porters, when they immediately decamped with them. The contents are very considerable.

Whitehall Evening Post
10–13 July 1784

The following intelligence is well worthy the public's notice:–
Alderman Pugh, who was afflicted with the Gout upwards of 20 years, and during his last fit, at the age of 67, September 1783, kept his bed ten months, unable to stir hand or foot, is now, to the utter astonishment of his friends, and particularly of the Faculty, who had pronounced him incurable, (indeed an instance of the like nature cannot be found in the annals of medicine) regarded by all who see him as risen from the dead; and for this surprising cure, scarcely to be credited by credulity itself, he is indebted to Mr. Buzaglo, of the Strand, who, in twenty-eight days, at an hour a day only, absolutely effected his cure, *without Medicine*, so that the worthy Alderman is now able to walk the streets, and ride a horseback, as well as he did at the age of thirty-five; and for that humanity and desire for the general welfare of mankind, for which he is universally distinguished, is willing and desirous to satisfy all enquiries concerning his own late desperate case, and also of many surprising cures of others to which he was witness. This remarkable and uncontrovertible instance of the infallibility of Mr. Buzaglo's method of curing Gout is the strongest and most convincing confirmation of its effect, and must have its due

weight on the minds of all those who have been taught to believe that pills, bathing, travelling, flannels, and patience, can cure the Gout.

General Evening Post
10–13 July 1784

The celebrated M. de Beaumarchais was last week stopped on the Pont-Neuf at Paris, and beat in a cruel manner, by four persons disguised, so that his recovery is doubtful. It is supposed that the four men were Dragoons in the service of a Northern Monarch, who is rather severely treated in a late publication, said to be published by M. de Beaumarchais.

General Evening Post
10–13 July 1784
[Beaumarchais in fact survived until 1799.]

The remedy to destroy or get quit of black beatles.—
Place a china bowl, or other glazed earthen bowl, in the kitchen or room, where the beatles are, in the bottom of the bowl place a piece of bread, bolster up the outside of the bowl with sand to the top, so as to make the ascent to the top easy. Our correspondent has caught many hundreds in a night, by placing several bowls on the floor of the room; whether all in his house were taken or destroyed, he cannot say, or whether the destruction they discovered of their brethren, drove them away, at present he sees none. Our correspondent had the three sorts lately described in our paper.

Morning Chronicle
15 July 1784

Two thousand copies of Cooke's Voyage to the Pacific Ocean were published the 4th of June, at 4 l. 14s. 6d.

each; the next day a thousand more were wanted, and since that time from fifteen to twenty guineas have been offered for a sett.—The sum thus raised, and 12,000 l. raised within the month for the Commemoration of Handel, do not speak a ruined nation.

Bath Chronicle
15 July 1784

Wednesday afternoon a swarm of bees, belonging to Mr. Tubb, farmer, of Denn-Court, near Oxford, having just taken flight, David Jones, his servant, who was mowing in the adjoining meadow, followed them, tapping his scythe with his whet-stone, when his foot unfortunately slipping, he fell upon his scythe, and cut open his belly in so shocking a manner, that his stomach and bowels rushed out; the latter of which were much wounded. All possible assistance, that his deplorable situation required, were afforded him, but in vain. He languished till the following night, and then expired in great agonies.

Bath Chronicle
15 July 1784

The scheme of employing felons on the fortifications, and off the dock-yards, in deepening the water, and removing shoals, will become general, hulks now preparing at Chatham and Sheerness for that purpose.

Bath Chronicle
15 July 1784

Plymouth, July 16.
Last Wednesday se'nnight there was a most dreadful storm of thunder, lightening, and rain, which never was equalled in the memory of man. The river Dart overflowed its banks, carrying away cottages, ricks of hay, sheep, &c. the

163

devastation it has occasioned is dreadful to the farmers; gravel and fish were washed from the river upon corn-fields and new mown hay, which were destroyed; the storm was universal over the northern parts of the county, and while it continued was terrible.

Bath Chronicle
21 July 1784

Extract of a letter from Hamburgh, June 15

A few days ago a singular and most innocent action occasioned the death of a young couple in a great city in Germany. The lady going to the church of the Augustin Friars, knelt down near a mausoleum, ornamented with divers figures in marble, among which was that of death, armed with a scythe. A small piece of the scythe being loose, fell on the hood of the lady's mantlet. On her return home, she mentioned the circumstance as a matter of indifference to her husband, who, being a credulous and superstitious man, cried out, in a terrible panic, that it was a presage of the death of his dear wife. The same day he was seized with a violent fever, took to his bed, and died. The disconsolate lady was so affected at the loss of her husband, that she was taken ill, and soon followed him. They were both interred in the same grave, and their inheritance, which was very considerable, fell to some very distant relations.

Norfolk Chronicle or Norwich Gazette
17 July 1784

His Royal Highness the Prince of Wales having been advised by his Physicians to Sea Bathing, we are informed from good Authority that his Royal Highness will set out on Monday next for Brighthelmstone: Mr. Weltjie, the Clerk of the Kitchens, and Mr. Gill, the Purveyor of the

Stables, are now at Brighthelmstone, preparing every Thing for his Royal Highness's Reception.

Public Advertiser
17 July 1784

[Brighthelmstone is now Brighton.]

On Friday evening died at the Bell Inn in this city, Joseph Losh, Esq; an officer in the 7th regiment of Light Dragoons. This amiable young gentleman fell a sacrifice to his notion of the use of strong exercise; for in one of the late hot days, he quitted his horse, when upon a journey, and walked from Ensham to Burford, which heated his blood to so violent a degree, that when he arrived here he was seized with a fever, which, after a few days illness, carried him off. The death of this young gentleman will be the subject of general concern in the regiment; where the elegance of his manners, and the liberality of his mind, had conciliated the respectful and affectionate regard both of the officers and men.

Gloucester Journal
19 July 1784

Sunday Morning as the Inhabitants of a Parish not quite twenty miles from Tyburn Turnpike, were crossing the Church-yard, in order to attend Divine Service, they were met by the Minister, who told them they might all go back again, as there would be no Service that Day.

Public Advertiser
20 July 1784

Sunday Morning a Fellow beginning to undress himself to go into the New River at Islington, a Constable told him he must not wash there, which the other insisted he would; and after some Altercation struck the Constable, who

165

immediately seized him and conveyed him crying and begging Pardon to Clerkenwell Bridewell.

Public Advertiser
20 July 1784

An air balloon descended at one o'clock yesterday se'nnight in the afternoon, in a hay field at Adlington, in Cheshire, to the great astonishment and terror of the Haymakers therein. When they had mustered up their courage a little, they drew near it, and found by a ticket pasted on it, that it had been let off, in Lord-street, Liverpool, at half past twelve o'clock the same day; having made a most rapid progress of upwards of 40 miles in one hour.

Leeds Intelligencer
20 July 1784

Lately died at Brookhill, in Ireland, Lovelace Love, Esq. This Gentleman was noted for his extraordinary bulk: he weighed upwards of sixty stone; his coffin measured seven feet in length, four across, and three and a half deep. His death was occasioned by his immense corpulence.

Parker's General Advertiser and Morning Intelligencer
20 July 1784

What must be the feelings of a philosopher on reading the following advertisement, which is copied verbatim from the SOUTH CAROLINA GAZETTE:

"NEGROES for SALE.

A CARGO of very fine stout MEN and WOMEN, in good order, and fit for immediate service, just imported from the Windward coast of Africa, in the ship Two Brothers."

General Evening Post
17–20 July 1784

London, July 20.
Friday a numerous Company of the Physical Profession had their annual Dinner at Chelsea. Just as they had sat down to Table, a Man of very genteel Appearance and polite Address joined them, and was supposed to have been invited; but immediately after Dinner he went into the Stable and ordered the Ostler to saddle a Horse belonging to Mr. Kinnard, Druggist in Holborn, with which he rode off unsuspected. The Sharper came on foot to the House, booted and spurred.

Jackson's Oxford Journal
24 July 1784

There is every reason to expect the present year will be the most generally plentiful in the memory of man. The crops of garden fruits are very great; the hay harvest has been amazing in produce and finely got in; the wheat and barley look very fine, the ears large and full, and very little blighted; the cyder counties are blessed in a burthen of apples and pears, superior in quantity and quality to their most sanguine expectations; so that the prices of cyder, perry, and malt, will shortly bear no proportion to what they have fetched for a long time past.

Bath Chronicle
21 July 1784

London, July 22.
Monday night some villains broke into Mr. Steele's, the Falcon alehouse in Falcon-street, Coppice-row, Clerkenwell. Unable to wake her husband, Mrs. Steele rose from her bed, and heroically pursued the villains to near forty yards from her house; and one of them would certainly have been secured had he not cunningly said that the naked woman in pursuit of him was a jealous wife, from

whose fury he was obliged to fly for having staid out till a late hour.

Leeds Intelligencer
27 July 1784

Sunday afternoon while six or seven lads were bathing in the arm of the Thames a little below Chelsea bridge, eleven constables came to the spot, and threw their clothes into the water, whereby several articles were lost, besides a watch out of one of their pockets. Admitting the boys to have been in a fault, that circumstance cannot justify the officers. The damage, and loss of their clothes, must be an injury to their masters or parents; and by wearing their wet apparel, the health of them may probably be endangered.

Yesterday a poor man belonging to Clerkenwell work-house fell down a cellar window in Turnmill-street belonging to Mr. Witts, and received so terrible a contusion on the back of the head, that he was taken to the workhouse in a coach speechless and insensible. While he lay bleeding a woman came out of the shop, and said it was impossible the man could be hurt, because, besides many blind men and women, she had known above a hundred children fall into the cellar without hurt.

Whitehall Evening Post
20–22 July 1784

Extract of a letter from Coventry dated July 16
"As soon as the news arrived here of the proposed tax on ribbands, the journeyman weavers assembled in the market place, and having first made a tall awkward figure which they called Mr. ——, they hung it on a gallows erected for the purpose with a silken halter, and afterwards consumed the whole in a large fire, amidst the applause of some thousands of people assembled on the occasion."

Whitehall Evening Post
20–22 July 1784

[The figure represented Pitt.]

London, July 23.

The celebrated Mrs. Thrale last week at Bath had the honour of giving her hand to Signor Piozzi, the singer. She was accompanied as far as Salisbury by her four blooming daughters as bride-maids.—Mrs. Thrale has settled 2000 l. a year upon the Signor during her life; but in case of her demise, the allowance is to be reduced to 1000 l.

Gloucester Journal
26 July 1784

[Hester Thrale (1741–1821), the friend of Dr. Johnson, had been married against her will to Henry Thrale, the son of a wealthy brewer. Gabriel Piozzi was an Italian Roman Catholic musician. Johnson was mortified at the news but his attempts to prevent her marriage to Piozzi were in vain.]

SUNDAY AMUSEMENTS

The favourable appearance of the firmament, the earth, air, and all that do therein inhabit, invited unnumbered thousands on Sunday into the fields.—Some sported their sweet persons and turned out their toes in the Beaux-walk. Others inhaled the dust on the Circular Road. Others twisted themselves into Tea-houses, which was attended with the consumption of Tea and Coffee, hot Cakes, Syllabubs, &c. &c.—Others smoaked the news of the week, while wife and the brats squalled over the fields.—Others displayed true gallantry, by handing the ladies over the stiles, by which means many a pretty ancle was exhibited.—Others spurred on their five shilling hacks in the Phoenix Park, and displayed wonderful feats of horsemanship, greatly different from any thing that Messrs. Jones and Parker can boast of.—Others, in martial phaetons, emulated the ancient method of fighting, while the ladies lappets, like signals of distress, intimated their fears of being in-turd before their death.

—In short, there was an immense superabundance of

pleasure, together with a most plentiful scarcity of religion,—Here ended the sixth Sunday after Trinity.

Magee's Weekly Packet, Dublin
24 July 1784

Oxford, July 24.
Wednesday Bumper Smith, a felon under sentence of transportation, who escaped from Oxford Castle on the 12th instant, surrendered himself by knocking at the Castle gate, and requesting to be re-admitted to his old apartments.

Bath Chronicle
29 July 1784

A letter from Dover says, that they had received an account there from Calais, that an English gentleman, supposed to be in a state of insanity, had shot himself in a room at the White Lion in that town; he came there about two hours before, in a diligence from Paris, has had no servant to attend him, and had only a few shillings in his pocket, after paying the post-boy, and no cloaths but what he had on; that several English gentlemen had viewed him, but he was not known to any one; however they paid the expences of his funeral.

General Evening Post
22–24 July 1784

A YOUNG GENTLEMAN MISSING

June 25, 1784
LEFT his friends yesterday, between the hours of one and two, a young Gentleman, who answers the following description. He is about five feet three inches high, of a

complexion remarkably fair and ruddy, round visage, large blue eyes, white eye-brows, and long light hair hanging loosely upon his shoulders. He was dressed in a dark chocolate-coloured coat with white sugar-loaf buttons, white striped dimity lapelled waistcoat, fustian breeches and white cotton stockings. He is supposed to be gone towards Portsmouth, or some other sea-port. All captains of ships, masters of inns, stage-coaches and coachmen are earnestly requested if they meet with such a person, to detain him, and give intelligence to Mr. Hargrave, at the Rainbow coffee-house, Cornhill; Mr. Longman, bookseller, in Paternoster-row; or Mr. Partridge, hosier, the corner of Tavistock-court, Covent-garden; and they shall be gratefully rewarded for their trouble. If the young Gentleman, upon reading this advertisement, will return to his afflicted parents, he will be most kindly received.

Gazeteer and New Daily Advertiser
26 July 1784

A BRICK MAKER

GONE away and left his work unfinished, which, by articles of agreement with Messrs. Hough and Pace of the city of Glocester, he was jointly bound to execute during the summer; A MAN, who calls himself BENJAMIN BROWN, a native of Shropshire, he is above the middle size, and lusty, wears his own hair, and is pitted with the small-pox; has also a particular look being near sighted, he usually wears a kind of plaid waistcoat with sleeves, and a round hat; he has a Welsh-woman with him, who passes for his wife, and a boy about ten years old who assists him in the business, he is supposed to be gone to Monmouth, or those parts.

N.B.   The above is inserted only as a caution to persons to whom he may apply, he being a man by no means capable or fit to be entrusted with the care of a brick-work;

171

on which account no reward is offered for bringing him back.

Gloucester Journal
26 July 1784

On Thursday evening last, a servant boy of Mr. Dimmery's of Dursley, in this county, took his master's horse out in the ground to feed, and being sleepy, lay down, tied the halter round his neck that he might not sleep too long, and composed himself; the horse taking fright, ran near a quarter of a mile with the boy, and bruised him in so terrible a manner, that he expired soon afterwards.

*Gloucester Journal
26 July 1784*

At a public Dispensary in Cumberland, 157 poor children were some time ago prepared for the small-pox, of whom 30 only were inoculated, so strongly prejudiced were the parents of the others against that salutary practice. Every one of those who had submitted to inoculation recovered without the least medical attention. Of the others (who had the distemper in the natural way) no less than 73 died.

*Whitehall Evening Post
24–27 July 1784*

This being appointed for a day of Thanksgiving on account of a General Peace, the House of Lords went in procession to Westminster Abbey, and heard a sermon preached by the Bishop of St. David's on the occasion; and the House of Commons went to St. Margaret's, and heard a sermon preached by the Rev. Dr. Prettyman.

This day at one o'clock, the Park and Tower guns were fired on the above mentioned occasion.

Whitehall Evening Post
27–29 July 1784
[The "General Peace" was that which followed the American War of Independence.]

Thursday se'nnight as Mr. Latham's son, a boy of about nine years of age, was selling his newspapers on the Exchange at Bristol, he was met by another boy, about 12 years of age, named Edward Williams, who not giving him the upper hand directly, the former took a small penknife out of his pocket, and stabbed the latter in his side, and leaving it there he ran off. The wounded boy was taken to the Bristol Infirmary, and is expected to recover. Young Latham is committed to Bridewell.

Whitehall Evening Post
27–29 July 1784

Paris, July 30.
There is a young stranger in this city whose language nobody here understands, but he is supposed to be a native of Otaheite; and probably the mystery will be soon explained by Mr. Bougainville, who has collected some words of the dialect spoken in that celebrated island. His features are open, and expressive of candour and sensibility, and, in short, he might be taken for the original from which Voltaire delineated the character of his sincere Huron. The Tragedian Larive has appointed him an income of 900 livres, and Madame Boursiere of Roulestreet, treats this stranger with the tenderness of a mother.

Public Advertiser
12 August 1784

[Otaheite is Tahiti.]

They write from Town Malling, in Kent, that Farmer Jackson, going from thence about Nine o'Clock on Wednesday Night, the 21st Instant was set upon about a Mile from that Place by several Men and Women, who pulled him off his Horse, and robbed him of Twelve Guineas and some Silver. The Women were for murdering him, that he might tell no Tales; but one of the Men said, it was Crime enough to rob him. They then turned his Horse loose, and made off.

Public Advertiser
30 July 1784

Yesterday se'nnight a most melancholy accident happened in the village of Hopton, near Yarmouth. As a girl of eight years of age was nursing her sister, an infant, in their father's cottage, in endeavouring to retire backwards to a chair which the girl imagined stood behind, she fell into a tub of boiling wort with the infant, who died almost immediately, but the girl lived till next day in great agonies.

Norfolk Chronicle or Norwich Gazette
31 July 1784
[Wort is an infusion of malt before it is fermented into beer.]

On Saturday Morning some Villains attempted to break into the House of Mr. Hett, Printer, in Wyld-court, Lincoln's Inn Fields; they broke the Sash of Miss Hett's Chamber, and removed the Blind, when the young Lady waking, ran to her Father's Room, who, calling to the Watch, saw the Rogues make off over the Wall before the House. By a long Tract of Blood which appeared on the Ground, it is thought some of them were much cut by the Glass on the Wall.

Public Advertiser
31 July 1784

Extract of a letter from Brighthelmstone, July 29

"The Duc de Chartres is every hour expected to arrive here on a visit to the Prince of Wales. His Royal Highness passes his time in the most agreeable manner. Music very much engages his attention. On the violencello he is said to have made great progress. Not an evening passes without a concert, at which he is accompanied by Mess. Cramer, Suck, and Shroder. The whole town is kept alive by the presence of the Prince. The nobility and gentry of the neighbourhood are every day making their appearance in this town. The ladies in particular croud to see his Royal Highness, whose affability and polite condescension are universally admired."

General Evening Post
29–31 July 1784

AUGUST

OLIMPIAN DEW.—C. SHARP, Perfumer, Fleet-street, London, respectfully recommends the Olimpian Dew to the Nobility and Gentry, assuring them, it will make the brownest complexion perfectly fair, clear, and beautiful, removing freckles, and every deformity from the skin, rendering it at the same time smooth, and elegantly pleasing (no perfume so sweet, none so delicate as Olimpian Dew, says the Queen of France). Gentlemen who use this article after shaving, if their faces are ever so tender, will find instant relief from its taking away pimples or scrophula; it makes the skin smooth and strong, whereby the operation of shaving becomes easy and pleasant, especially when performed by SHARP'S Concave Razors. His Alpine Shaving Cakes, his Metalic Razor Strops, his curious Pocket Shaving Cases, and Lavender water, drawn from the flowers, are articles superior to every thing of the kind. Sharp's Cypress Hair Powders, sweet Pomatums, and the new very curious Cyprian Wash Balls, sold only at the ROSE, in Fleet-street. N.B. The Chinese Gloves, should always be worn at this Season.

Morning Post
August 1784

Lewes, August 2.
At five o'clock on Monday morning last, the Prince of Wales mounted his horse at Brighthelmstone, and rode to and from London that day. His Royal Highness went by the way of Cuckfield, and was only ten hours on the road, being four and a half going, and five and a half returning.

Whitehall Evening Post
31 July–3 August 1784

Four Ladies, a few days since, went up in an air balloon at Rouen, and were landed in about an hour and a half sixteen miles from that city.

General Evening Post
31 July–3 August 1784

The following very audacious robbery was committed on the road between Dock-Head and Rotherhithe, on Monday evening. As Mr. Burchet, sail-maker, with his wife and sister, were returning home from town, four fellows rushed out from the rope-walk, and stopped the coach; two of them got inside (while the others kept watch) and rifled the pockets of Mr. Burchet and the other ladies of cash, &c. to the amount of 11 l. One of the robbers asked Mr. Burchet for his watch, who answering that he had left it in London, the villain put a knife to his throat, and one of the fellows of the coach called out with horrid execrations to murther him. Mrs. Burchet, alarmed for her husband, took a purse containing eleven guineas, which she had concealed in her bosom, and gave it to the villain. They then quitted the coach, bidding the driver go on; but one of them coming again up to the window, fired a pistol at Mr. Burchet, the ball of which struck him on the thigh, but having a rule in his pocket, it luckily turned it off, so that it did not penetrate.

Gloucester Journal
2 August 1784

At Gloucester assizes . . . received sentence of death . . . Henry Dunsdon and Thomas Dunsdon, natives of Fullbrook, near Burford, two desperate fellows, who had long been a terror to the country where they lived. They were ordered to be executed on Friday, and their bodies to be hanged in chains on Capslodge Plain, near Whichwood forest, the spot near which they had shot William Harding, who attempted to apprehend them.

Bath Chronicle
5 August 1784

Monday night a lad, about thirteen years old, was committed to New-prison by Peter Green, Esq; charged with being concerned in divers robberies. He is very small for his age, and it was his custom to get between the bars of windows, &c. and let his accomplices into the houses.

General Evening Post
3–5 August 1784

London.
Last night, about half an hour past ten, an extraordinary *meteor* appeared in a direction from West to East. It was seen at five distinct periods, and illuminated every part of the hemisphere with effulgence equal to the light of the sun, but with a *blue* cast. A violent rumbling was produced in the air for several seconds after the *light* disappeared.

Whitehall Evening Post
3–5 August 1784

With pleasure we inform the public, that Health and Strength are daily restored, and the following disorders effectually cured, at a trifling expence, without medicine, bathing, sweating, or journies to the Continent, viz. the gout, rheumatism, palsey, lameness, nervous complaints, debilitated constitutions; weak, wasted, and contracted limbs; corpulency, bad digestion, &c. The certainty of success is supported by a list, which is given gratis to ladies and gentlemen only, at Mr. BUZAGLO's, opposite Somerset-house, Strand, of 159 surprising cures in similar cases, performed on many of the most distinguished personages; whose testimony will confirm that their cures were effected by muscular exercise only, after all physic and bathing had failed, and pronounced incurable by the most eminent of the Faculty. Mr. BUZAGLO at first sight tells every patient the benefit he has to expect; which generally surpasses his most sanguine expectations. One week's exercise in warm weather, is found preferable to six in winter. Patients in general should apply for relief in the intervals of the fits, whilst they have the use of their limbs; and not wait till they are laid up helpless.

Whitehall Evening Post
5–7 August 1784

The *Duc de Chartres* confesses himself fairly vanquished by the *Prince of Wales*. The Duke went up in his balloon to an immense heighth, and made the experiment of flying among the Clouds – He presented a French picture of the Westminster Scrutiny, for after being buffeted – turned over head – twisted – and made the sport of the wind – buried in clouds – and out of sight for three quarters of an hour, he was forced to come down exactly *where he set out*.—The Prince of Wales, when he heard of his achievement, to shew him that we had no occasion for air balloons to *outstrip* the *winds* in England, mounted his horse, and rode one hundred and twelve miles in *eight hours and a half*.

General Evening Post
5–7 August 1784

[The Duc de Chartres, later Duc d'Orleans, was the father of Louis-Philippe of France.]

Extract of a letter from Dublin, July 27

"Tuesday last a journeyman silk weaver was taken in New-street by a mob, charged with being an informer:– they led him through Malpas's-street, Mill-lane, Sweeny's lane, to the Weaver's-square; where they stript him, and bedaubed him with dirt (the tar being all used) they then led him through Brown-street, and so on to the Canal, where they put a rope about his neck, and were going to drown him. A report having got amongst them of the approach of the military, they made a precipitate flight, leaving the object of their vengeance behind."

Whitehall Evening Post
5–7 August 1784

Corke, July 22.
On Sunday last Owen Reardon, in consequence of an old quarrel, about four years ago, with Daniel Bohely, pursued the latter, in the Town of Macromp, to execute a capias. Bohely, who was aware of him, in attempting to effect an escape, was shot through the body and expired. It is somewhat remarkable that the same ball killed two geese and a duck.

Morning Post
10 August 1784

[A capias is a writ authorizing arrest.]

Dublin, August 2.
Barrington, the *first* of his profession, is again let loose upon the public; he was liberated from Newgate on Tuesday last, and now roams at large. It therefore behoves the public for their own safety, to be upon their guard against the *polite condescension* of this *finished* pick-pocket.

Morning Post
10 August 1784

London, August 10.
The following extraordinary circumstance may be depended on as a fact:—Three swarms of bees having taken their residence between the rafters and leads of the

180

Right Hon. the Earl of Exeter's library at his seat at Burleigh, the bees were rendered tractable and compleatly settled in three different hives, and an amazing quantity of honey taken away last week by Mr. Wildman, of Holborn, who had been sent for by his Lordship for that purpose; after which Mr. Wildman made several experiments with the bees, such as making them march at the word of command, &c. much to the astonishment of the Nobility present.

Jopson's Coventry Mercury
16 August 1784

London, August 12.
Tuesday a relation of Mr. Cole's, of Fontmill, Dorset, not knowing any person was in Mr. Cole's garden, discharged a gun at some birds in his pease. Unfortunately a servant of Mr. Cole's child, an infant in her arms, was behind the pease, and the contents lodged in the servant's breast, and the back and head of the infant, both of whom now lie dangerously ill; though by the timely assistance of two surgeons, who extracted the shot, there is some hopes of their recovery.

Shrewsbury Chronicle
14 August 1784

London, July 31.
The following extraordinary account of a lunatic's happy recovery, may be depended upon for fact.—Above six years since a seafaring person was taken into the Asylum for Maniacs at York; During the space of five years and six months he never expressed any desire for sustenance, and was fed in the manner of an infant. The servants undressed him at night, and dressed him again in the morning; he never spoke, and remained with his body bent all day, and was regarded by all about him as an animal nearly converted into a vegetable. About the middle of May 1783,

he suddenly astonished the people around him, with saying "Good morrow to you all." He then thanked the servants for the care they had taken of him, and appeared perfectly sane. A few days after he wrote a letter to his wife, in which he expressed himself with great propriety. On the 28th of May following he was allowed to leave the hospital, and return to his family; and has now the command of a ship in the Baltic trade, and is in the full enjoyment of perfect health, both in mind and body. This very singular case is attested by Dr. Hunter, of York, F.R.S. in a letter to Dr. Percival, of Manchester; also by the servants now at the Asylum in York.

Shrewsbury Chronicle
14 August 1784

Bath, August 11.
The New Mail Coach has travelled with an expedition that has been really astonishing, having seldom exceeded thirteen hours in going or returning from London. It is made very light, carries four passengers, and runs with a pair of horses, which are changed every six or eight miles; and as the bags at the different offices on the road are made up against its arrival, there is not the least delay. The guard rides with the coachman on the box, and the mail is deposited in the boot. By this means, the Inhabitants of this city and Bristol have the London letters a day earlier than usual.

Gloucester Journal
16 August 1784

On Monday night a sharp skirmish happened between some revenue officers, assisted by a party of soldiers, and a body of smugglers, at Angmering, in which several of the smugglers were shot through their clothes, but no lives lost. The officers came off victorious with about 200 casks of liquor, and a chest of arms.

Bonner and Middleton's Bristol Journal
14 August 1784

On Wednesday the 4th instant was launched from the Bowling-green in Wisbech by the Sieur Hermon Boaz, an air-balloon of eighteen feet nine inches in circumference, containing 607 gallons of inflammable air. The concourse of people of all ranks assembled on the occasion was inconceivable. It was filled in presence of the spectators, and after being suspended by a cord at about the height of 100 yards (for some time) it was liberated, and rose to an amazing altitude, where it became stationary, and after remaining in view more than 30 minutes, it took a S.W. course till it lost the reach of human eye. The day being fine added much to the brilliancy of the spectacle, which was truly and magnificently grand.

Norfolk Chronicle or Norwich Gazette
14 August 1784

The following extraordinary circumstance was communicated to us in a private Letter from Scotland:

"About the end of June last a poor woman died in the hospital at Aberdeen, and was buried in the church-yard in the neighbourhood. A company of young surgeons agreed with the grave-digger to set some mark on the grave as a direction for them; but some person, in order to disappoint the grave-digger's employers, moved the signal to another grave, that of a woman who had been buried about three or four months. The party came, and, directed by the mark agreed upon, dug up the grave, drew out the coffin, and carried it home. But upon opening it a vapour like flame of brimstone came forth, and suffocated them in an instant. Two women also going past the room fell dead. It is said that eleven persons thus perished."

Whitehall Evening Post
12–14 August 1784

A vessel from Greenland, arrived at Hull, has brought over among other articles, seven very large bears, two of which are nearly white; they are reckoned a great curiosity. One of them is to be presented to the King.

Parker's General Advertiser and Morning Intelligencer
16 August 1784

Lately died at Derby, aged 104, Thomas Smith, usually called Dr. Smith, (a cow-doctor) very famous in his profession, who also kept cows as a milkman. He was a stiff, middle-sized man, and retained all his senses, stature and complexion to the last, and never used spectacles. He was like a nonpareil that had endured a long winter, rosy and plump, though shrivelled with long keeping. He loved ale, and in his time of prosperity had been used to drink five or six quarts a day of it.

Leeds Intelligencer
17 August 1784

[A nonpareil is a fine variety of apple.]

Wednesday Evening last a poor Man named Fisher, was unfortunately drowned while drawing for Salmon, in the River near this City.—It is somewhat remarkable, that the above Person had a Brother who unhappily lost his Life, a few Years ago, in the same Place.

Adams's Weekly Courant, Chester
17 August 1784

On Wednesday last a cricket-match was played in Heath betwixt the young gentlemen of Pontefract, and the young gentlemen of Wakefield, which was won easy by the former.

Leeds Intelligencer
17 August 1784

Doctor Mesmer has received orders from the French government, not to open any more subscriptions, nor sell his secret, under pain of being severely punished. One of the late victims of animal magnetism, is the Marchioness de Fleury, lately buried in the church of Eustache. She died at the Alchymist's house, in Cocqueron-street.

Parker's General Advertiser
19 August 1784

Monday an immense concourse of people assembled on Blackheath to see a battle, for a sum of money, between the famous Death and one Johnson a ticket-porter. Death came to the spot in a hackney-coach; but refusing to fight, the populace were so enraged as to threaten him with vengeance unless he faced his antagonist, which at length he consented to do, but yielded to his superior strength and dexterity in a few minutes. Death got into the coach again; but the mob followed him, dragged him out of the carriage, and compelled him to stand another bout, in which he received a very severe drubbing.

London Chronicle
17–19 August 1784
[*Parker's General Advertiser and Morning Intelligencer* adds: "Sharpers, pick-pockets, and in short thieves of all descriptions were so numerous on this occasion, that several publicans in the neighbourhood refused to serve any liquor, but kept their houses closely shut up till the rabble had dispersed."]

185

After a light fingered journey through Wales, and some pickings up at Chester, the right noted Mr. Barrington, otherwise Waldron, arrived in town, on Thursday morning. He is perfectly recovered from the gaol distemper, which he caught at the little green near the Linen hall, in Dublin, and has got the use of his thumbs, notwithstanding the screws have disfigured them much. He went immediately after his arrival to the handkerchief hotel in Field-lane, where he had a levee in the evening, at which most of the coat and breeches pocket plenipotentiaries were present. This day he means to attend the House of Lords, give his assent to the tax on light, and join with Parliament in emptying the pockets of the Public to fill the coffers of adventuring individuals. He attended the opening of the present Parliament, and on the first day borrowed a timepiece from Alderman Townshend, that he might be regular in his motions about Mrs. Siddons.

London Chronicle
19–21 August 1784

The noted Mr. England is now at Spa, where he lives in an elegant style, and is said to be much caressed by foreigners who visit that place of fashionable resort.

General Evening Post
19–21 August 1784

At the Theatre Royal in the Haymarket on Wednesday evening, when the house was uncommonly crowded, a Gentleman going into the front boxes suddenly missed his watch, and accused a genteel young man, who stood near him, with the robbery: the latter, with great warmth, denied the charge; and, after a long altercation, the watch in question was found in the owner's coat-pocket, though how it came to be there no one pretended to determine.

General Evening Post
19–21 August 1784

On Tuesday night, as Mr. Pitt was on his return to town from Mr. Jenkinson's seat near Wandsworth, the postillion mistook the way, and got so bewildered, that Mr. Pitt was obliged to leave the carriage, and go to the next farmhouse to ask the way to the great road to town. On his approaching the house, the dogs began barking, which alarmed the farmer, who got up, and presented a loaded gun against Mr. Pitt, telling him if he approached any farther he would shoot him. Mr. Pitt remonstrated for a considerable time, and endeavoured to persuade the farmer of the purpose of his business; but his arguments tended more to rouse the resentment and suspicion of the countryman, that he was either a highwayman or house-breaker. He accordingly fired, and the bullet went through the breast of Mr. Pitt's coat, but providentially did no mischief.

Norfolk Chronicle or Norwich Gazette
21 August 1784
[Charles Jenkinson (1727–1808), later Earl of Liverpool, was President of the Board of Trade under Pitt.]

Account of the Robberies committed by JOSEPH RADLEY, not eighteen years of age, who was executed at Aylesbury, on Thursday, Aug. 5, 1784.

		£.	s.	d.
1.	From Councillor Dallas, in Kensington Gardens	4	14	6
2.	From Earl of Buckinghamshire, ditto	36	15	0
3.	A clergyman and his lady, ditto	7	7	0
4.	An old gentleman, ditto	1	8	0
5.	Another person, ditto, a watch and 2s.– Returned			
6.	Barnet Road, two ladies in a post-chaise	26	5	0
7.	Ditto, two ladies and one gentleman, in a post-chaise coming to London, two twenty pound notes, 17 guineas and a half, 19 shillings, two Spanish dollars,			

three pocket pieces, lady's gold watch, a silver one, and some trinkets, amounting in the whole, to about	75	0	0
8. Between Twyford and Reading, two gentlemen in a post-chaise	5	5	0
9. Mr. —— of Argyle-street, and his lady in a coach	17	5	0
10. Near Bagshot Heath, a gentleman in a post-chaise	3	3	0
11. A Quaker, in a post-chaise, near Henly, of a watch, &c.	3	3	0
12. Two foreigners in a post-chaise, on the Bath road	16	16	0
13. Forged upon a certain Lady, in keeping by Lord ——.	17	0	0
14. Feather-bed lane, near Stoken Church, three ladies in a post-chaise, an enamelled ring, one gold ditto, and 10s. – in the whole	1	5	0
15. A man near Epsom, of	0	2	6
16. Near Kennington Common, a gentleman and two youths in a post-chaise, in gold and silver, about	3	0	0
17. Barnet Road, from a gentleman and two ladies, in a coach, a gold watch, &c.	4	14	6
18. Ditto, the same morning, an old clergyman	2	10	0
19. Epping Forest, a gentleman and lady in a coach	12	10	0
20. Remnan Common, near Henley, four officers, in a post-chaise	19	19	0
21. Park-lane, Hyde Park, a gentleman, in a coach	7	0	0
22. An old lady, in her coach, near Dunstable	26	5	0
23. Bath road, near Burnham, for which he was tried and condemned, for robbing two ladies of a watch, with a gold seal, a small picture, a ring, and one guinea	4	0	0
	£308	8	6

After his being apprehended for this last robbery he made
his escape, and was at large five weeks, during which time,
he committed trifling robberies, and also several others, he
said, which were trivial, and not worth mentioning.

Norfolk Chronicle or Norwich Gazette
21 August 1784

On Wednesday last as a boy was passing through Maiden-
lane, at the bottom of Gutter-lane, Cheapside, he was
robbed by a man of a bundle. The boy calling out, some
people came to his assistance, and securing the culprit,
carried him to Goldsmith's-Hall pump, where he underwent a most severe discipline. Not thinking this a sufficient
punishment, they beat him in a cruel manner, and by a
blow with a stick, the unhappy wretch was deprived of a
eye. He was the next day found dead in Queen-street.

Norfolk Chronicle or Norwich Gazette
21 August 1784

Monday last Witton, who was tried at the last assizes for
stealing eight guineas from the landlord where he was
quartered at North Walsham, and acquitted, was taken
from the castle and tried for desertion; as also another
soldier for robbing the waiter at the Angel inn in
Yarmouth of some money, were conveyed to a field near
Coltishall, where they were met by that part of the
regiment quartered in that neighbourhood, where the
former received 700, and the latter 500 lashes.

Norfolk Chronicle or Norwich Gazette
21 August 1784

On Wednesday last a gentleman undertook, for a considerable bett, to walk from this city (Norwich) to Yarmouth

and back again in fourteen hours, which he did two hours within the time limited.

Norfolk Chronicle or Norwich Gazette
21 August 1784

Last week died at Wilsford, near Sleaford in Lincolnshire, Mr. John Forster and Martha his wife, both aged 84 years to a day. What is most remarkable, they met on the 9th of August, in the year 1724, at a country wake, and in the course of conversation, it came out that they were both of an age, on which they agreed to make their birth-day their wedding-day, and accordingly were married the next day; they lived together perfectly happy, and were both taken ill but a short time previous to their dissolution. They were on Saturday interred in one grave, and in one coffin, with a plate on the lid, expressing the extraordinary circumstance, of being born, wedded, and dying on the same day of the month.

Norfolk Chronicle or Norwich Gazette
21 August 1784

Saturday afternoon about five o'clock, a clergyman was found, with his throat cut in a most shocking manner, behind a hay-stack in a farm-yard near the Small-Pox Hospital at the bottom of Gray's-Inn-Lane. He was very decently dressed, had a gold watch in his pocket, and nine shillings in silver, and a gold-headed cane by his side. On searching his waistcoat pocket, a paper was found, signifying his abode, and where he had a desire to be buried.

Bonner and Middleton's Bristol Journal
21 August 1784

London, August 19.
The following curious method of preventing the dangerous

consequence of the bite of a viper, is communicated in a letter from Sclavonia, dated the 29th ult.

"A girl was stung in the arm by one of those venomous creatures: her father instantly dug a deep hole in the ground, sufficient to take in the girl's arm entirely, and then covered it all round with the earth he had taken up. In this situation she remained for 24 hours; her father all the time watching by her, to prevent her falling asleep; thus he saved the life of his child, who never felt the least effect of the bite, and is now in perfect health."

Ipswich Journal
21 August 1784

On Wednesday a clergyman was committed to the Wood-street Compter by Alderman Hart, on the oaths of several persons, for feloniously stealing two fowls from the Cock of Snow-hill; before he committed the fact, he was appointed to preach next Sunday at the Chapel in Wood-street Compter.

Whitehall Evening Post
19–21 August 1784

London, August 24.
The narrow escape of our young Minister on Tuesday evening has occasioned much whimsical conversation. The farmer who fired at him has been blamed by those who disliked the new taxes, for not taking a better aim; the gunsmith has been censured for making a piece so uncertain in its direction; and the man who cast the ball has been condemned for not giving it its usual fatality. Such have been the remarks of his severe enemies; while on the other hand, the jocular have amused themselves with the idea, that a young Gentleman who presumed to direct the affairs of England, was so unacquainted with the country that he could not direct his post-boy in the right way from Secret Influence-Hall at Wandsworth, to

Nominal Importance Place at London, but was necessitated, in imitation of the TEMPLE where he worshipped, to proceed by a back-road.—Nor has it escaped the sarcasms of the witty, that the affairs of Britain should be placed in the hands of a youth who has been suspected by an honest farmer of an intention to commit the joint offences of burglary and robbery. We trust, however, that this singular occurrence will be a warning to this aspiring Statesman, that whenever, through the errors of inexperience, he attacks the rights of Englishmen, or justly alarms their fears, he must expect their manly resistance.

Bonner and Middleton's Bristol Journal
28 August 1784

Died at Mundole in Scotland, John Thomson, day labourer, aged 107, who had by his first wife 28 children, and by a second wife 17; was father to 45, grandfather to 86, great grandfather to 97 and great-great grandfather to 23, in all 251. And what was very surprising, he retained his senses, and followed his usual employment to the day preceding his death.

At Matlock, Ann Clowes, widow, aged 103. She measured 3 feet 9 inches in height, and weighed about 48 lb. The house she resided in was as diminutive (in proportion) as herself, containing only one room about 8 feet square.

Bonner and Middleton's Bristol Journal
24 August 1784

The following may be depended on as the origin of the fashion of the little round hat, worn at present by our bucks and *petit maitres*. Monsieur le Comte d'A—— being out in a field near Versailles, where a very pretty brunette was milking her cow, and singing a *sans souci* to each press she gave the paps, he insisted on, and took a kiss. The lass returned the salute with a courtsey, and said with a smart

192

air to the Count: "Sir, if you mean to be familiar in my dairy, you must accustom yourself to bearing the burden of its furniture." And so saying, she put the skimming dish on his head. This story soon got abroad, and as nothing is so common in France as to create a fashion from the most trifling incident, every man of the gay circle immediately got a hat as nearly resembling a *skimming dish* as possible; and it soon got the name of the *Milkmaid's Frolic*.

General Evening Post
24–26 August 1784

London, August 24.
Friday Afternoon a Man who lodged in Catharine-Wheel-Court, Snow-Hill, sent for a Hair-Dresser, and while the Man was dressing him, the Landlord of the House, who is Guard to a Stage-Coach, came in, and laid down his Pistols upon a Table; the Hair-Dresser having done, the Person he had been dressing got up, and taking one of the Pistols, asked him if he would like to have the Contents lodged in him, when by some means the Pistol went off, and two Balls passed thro' the Hair-Dresser's Body, who was carried to St. Bartholomew's Hospital, without Hope of Recovery. The Man immediately absconded.

Jackson's Oxford Journal
28 August 1784

ON EMIGRATION

AMERICA is in many instances the most extraordinary country in the world, and ought to be perfectly well understood before any persons emigrate to it. There is a party necessarily in this kingdom, who greatly and interestedly advise emigration. On the contrary there are others who on every occasion ridicule the idea. The truth lies between them, and ought to be well understood.

Living in an American town is, all things considered,

dearer than living in England; and it is impossible to live in the country without building a house and offices, and planting a garden and orchard, and cultivating some land: all this is labour; and labour is dearer than in any country in the world; so that the only resource is buying all this ready done, for which a considerable sum of money is necessary. But I admit that 5000 l. may thus be expended to better advantage than any where else. It is not so with larger sums, nor yet with a small one of 500 l. or 1000 l.

But a healthy labourer landed there with 1000 l. or even with 50 l. who will establish his hut in the woods, by a week's work, and lays his money out in cows, sows, mares, &c. to turn into them, will sooner acquire a fortune than in any country in the world. But then it is to be remembered that labourers have no such sums, that the freight is not discharged under two years hand-servitude, and after that, incredible hardships are to be encountered to get a flock of cattle together; all which makes a poor man's lot not enviable, however well his son may succeed. In a word, it is highly eligible only for a countryman with 100 l. or a gentleman fond of a rural residence with from 4000 l. to 6000 l. To all the rest it is misery and ruin.

An AMERICAN

General Evening Post
24–26 August 1784

Bath, August 25.
Saturday the 14th curt. was executed at Dorchester, Wm. Cottman, for stealing a trunk, containing 12 l. in gold and silver, a gold ring, and other articles, the property of his aunt. At the place of execution he behaved in a manner suitable to his unhappy situation, acknowledging his guilt, and particularly recommended it to the young to abstain from bad company and lewd women, which he said was the cause of his untimely fate. He was only 23 years of age.

Public Advertiser
27 August 1784

To the admirers of the wonderful Productions of Nature
To be seen alive in a Caravan in the Horse-Fair, during the
time of the Fair, a most astonishing Creature called the
Ethiopian SATYR, or real Wild Man of the Woods.—It
may be justly asserted that this animal is of a different
Species from any Creature ever seen in Europe, and seems
to be the link between the rational and brute Creation. It
was brought from the Desarts of Abyssinia in Ethiopia
Superior, to Amsterdam in a Dutch ship, and purchased
by the Proprietor for a large sum.

This astonishing Creature, when he stands erect, is
near five feet high, and in many respects is a striking
resemblance of the human species. His Ears are small, but
have large apertures, so that he is extremely quick of
hearing; his face is black with a white circle round it,
which resembles a mask, his forefeet are like the arms and
hands of a man, and grow gradually taper till they come to
the wrist, and he uses his fingers with surprising facility,
his body is covered with a fine long hair, perfectly smooth
on the surface; he sits in a chair in a very pleasing and
majestic attitude, to receive and eat his food; he is very
affable and obedient to the commands of his keeper, who
can even sleep by his side with safety. This wonderful
creature is a fine display of nature's amazing productions,
and is allowed to be the greatest curiosity ever exhibited in
Britain.

And as this animal has not been taken notice of by
Linneus, *Buffon*, *Johnston*, and *Gesner*'s Natural Histories,
it is certain that he is the first of this kind that was ever
brought to Europe.

Bonner and Middleton's Bristol Journal
28 August 1784

NO MONEY – NO MEMORY
An Anecdote

PIOVANO ARLOTTO; a famous Italian Priest, and a
great traveller, being on the point of embarking on a

voyage, was solicited by several of his friends to purchase a variety of things in the country he was going to visit. The curate received all their commissions with great politeness, put the memorandums in his pocket-book very carefully, and promised to oblige every friend.—At his return they all crowded round him to receive his purchases; but, to their surprise, he had only executed one single commission. This partiality affronting all the rest, he made his apology in the following speech: – "Gentlemen, when I set sail, I laid all your memorandums on the gallery of the ship to peruse them, that I might put them in order, to be executed regularly; when suddenly a squall arose, which blew them overboard, and it was impossible for me to remember their divers contents."

However, replies one of them, you have brought Mr. —— his silks. Very true, says Piovano; but the reason is, that he inclosed in his memorandum a number of ducats, the weight of which prevented it from blowing away along with yours, not being so light; so that I had the means of remembering what he ordered.—A word to the wise is sufficient; it is trouble enough to execute commissions, without adding to it the inconvenience of advancing the money, and raising an account, when the obligation is conferred not received.

Whitehall Evening Post
26–28 August 1784
[Arlotto Mainardo (1396–1484) was curate or piovano of S. Cresci di Maciuoli, near Fiesole.]

Newcastle, August 28.
A labouring man who lives in Gateshead, finding his wife, as he thought, indulge herself much too liberally in the article of tea, concerted the following *ingenious* method of deterring her from the use of it in future. In her absence a few days since, he mixed a quantity of gunpowder with her tea, in hope she would drink it in that state; but she having had occasion to apply to it before day-light the next

morning, on looking into the cannister, some of the powder unfortunately fell upon the candle which communicated to that in the inside, and caused such an explosion as to wound her face, hands, &c. in a most shocking manner; she was admitted an out-patient of the Infirmary, and is now, we hear, likely to recover.

Public Advertiser
2 September 1784

Wednesday night a fire broke out at the White Swan public-house, the corner of King James's-stairs, Wapping, which consumed the same, and did considerable damage to the house adjoining. This accident was owing to the carelessness of the servant maid, who, having put a child about four years old to bed, left the candle burning, which communicated to the curtains, and the infant was unfortunately burnt to death.

Bonner and Middleton's Bristol Journal
28 August 1784

AUGUST 27, 1784

BROKE out of Witney Bridewell, on Wednesday Night, the 25th Instant, RICHARD EDWARDS and GEORGE COX, charged on a violent suspicion of stealing three Horses.

Richard Edwards is about 25 Years of Age, five Feet ten Inches high, long strait black Hair, long Visage, dark Complexion, and thick Lips; had on when he broke out a narrow-ribbed Fustian Frock and Waistcoat, clean Leather Breeches, and a Pair of high shoes.

George Cox, about 35 Years of Age, about five Feet seven Inches high, thick made, Large Feature, black Hair, hanging down his Forehead, very thick Lips, with a down Look; had on an Oil Case Hat, brown Fustian narrow-ribbed Frock, Velveret Waistcoat, with black and red

Spots, greasy Leather Breeches, and a Pair of Boots.

They were seen on Friday Morning about one o'Clock, near Ensham, with their Irons on.

Whoever will apprehend and secure them, shall receive a Reward of TWO GUINEAS for each of them, by giving Notice to John Jeffrey, Bridewell Keeper, of Witney.

Jackson's Oxford Journal
28 August 1784

Wednesday, agreeable to a sentence of the Magistrates of Glasgow, Annabella Wardrobe, a notorious baud, and disturber of the neighbourhood, stood on the tolbooth stair-head and was banished the city, by tuck of drum, for seven years under the usual certification.

Caledonian Mercury, Edinburgh
28 August 1784

["Tuck" is a Scottish word for a beat or a stroke.]

The celebrated hymeneal Dr. Graham has again experienced the fickleness of fortune. A few months back he was in prison without a shilling, and now he is living in splendour and rolling in his chariot at Manchester.

Ipswich Journal
28 August 1784

ANECDOTE

The late Sir Robert Henley, who was commonly pretty much in debt, walking one day with two or three other Gentlemen in the Park, was accosted by a Tradesman, who took him aside for a minute or two; and when the Baronet rejoined his company, he seemed to be in a great passion, which his friends taking notice of, asked what was the matter? "Why the rascal (said he) has been dunning me for the money I have owed him these seven years, with as much impudence as if it was a debt of yesterday."

London Chronicle
28–31 August 1784

About a fortnight since, as the son of Mr. Pendercross, near Swaffham, in Norfolk, was returning from a neighbouring village in a cart, with some pigs, he was struck by lightning, the effect of which was, that when the father, who was on horseback, overtook the cart, he discovered his son lying at the bottom of it apparently dead; but in about a quarter of an hour the young man began to shew signs of life, and next day was perfectly recovered. It is remarkable that no alteration was discoverable in his outward garments, yet his shirt from the right shoulder to the hip was tinged with several lines of pale yellow.

Morning Chronicle and London Advertiser
30 August 1784

A correspondent is informed, that, about ten days ago, a man being detected in some petty theft, he was seized by the populace, who immediately conducted him to the pump, where they administered the ablution practiced upon such occasions; and from whence they led him from pump to pump, till at length, exhausted by the severity of the discipline, the poor wretch dropped down in or near Cheapside, and expired. The circumstance not being mentioned in any of the publick prints, it is hoped, for the sake of common humanity, that the report is without foundation. However the state of the case may be, it certainly is highly incumbent upon Magistracy to interfere, to prevent the administration of justice from being assumed by a lawless rabble; who are, in general, as unable to discriminate between the nature of the crimes, as they are incompetent to the proportioning of punishment to the guilt of the criminal. In the present case, (if the fact be as before stated, and it certainly merits an enquiry) a fellow subject underwent the punishment of death for an offence not *legally* proved; and for which, if legally proved, the laws of his country would only have subjected him to a whipping, or a banishment for a term of years.

Morning Chronicle and London Advertiser
31 August 1784

Yesterday se'nnight at night, a bet of one guinea was decided between two tradesmen at Stamford: The bet was, that a servant man belonging to one of them, could eat a plumb pudding of 8 lb. weight within an hour; but the man gave up when he had eat the *small* quantity of 5½ lb.

Leeds Intelligencer
31 August 1784

The following manoeuvre was played off within these few days: A vacancy happening about three weeks since for master of the school at Leek, in Staffordshire, a person of character and learning was elected, not without some opposition from other candidates. Soon after he had been comfortably settled in his place, he received a letter from London, signed with the name of a respectable gentleman, declaring the mastership of the Welsh school in Gray's-Inn-Lane was vacant, and as the salary was much superior to that he enjoyed at Leek, if he thought it worthy his acceptance, the place should be reserved for him. The unsuspecting schoolmaster with too much precipitation, it is acknowledged, went to the Trustees, and resigned his office in favour of one of the former candidates. On his arrival in town last week, no person of the name signed to the invitation was to be found in the neighbourhood of St. Paul's, from whence the letter was dated; nor had there been any vacancy in the school above-mentioned!

Whitehall Evening Post
28–31 August 1784

A gentleman who has lately been travelling through Buckinghamshire, was surprised out of his sleep, in the middle of the night, by a loud hand-bell ringing; after resting a little, a *poetical* watchman (Philomela like) sung through his nose the *very elegant and curious* stanzas, in which is the most solemn appeal to his sleeping friends:

> As God Almighty is my Judge,
> About this town I here do budge;
> And while my masters are asleep,
> Their housen and their goods I keep;
> And there's NO man can do NO more,
> Than go about from door to door.

After which he bawled still more vociferously to tell them it was three o'clock and a cloudy morning.

Whitehall Evening Post
28–31 August 1784

SEPTEMBER

A POINTER DOG LOST

Went off, last night, from Parkside, near the Gibbet Toll, on the road leading from Edinburgh to Dalkeith, A LARGE WHITE POINTER DOG, with liver-coloured spots upon his body and ears. The Dog is young, and in high spirits, and answers to the name of NERO. He had a bit of rope about his neck when he went off, and was a good deal marked with pitch, having come lately from England on board of ship.

It is intreated of any person who may have found the Dog, to return him to Colonel Lumsdaine at Parkside; and a handsome reward, and any expenses incurred will be paid, if required. And if the Dog is found, after this notice, in the custody of any person, he will be prosecuted as the law directs.

Caledonian Mercury, Edinburgh
1 September 1784

DESERTED

From his Majesty's 63d (or West Suffolk) Regiment quartered at Stirling, on the morning of the 29th of August. ROBERT STEWART, drummer, 5 feet 3½ inches high, 18 years of age, fresh complexion, long visage, grey eyes, fair hair; was born in Burry St. Edmunds, in the county of Suffolk, and by trade a wool-comber.—He went off in his regimental coat (green, faced with red) white waistcoat and breeches.

Also, at the same time, and in the same uniform, JOSEPH MULLY, drummer, 5 feet high, 15 years of age, swarthy complexion, round visage, grey eyes, brown hair; was born in the parish of Norton, in the county of Suffolk, and by trade a barber.

Whoever apprehends the above deserters, and lodges

202

them in any of his Majesty's jails, or guard-houses in Great Britain, shall receive the sum of TWENTY SHILLINGS Sterling for each, over and above the allowance made by act of Parliament, on applying to Lieutenant-Colonel Wemyss, commanding the regiment at Stirling, or to Messrs. Meyricks, agents, Parliament-street, London.

Caledonian Mercury, Edinburgh
1 September 1784

Yesterday morning the following malefactors, convicted in July sessions, were, in pursuance of their sentence, executed on a scaffold erected for that purpose before the door of Newgate, viz. Richard Edwards, for assaulting the Hon. Keith Elphinston, near the Theatre in the Haymarket, and forcibly taking from him a gold watch, gold seal, &c. Robert alias John Moore, for assaulting Mrs. Arabella Jeffreys near St. James's Gate, and snatching from her head-dress a cluster diamond pin; John Codd, for a street robbery on Samuel Ellison; William Holmes, for a burglary in the house of Adam Hamilton at Enfield; John Shelley, alias Sharley, alias Sherlock, for being concerned with others in rescuing and carrying away 350 lb. of tea, which had been seized by an Excise Officer; and James Napier, convicted the sessions before, for assaulting the Hon. Albinia Hobart, near the Opera-House, and taking from her person a diamond ear-ring, by tearing the same from her ear, but which slipped out of his hand, and fell into her handkerchief. Having attended Divine Service in the Chapel, the unhappy men appeared on the scaffold at twenty-five minutes before seven; and after being tied up, they joined the Ordinary in fervent devotion. The prayers being over, Mr. Villette took them each by the hand, and having respectively recommended them to Almighty Mercy, went off the scaffold, when John Codd gave a handkerchief to the deputy executioner, who at the convict's desire delivered it to a person in the crowd. The platform dropped a few minutes before seven, when Codd, in consequence of the noose having slipped from under the ear to the back of the neck, writhed his body and struggled near ten minutes after his fellow-sufferers appeared to be quite dead. They were stout well-made young men, the oldest not appearing to be more than four or five and thirty, and decently dressed. Sherlock wore a new suit of mourning.

General Evening Post
31 August–2 September 1784
[The Ordinary was the chaplain who attended those condemned to death, especially the chaplain of Newgate.]

Anecdote of the late Duke of Cumberland

HIS Royal Highness was one day playing at billiards at a public table, in company with several Gentlemen, and frequently laid his snuff-box down whilst he played; it was a box of exquisite workmanship, and great value, and was presented to his highness by one of the German Princes. The box suddenly disappeared; his Highness searched all his own pockets in vain: it was certain nobody had come into or departed from the room since the box had been seen; it was therefore proposed that every Gentleman present should be searched, which was agreed to by all but one, a Lieutenant of the guards, who swore that no man living should search him, and that whoever offered to touch him, should do it at his peril. This declaration, in a manner, identified the thief; and the Lieutenant, beginning to find himself roughly treated, requested permission to speak to the Duke in private, to which his Highness readily assented and retired with him into another room. The Lieutenant then informed the Duke, that he had been many years in the army and had served his King and Country faithfully, but was not fortunate enough to meet with an advancement which his services and long standing in the army entitled him to expect, and that having a large family, he was consequently poor, but not poor enough to forfeit the character of a man of honour. He had that day, he said, ordered a chicken at a Tavern for his dinner, and not having eat it all, he had wrapped up the remainder in paper, and having that in his pocket (which he showed the Duke), was his only objection to be searched, knowing that he must cut a ridiculous figure if it were produced before the Company. His Highness could not but heartily laugh, and at the same time pity the poor Lieutenant, whom he re-introduced to the rest of the Company, assuring them that the Gentleman was intirely innocent of the charge. The box, however, could not be found, and the company retired wondering at the incident; the next day, however, the Duke found it in the *lining of his coat*, of which he took care to inform every individual of the company with whom he had been playing; and it ought to be remembered, to his honour, that he immediately advanced the poor Lieutenant into such a position in the army, as to render it totally unnecessary for him to carry *cold chicken* in his pockets for the future.

Norfolk Chronicle or Norwich Gazette
4 September 1784

[William Augustus, Duke of Cumberland (1721–65), was the second son of George II. He commanded the English army at Fontenoy and Culloden.]

Mr. Lunardi's grand ENGLISH balloon which has for some time past been floating for the inspection of the curious, at the Lyceum, near Exeter Change, London, is expected to ascend some time this day with the proprietor and another gentleman. The size of this large machine is a perfect sphere or globe of about 33 feet in diameter, and 102 feet in circumference, it contains 18200 cubic feet of inflammable air, and [is] composed entirely of oiled Silk.—The gallery contains one pair of wings, which are raised high, and move horizontally for the purpose of increasing the motion it receives from the wind; also one pair of oars which will move vertically; and are meant to raise or depress the balloon at the pleasure of the aeriel travellers.

Norfolk Chronicle or Norwich Gazette
4 September 1784

205

A few days since as a boy, servant to a Mr. —— of St. Martin's-lane, button-seller, was going with a parcel of buttons of about 10 l. value, to the Swan with Two Necks in Lad-lane, to be sent by the Norwich coach, he was accosted in Holborn by an elderly looking gentleman, standing under a gateway as it then rained, who desired him to call a coach, one not being in sight, which the boy refusing on account of his load, the gentleman repeated his intreaties, and tempted him with the offer of 6d. for his trouble, and to remove the objection of his load being a burden to him, pointed to a small shop, where he said the master would take care of it till his return. Urged by these considerations, he accordingly obeyed; but when he returned with the coach he found that the sharper had in his absence imposed on the man in the shop, and obtained from him the parcel, with which he had made off. When the boy returned to his master, and acquainted him with the transaction, not having just then time to enquire into the particulars, he ordered his servant to make up another parcel as before. In going through Long acre, he accidentally met a man, with a parcel exactly resembling that of which he had been defrauded; upon charging him with being concerned in the fraud, and persisting, notwithstanding the man's repeated denial, in his charges against him, a crowd soon gathered round them, when a gentleman, interesting himself in the situation of the boy, ordered some of the by-standers to procure a coach, into which he put the two disputants, the parcels in question and accompanied them himself to the boy's master in St. Martin's-lane, where, upon examination, it appeared that the parcel which the boy had so positively affirmed to have been his, to the great surprise of all present, was found to contain contraband lace, to the amount of 1000 l. one-half of which falls to the share of the boy.

Norfolk Chronicle or Norwich Gazette
4 September 1784

Yesterday being the first of September, all the gunners who could escape from behind their desks and counters, went out armed against all the partridges they could find. But unaccustomed to game they were often imposed upon. Some shot at sparrows, some at crows, some at magpies, and some at chickens, ducks, turkies, geese, cocks, hens, and water wagtails by mistake. Many burned their fingers with the priming, others singed their eye-brows, and several so overloaded their guns, that they burst, wounding the hand of the poor stunned sprawling sportsman, and leaving him a butt of ridicule to whoever saw him. About Blackheath, and at all the avenues leading to the town, a variety of higglers had placed themselves, with game chickens, and brown ducks, and some partridges for the more knowing shopkeeper and apprentice, which they sold at a high price to the returning empty and tired gunners, who out of the 1700 yesterday that went out, did not among the whole kill more than two brace of birds. Hundreds of rabbits were sold as hares, and numerous ducks and chickens disposed of as partridges, which, when brought home were dressed, and eat as real game, most of the families not knowing the difference between a rabbit and a hare, or between a duck and a partridge.

Norfolk Chronicle or Norwich Gazette
4 September 1784

[Higglers were itinerant dealers.]

For the HOOPING COUGH.—Take emetic milk of squills four ounces; simple cinnamon water, syrup of diacodiam of each one ounce; mix it and let the child take a table spoonful till it operates as a gentle puke, which is to be repeated for three days; after which a dose or two of Turkey rhubarb generally completes the cure.—If convenient the patient should either change his abode or take the air.

RECEIPT for the AGUE.—Take of the best bark in fine powder, half an ounce; Venice treacle, two drachms;

lemon juice, as much as will make a very soft electuary: It is to be divided into three doses, and taken for three nights together in warm ale, going immediately after into a warm bed.

Bonner and Middleton's Bristol Journal
4 September 1784

Thursday a black hailed a boat at Wapping New Stairs to cross the water, the waterman would not take him in, and called him names, and struck him with his oar, upon which a battle ensued, when the black throwing him down, stamped on his body, and killed him on the spot. He was secured and sent to Whitechapel Roundhouse.

Parker's General Advertiser and Morning Intelligencer
4 September 1784
[Whitechapel Roundhouse was a lock-up.]

Extract of a letter from Paris, August 16

"An event lately happened at the Palais Royal, which proves how little some men value the life of a fellow-creature. A man richly dressed, going heedlessly along, happened to hit against a labourer who was carrying two pails of water in equilibrium on his shoulders; the shock of the pails occasioned some water to fall on this person's clothes, who, irritated at finding himself wet, drew his sword and gave the unhappy labourer three stabs, who died of his wounds two hours after. The murderer was carried before the Commissary, and from thence to the Grand Chatelet."

Parker's General Advertiser and Morning Intelligencer
4 September 1784

Yesterday the Right Honourable the Lord Mayor, attended by the Sheriffs, went to Smithfield, and proclaimed

Bartholomew Fair in the usual manner. In their way they partook of a cool tankard with the keeper of Newgate. After the proclamation was over, the usual entertainments of the place began.

The following august personages, viz. his Most Christian Majesty, the Dauphin, the Count de Grasse, the Prince of W——s, Lord R——ney, King Pippin, Patient Grizzle, Fair Rosalind, Punch, Harlequin and Pantaloon, Cupid and Columbine, seventeen monkeys and a giant, with several learned dogs and horses, arrived early yesterday in Smithfield, the place of their annual randevouz; and about Two in the afternoon, after the Lord Mayor had proclaimed the Fair, a very grand concert of salt-boxes and trumpets, with drums, fiddles, and French-horns, commenced — Several favourite airs were sung by young ladies admirably, calculated to charm the senses! — But alas! that prince of mimics, and mirrir of mirth, Sir Jeffery Dunstan, was not there: The poor gentleman has the misfortune to be in prison for not having had resolution enough to resist the attractions of a silver spoon that stood in his way! — But there are *other* fools who supply his place with great satisfaction. In short, Bartholomew Fair never wants fools. A *logical* horse, with the finest faculties was in want of a master this year; and therefore the following advertisement was fixed on the gate of the George Inn:—"To be sould or lette during the fare, the famous larned Horse that was the proparty of the late Henry Hinton, diseased. If not sould or lette, to be raffled for the last day of the fare at the George Inn."—A Correspondent was sorry to find one part of the fair continued. The puppet-shews do no harm; nor do the interludes, the tragedy heroes and heroines being as inoffensive as the gingerbread queens. The objectionable part of the amusements is the riding round the Fair in coaches, which are exceedingly dangerous, and occasion many accidents.—It is hoped the Lord Mayor, who always reads this Paper, will order the coaches to be suppressed.—In the fair of this year are Palmer's company, who give "The Poor Soldier"; Hall, who performs "As you

209

like it"; and Hyllyard's, who give a Pantomime.—The noted Flockton, the notorious Jobson, and others as usual.

Public Advertiser
4 September 1784

MORE NEWS FROM BARTHOLOMEW FAIR

The eye was at first engaged with the different collections of *beastesses*, properly scattered along the railing which incloses the sheep-pens. The masters of these terrible animals took infinite pains to worry them with poles and sticks, that the spectators might be struck with the beautiful languages of the lion and bear; there were likewise, near the same spot, innocent dancing dogs, leaping monkies, and birds with strange heads but beautiful feathers.

The elegant part of the entertainment was confined to a few booths. At the Lock and Key, near Cloth-fair, a select company performed the musical opera of *The Poor Soldier*, with Columbine's escape from Smithfield. Mr. Flockton, whose name can never be struck from off Bartholomew roll, had a variety of entertainments without and within. The King's conjurer, who takes more from out the pocket than he puts in, made the lank haired gentry scratch their pates—the walking French puppet-show had hired an apartment, with additional performers; Punch and the Devil, in his little moving theatre, were performing without doors, to invite the company into the grand Theatre.—Two men, in a very large balloon, made of sail-cloth, sat smoking their pipes and drinking grog, with their heads popped out from two round holes, acquainting the spectators they were to set off at eight o'clock to visit the little man in the moon, and should be with them at twelve o'clock on Saturday, when the company might be assured of hearing the reception they met with—for we are told, "The man in the moon loves claret, &c."

Men with wooden mummies in shew-boxes were found

210

straggling about the fair—tall women in cellars, dropping upon their knees to be kissed—dwarfs mounted on stools for the same civil purposes—and men without arms, writing with their feet.

Nor must we forget the fair sex, who with their flashmen, rolled to the spot from Rosemary-lane, Chick-lane, Duck and Giblet-lane, Field-lane, &c. &c. They paid the first visit to their acquaintance of the savory parlours—"All fat and good oh—step in and grease your chin oh," was the cry. Their language was simple, but plain, "D——n your eyes, Peg, tip us half a dozen of brown relishers, or I'll upset your pan, blow me—Hand us over the yellow sneezums, or I'll twirl the pot in your eyes."

The public-houses in the neighbourhood were full from top to bottom. The cook-shops had plenty of customers— at one house in particular, there was a man who sat in a corner of the room, not much in size less than an elephant, with a stomach like a tyger—he kept shovelling in beef and cabbage, half a pound at a throw, for upwards of an hour; whilst others diverted themselves with varnishing their chins with pig fat; nor must our Correspondent forget an old Snuffletonian whose nose was so lost in his cheeks, you would swear his head had been troubled with an earthquake; he undertook to amuse the company with speeches from plays. The evening's entertainment was, as usual, complete with riots, confusion, and picking of pockets.

On Saturday evening last a boy about 14 years old, amusing himself with blowing up sausage-pans, at last blew himself up, and was taken home to his parents in White-cross street with a temporary loss of sight;—another boy run over by a coach and much bruised;—and two well-dressed women ascending the steps into Flockton's booth, had their pockets cut off, and were therefore obliged to return without gratifying their curiosity.

Public Advertiser
6 September 1784

211

The Society of *pickpockets* had a numerous meeting last night to consider of the supplies for the ensuing year, when it was agreed upon to *transfer* the handkerchief *stock* and *reduce* the number of *pigtails* during Bartholomew Fair.

Public Advertiser
5 September 1784

The Jews, like Rats out of a building falling to ruin, have been for some time on the move for Holland.

Certain moveables, accompanying the afforesaid Jews, will no doubt make them welcome every where.

Public Advertiser
5 September 1784

Take care of your pockets.—The people of this country are now, since the fine weather commenced, so completely air-balloon-mad, that nothing is to be seen or heard in the streets, about dusk, but "See the air-balloon!" And indeed, the exhibition is abundantly common, as five or six may often be seen dancing above our heads at one instant, like so many *Will-o'-the-Wisps* transported from a terrestrial to an aerial station. The well known *Slight of Hand Club*, who live by an attention to the signs of the times, take every possible advantage of this temporary delirium; and while the eyes of the multitude are soaring among the clouds, their fingers are diving with great dexterity to the bottom of every pocket within their reach.

Public Advertiser
6 September 1784

On Thursday last at two o'clock a balloon was launched from the inner court of Berkeley Castle, which rose to a very great height, and was visible for a quarter of an hour. The same afternoon it was seen to descend in a field where

212

some people were reaping, near the Smith's-shop, in the parish of Kingscote, about ten miles from Berkeley. The reapers were so much terrified, that they could not for some time be prevailed upon to approach it.

Gloucester Journal
6 September 1784

A very elegant coach, made in London, for a nobleman at Dublin, was landed at the Custom-house of that city about ten days ago. On its way to the nobleman's house it was stopped by a numerous mob, who smeared it with tar, then feathered it, after which, having drawn it through several streets, they pulled it to pieces, and carried it off for firing.

Jopson's Coventry Mercury
6 September 1784

The Nobleman's carriage, lately tarred and feathered by the Dublin mob, is said to have been belonging to Lord Muskerry. It was the beautiful and magnificent coach not long since sent over by Hatchert.

The quarrel to Lord Muskerry is not on any political or personal ground, but merely the offence his carriage has given the non-importation agreement!—The agreement, by the bye, did not take place till two months after the coach was landed in Dublin; so that here is a disorder, not more full of barbarism than blunder!

Morning Chronicle and London Advertiser
6 September 1784

Yesterday evening a great riot happened at a house near Cloth-fair, in Smithfield, the upper part of which had been lett to the master of a show. The strollers not performing the Poor Soldier to the satisfaction of the spectators, they pulled up the benches, and attempted to set fire to the scenes. Some parts of the scaffolding tumbled down, by which two children were dangerously hurt, a woman's arm was broke, and several others received considerable injury.

The avenues to Bartholomew-Fair have, from a lawless mob, been almost impassable during the continuance of that scene of confusion and riot, to the great disturbance of the inhabitants, and such persons who have business in that quarter of the town.

Last night a number of disorderly fellows, called Lady Holland's Mob, committed several outrages in Smithfield, knocking down every man, and tearing the cloaths off almost every woman they met. They attacked two gentlemen in Pye-corner, about ten o'clock, robbed them of their watches and near eleven pounds, and did a great deal of mischief wantonly, as they proceeded down the Old-Bailey.—Two of them were seized by the watch; but rescued directly afterwards.

Yesterday morning at five o'clock, ninety-six male convicts, ordered for transportation, were conveyed by Mr. Akerman, with proper assistants, from Newgate to Black-Friars stairs, where they embarked on board a lighter, which fell down the river to Woolwich; at which place Sheriff Skinner (who has been much indisposed) met them, and saw them put on board the Censor transport, bound for North-America. These people seemed totally unconcerned at their unhappy situation, and sung and behaved with great insolence during their passage.

General Evening Post
4–7 September 1784

INHUMANITY – A FACT. Sunday evening last, about six o'clock, a boy about thirteen, whose appearance indicated something above the common rank, and whose countenance and dress claimed respect, being in a hurry, and having overstaid his time, got up behind a chariot which came out of a bye lane into the main Edgware Road, and proceeded towards London. The boy got up, nearly as

214

the writer of this paragraph can calculate, about four miles on the other side of Tyburn turnpike; and he had rode about a quarter of a mile, when the lady in the carriage, looking through the glass behind, perceived him. She and the person along with her, for we cannot call him a man, bawled out to the coachman, "Drive as fast as you can to prevent the young gentleman's getting down, and *cut away* at him." The coachman did so, and in consequence the poor lad received a smack of the thong, or rather a jerk of the whipcord, which took his eye out of the socket, the optic nerve being cut across. A gentleman in a phaeton saw the transaction, took the boy up in his carriage, and carried him home to King-street, Soho. The man in the chariot was about *fifty*, wore a wig, and was dressed in green. The coachman had on a dark green livery, lined with red, red waistcoat and breeches, a silver-laced hat, was about twenty-five, thin made, with a sallow hanging look. The woman in the carriage was elderly, and had on a white bonnet. The horror of the act, which at first caused a ghastly grin on their countenance, at last came home to them, and they were so terrified, that they ordered their coachman to turn down the next lane, on the same side of the road as that on which they came out, and by that means made their escape. The horses which drew the chariot were long-tailed blacks.

Public Advertiser
9 September 1784

London, Sept. 9.
On Friday the 20th ult. two boys at Tunbridge Wells went into the fields to shoot small birds, and as one of them was going over a gate, with the gun under his coat, to keep it from the rain, it suddenly went off, and lodged the whole contents in the bowels and thighs of his unfortunate companion; and though all possible assistance was given, he expired in a few hours; the other lad (a youth about fourteen years of age) was so deeply depressed and afflicted

by being the cause of the unhappy accident, that he attempted to put an end to his life, by stabbing himself with a knife but the wound did not prove mortal.

Bonner and Middleton's Bristol Journal
11 September 1784

A letter from Framlingham, in Suffolk, says, that the smugglers are become so outrageous for want of business that they plunder every house they come to; and it is generally believed that the military must be called in to drive them out of that part of the country.

General Evening Post
7–9 September 1784

Extract of a letter from Bath, Sept. 6

"On Sunday evening died, at her grandfather's house in Belmount, Miss Maria Linley, the eldest unmarried daughter of Mr. Linley, of Norfolk-street. Miss Linley was with her father and mother here on a visit to her relations. Her illness was a violent and rapid fever, occasioned by cold after dancing, which put a period to her life on the 10th day, and in the 20th year of her age."

General Evening Post
7–9 September 1784

Portsmouth, Sept. 10.
On Monday night the Chaplain of the Elizabeth man of war was topped near Kingston by a man and his two sons, and robbed of a gold watch, and a considerable sum of money. Being immediately pursued by several persons, the father, on their coming up to him, endeavoured to fire a pistol at them over his shoulder, but not lifting high enough, shot himself in the shoulder, by which means he

216

was taken. The next morning one of the sons was apprehended in the dock-yard; but the other has hitherto escaped.

Public Advertiser
14 September 1784

Winchester, Sept. 11.
Muddle, who was committed to our gaol for robberies near Ringwood, is lately dead, having destroyed himself by an inflexible resolution to abstain from all sustenance.

Gloucester Journal
20 September 1784

London, Sept. 11.
Sir Joshua Reynolds, about ten days since, received notice in form of his appointment to the department of Portrait-Painter to his Majesty. The salary of this situation, with the other advantages arising from it, produce nearly an income of a thousand a year.

Bonner and Middleton's Bristol Journal
18 September 1784

Peruque à la Bouches perpetuelles,
Or PERUKES that never require Dressing.
TREMLET's new invented Bag or Queue Perukes, likewise Bob Perukes, for Clergymen, Hunting, Shooting, &c. Perukes made in the genteelest taste, and superior to any other kind of Perukes, for neatness, elegance, and convenience, endure all weathers, never disorder, therefore require no dressing as others do, which when the curls fall are frequently pinned up in a very awkward and inelegant manner; the utillity of these Perukes is so great to Gentlemen who travel, or reside in the country, they need only be seen and understood to recommend them. All

217

orders punctually executed, and Gentlemen on sending a Peruke (carriage paid) fitted in the best manner, by their humble servant

F. TREMLET.

No. 8 St. Clement's Church-yard, Strand.

N.B. As some Gentlemen at a distance from London have been desirous of having my Perukes, but are doubtful of not being suited, I assure these Gentlemen, that if not suited, another may be made, and the expence of returning fall on me.

General Evening Post
9–11 September 1784

Last Tuesday night, between eight and nine o'clock, a gentleman walking from Whitechapel church to the 'Change, counted no less than seven balloons, with lights to them, floating in the air, one of which fell in Whitechapel.

Public Advertiser
11 September 1784

London, Sept. 11.
On Monday night an air-balloon took fire and fell in a field at Whitton, near Twickenham, belonging to Mr. Haugton, a butcher in Bearbinder-lane, and set the stable on fire, within a few yards of his corn-stacks; the wind blowing brisk the flames would soon have communicated to them, had not some people immediately ran and extinguished them.

Bonner and Middleton's Bristol Journal
18 September 1784

The present rage for air-balloons has encouraged a projector to endeavour at a revival of the art of flying; in order to which, he is said to have applied to a prelate equally celebrated for the soundness of his religious

218

principles, as for his learning and critical abilities, to grant him permission to make an essay of his art from the top of his (the prelate's) cathedral: the good father answered him, that he could not grant his desire, it being quite contrary to his inclination for though he would do everything in his power to incite people to come to church, his conscience would not permit him by any means to encourage them to fly from it.

Norfolk Chronicle or Norwich Gazette
11 September 1784

The following singular circumstance happened last week in Worcester:—A man who had been some years abroad returned lately, and hearing that his wife cohabited with an acquaintance of his, a chimney sweeper, he went to their place of abode, and demanded her; but the sable knight of the brush, unwilling to part with what he considered a valuable acquisition, proposed a legal transfer by purchase, to which the husband agreed, and writings being according-ly drawn up, and presented to a lawyer for inspection, who pronounced them invalid, and advised the parties, as a mutual security, to have the woman taken by her husband, with a halter round her neck, to a public market, and there exposed for sale. In consequence of this, the woman walked in form to the beast market on Saturday, and was there purchased by her paramour for a Guinea. This done, the parties retired, each seemingly well satisfied.

Bonner and Middleton's Bristol Journal
11 September 1784

Saturday se'nnight died, at Esher, in Surrey, Mr. Ebenezer Bramble, many years master of the Academies at Brentford and Isleworth.

Public Advertiser
13 September 1784

219

Saturday evening last was the grandest balloon evening the town has yet had: A correspondent counted no less than thirty-two balloons. Tower-Hill was twice illuminated with descending ones, to the particular gratification of several hundred *rational* beings!

The Balloon Mania, it is feared, will not subside, till some fatal calamity shall be the result of it. One of these balloons, filled with spirit of turpentine and other matter of that kind, falling last Friday night on the leads of a house in Tottenham-court Road, the leads melted by the fire.—Who then will say there is no danger attending these balloons?

Friday a complaint was laid before the Lord Mayor, relative to the danger that may ensue from the air-balloons which are every night sent up in different parts of this city, and his Lordship promised that he would lay the matter before the Court of Common Council to-morrow. . . .

Saturday morning an air-balloon, of very large extent, was found in a field between Pancras church and White-conduit-house; by a label fixed to it, it appeared to have been launched at Uxbridge on Friday night at nine o'clock.

On Tuesday evening a very serious accident took place at the Rev. Henry Bate's in Essex: That gentleman had procured an air-balloon for the entertainment of the country-people, and gave orders that a cannon should be fired for the purpose of giving notice. In preparing the charge for the cannon, a spark from a match fell upon two pounds weight of gun-powder, which blew up and burned the face of the coachman and a boy in a most miserable manner.

The following facts are offered to the public, not without hope that they will contribute to the safety of our fellow-creatures, by discouraging the present practice of launching balloons. Within these few days more than fifty have been sent off from Westminster and its vicinity, one of which fell on the top of a timber-merchant's house, near Cuper's bridge, and continued burning until a person gave notice to the servants, who happily extinguished it before it had done any material mischief; and on Thursday evening last a balloon fell in Jennings's Garden, near Westminster bridge, which blazed very fiercely for many minutes, and was at last extinguished by force. On examination, it appeared to be composed of a large piece of sponge, dipped in spirits of turpentine, which undoubtedly would have continued on fire for a great length of time. Will Englishmen any longer sacrifice humanity to a momentary and useless curiosity?

The increase of air-balloons has considerably lessened the market for pocket handkerchiefs in Field-lane, &c. the shops being nearly over-stocked, owing to the facility with which the industrious manufacturers of these articles are able to work while crowds stand gaping in the streets.

Public Advertiser
13 September 1784
[Sir Henry Bate or Bate-Dudley, vicar of Fambridge, Essex, was editor of the *Morning Post* 1775–80.]

We hear that the inhabitants of London and Westminster are in great trepidations for the event of To-morrow, the day fixed on by Signor Lunardi and Monsieur Soleil for their visit to the stars. The absence of the two grandest luminaries must inevitably leave the regions of this metropolis in an eclipse for some time, but it is most earnestly desired that the Messieurs abovementioned will manage their excursions with so much judgment as to save many thousands of their fellow creatures from the dreadful consequence of an earthquake in their absence.

Every person not infected with the Balloon influenza must be happy to find that a Court of Common Council will consider on a means to check its alarming progress. It is amazing that it should be conceived that the Chief Magistrate cannot easily do this. The throwing of a squib in a street is reckoned a very dangerous nuisance, and is punishable by a fine of twenty shillings by act of parliament: But can it be supposed that this act is confined to *squibs*? It extends to all fireworks, and consequently includes *Balloons*, or any other instrument, whatever be its name.

By barring and bolting our doors, and the confidence we place in the care of our neighbours, we think ourselves secure from thieves and fire: but what security is there against a *Balloon?*—Can there be a stronger instance of folly than by giving half a crown or three shillings for one of these baubles, that only gratifies the sight for a few minutes, and endangers the whole community?

Public Advertiser
14 September 1784

On Monday the following accident happened at Whitwell Farm, in the parish of Whitwell: As a son of Farmer Harley, a fine lad, about 15 years of age, was chaining a young horse down in the field to keep him within a small compass, and stroking him, the horse being tickled, kicked him on the stomach, and killed him on the spot.

General Evening Post
11–14 September 1784

We are assured that the following singular instance of good fortune is an indisputable fact.—In the very inclement part of the season two winters ago, about three in the afternoon, a poor girl stood curtseying at the kitchen window of an elderly gentleman in a populous village near this metropolis, dinner being just carried down to the servants. The gentleman observing the distressed object, rang his bell, and ordered the servant to give her some food, and (it beginning to snow pretty smartly) to take her into the kitchen, that she might warm herself, and fill her belly at the same time. When she was going away, after having been plentifully regaled, this good Samaritan (the weather strongly prognosticating a stormy night) ordered her a bed for the night. Next morning the servants, by their master's direction, dressed her in a decent manner, and she was taken into the parlour to thank her kind benefactor, expecting then to be discharged from his hospitable roof. But, instead of dismissing her, he insisted on her staying in the family, and sent for the proper trades-people to fit her to appear therein. In short, by her prudent and decent behaviour, she soon gained such an ascendance over him, that he gave her the entire management of his house. In about a twelve-month after he was taken ill, and his regard for her was so much augmented, that he would not receive any thing from any one but her; and finding himself grow worse, he sent for a lawyer, and left her all he was worth. At his death, which happened soon after, she found herself in possession of several thousand pounds, besides plate and furniture. She is since married to a gentleman of fortune, and now rides in her carriage.

Public Advertiser
15 September 1784

Anecdote of a Paddy.—During the late war one Fall was carpenter to a man of war. One day, as they lay at anchor in the Downs, the Captain sent him on a message to a Dutch ship which happened then to pass them. Fall foresaw from certain circumstances, that he should be baulked, by this incident, of his dinner. His messmates therefore promised to save him a portion of whatever they cooked for themselves. He then shewed them a place of security in which his dinner might be deposited. His servant was an Hibernian, whom he charged to take special care of whatever was allotted for his use. He trusted the fellow at the same time with a bottle of wine, calling it poison for the rats, that no trick might happen to it in his absence. This he desired might be kept till he returned, as he pretended to be afraid of trusting the application of the poison to any but himself. He conjectured right. The Mynheers suffered him to return as empty as he went. He was consequently very hungry. On being told what was reserved for him, he immediately ordered the mess to be

223

brought in. The Irishman then began a whimpering and muttering to himself, and owned, "he had been tempted to take it, in hopes his master might dine abroad. But you rascal" said Fall, "since the victuals are gone, where is the bottle of stuff, which I desired you to keep for the rats?" "O, Sir," said Paddy, crying most bitterly, "I was so afraid of looking your honour again in the face, that I had no other way of getting out of the scrape, than by drinking the poison."

Morning Chronicle
16 September 1784

London, Sept. 16.

LUNARDI'S AERIAL EXCURSION

To combat the prejudices of a nation, and the incredulity of mankind, especially when deterred by examples of resentment in consequence of deception or misfortune; when awed by the danger incurred in the experiment, and the uncertainty of success in the project, must certainly require the greatest effort of human resolution to encounter. Whilst we were recollecting the occasion, which collected at least one tenth of the inhabitants of the metropolis within the optical powers of an individual, we cannot help indulging ourselves in these eccentric reflections. The aerial voyage, which has long been proposed by Mr. Lunardi, was appointed for yesterday, and perhaps the English nation never witnessed, upon any occasion whatever, such a number of persons being collected together as were to be seen within the environs of Moorfields; not a plain, or an eminence, a window, or a roof, a chimney or a steeple, within the sight of Bedlam, but what were populously thronged.—About half past one o'clock, the Prince of Wales arrived in the Artillery Ground, viewed the apparatus of the balloon and retired to the Artillery-House, which was principally occupied by his suite, and the persons who had liberally paid the adventurer for their admission.

The operation of filling the balloon was carried on under the inspection of Dr. George Fordyce, during the whole of the preceding night. The materials of the rarefied air were zinc, oil of vitriol, and steel shavings. About a quarter before two o'clock the balloon was sufficiently filled and closed, and the gallery and other apparatus prepared to be suspended; but on Mr. Lunardi, and his intended companion, whom we understand to be Mr. Biggen, a young gentleman of fortune and enterprise, having taken their situation and finding that the machine was unequal to their weight, it was determined that Mr. Lunardi should ascend alone. A cannon having been fired as a preparatory signal, Mr. Lunardi embraced his friends, and all matters being adjusted, a second cannon was fired as the signal of ascension. Insensible must that heart be which did not feel itself anxious and interested at that moment for his fate. About five minutes after two o'clock, the machine was launched; and after having mounted about twelve yards, reclined to its native earth. Mr. Lunardi took his seat in the gallery with great composure and confidence on the balloon's being launched; but finding himself too equally poized, he readily discharged a part of his ballast, which consisted of small bags of white dry sand, and by that means relieved his weight, and caused a regular and most beautiful ascension. After he had cleared the building, subject to the direction of the easterly wind, he saluted the populace with great elegance and gallantry, by waving a blue flag, which he had taken for that purpose, and seemingly bidding them a friendly adieu. The gallery was formed of an upright four-feet square, and netted with a strong cord, about breast high, but quite open at the top. After this salutation for the space of five minutes, he dropped his flag with an air of security, and having seated himself, took to his oars; but soon after one of them came down, which alarmed his friends for the consequence. Steering at this moment due west, he suddenly tacked towards the north, and with little variations, according to the altitude which he obtained. Till he seemed by degrees to establish that direction, his progress seemed exceedingly elevated and swift, although the balloon appeared to be under masterly management. We viewed this object, nevertheless, distinctly for one hour and twenty minutes, with a mixture of anxiety and delight, not unallayed, by a friendly dread for ultimate effect. Mr. Lunardi afterwards lowered himself towards the earth near Barnes, but not approving the situation, and finding he had command of his machine, he discharged a part of his ballast, and pursued his course until he arrived over Collier's-hill, five miles beyond Ware, in Hertfordshire, at 25 minutes past four o'clock. His companions in this adventurous voyage were a dog and a cat, the latter was destroyed, and the dog was almost spent by the difference of climate through which they passed.

Mr. Lunardi seemed quite benumbed with the cold he had suffered in the upper regions; the thermometer, by his account, was six degrees below freezing point; and the gallery was covered with a coat of ice.

Bonner and Middleton's Bristol Journal
18 September 1784

It is supposed there were not less than five and twenty hundred pick-pockets, on Tuesday last, properly dispersed in the neighbourhood of Moorfields, and at their labour— the notorious Count Dive, alias Smirk Barrington the pick-pocket, was within the gates, and got safe off with his plunder.

Morning Chronicle
17 September 1784

London, Sept. 18.
Mrs. Saunders, widow to an upholsterer of that name who formerly lived in Goodge-street, was so terrified at the fall of Mr. Lunardi's oar which she took for a human body, that she was suddenly taken ill, and, in spite of all medical assistance, expired early the next morning.

The great success that attended Mr. Lunardi in his aerial voyage with the flattering approbation he has received from the public, has so inflamed the zeal of the aerostatic adventurers, that in the course of a few days, it is publicly said, no less than four of these machines, with each of them two travellers, are to be launched.

Bonner and Middleton's Bristol Journal
25 September 1784

Wednesday the populace took the horses from the coach of the Right Hon. Charles James Fox, in Old-street, and substituted themselves in their places; but lest he should be too much elated, contrived to pick his pocket of a valuable gold watch. This seems to be intended by our sovereign lords the mob, as an humble imitation of a circumstance in the triumphs of the heroes of ancient Greece and Rome; which was this, whilst the conqueror was receiving the repeated applauses of his countrymen, an officer attended him in his triumphal car, who to prevent his pride from being puft up too much, continually admonished him to remember, "he was but a man."

Public Advertiser
18 September 1784

Anecdotes of the late Sir Philip Cravenleigh
This gentleman had a very good estate in Shropshire, the income of which he spent in gratifying his own humours, which were original and extraordinary. He built a house, which contained every thing that other people erect offices for, barns, granary, stables, cowhouse, piggery, dairies, pigeon-house, parlours, bed-chambers, and drawing-room, all surrounded one great court. His own bed-chamber was next the barn, because he liked the noise of the flails at five in the morning. He was always adding to this ark, for every wench that brought him a boy had an apartment for life; and the number of his natural children living under

227

his roof at once exceeded forty. His great amusement was farming, keeping 1000 acres in hand, and the whole produce of the farm was eaten up in the family, but he would on no account permit one penny to be laid out for any article the farm produced, such as wheat, malt, hops, meat, butter, milk, cheese, cyder, &c. and he extended this to wine, till he sent one of his sons, bred to the garden, to France, to learn the art of planting and dressing vines; after which he planted a vineyard, and then drank wine, good, bad or indifferent, as it happened. Honey he eat instead of sugar, which he would never permit any more than tea, to come into his doors. They were once, from a wasteful consumption, two months without bread. He would not suffer a single loaf to be bought, but made all live upon potatoes instead of it. He was kind and good-natured, unless any one offered to oppose his will, in which case he was steady, determined, furious, and inexorable, and governed near 100 in family like a sensible, stern Bashaw, that was good humoured and pleasant; and never had freaks of ill-nature if he met no opposition, which he always took care to crush as soon as it appeared. He was very charitable, and much beloved.

Public Advertiser
18 September 1784

Anecdote of an honest STOCK BROKER

Some time since a Countryman, having a legacy left him was advised by an acquaintance to get into the stock-jobbing business, assuring him that large fortunes had been made in that line. The Countryman being struck with the thought of increasing his fortune, desired his friend to recommend him to some person acquainted with the public funds; accordingly Mr. L—— was named. The Countryman, in a few days repaired to town, and on enquiry at the Bank, was introduced to the honest Broker; when, after telling him his tale, Mr. L. asked the sum he was in possession of. The Countryman replied. "Five thousand pounds." "What business have you followed?" He answered, "Farming." "Then (says he) go on Monday next to Smithfield, and buy pigs with it."

"Pigs! Pigs!" replied the Countryman, "Lord, Sir, I never dealt in pigs."

"Then" says the Broker "let this be the first time, for there you will be sure of a *squeak* for your money, but I'll be d——d if you have even that here."

Norfolk Chronicle or Norwich Gazette
18 September 1784

Wednesday se'nnight the Lord Bishop of Bristol confirmed at Shaftesbury 1604 persons. It was a general observation that a greater number of handsome women was scarcely ever seen in one country town who, without the aid of ornamental head-dress, (which the Bishop would not admit of) appeared in all their natural comeliness.

Sunday the 5th instant his Lordship confirmed 1382 persons in the church of Sherborne. . . . It is considerably more than 20 years since the last confirmation took place, but his Lordship intimated his intention of confirming again, throughout the whole of his diocese, at the expiration of three years. His Lordship confirmed upwards of 1700 persons at Blandford, and vast numbers at Bridport, Cerne, and other places.

Bonner and Middleton's Bristol Journal
18 September 1784

London, Sept. 14.
Last week was married at St. Hillary, near Marazion, amidst a numerous concourse of people, a girl who goes by the name of the Irish Fairy, being only thirty-four Inches high. She had travelled for some years in company with a man who calls himself the Irish Giant, and both together exhibited a striking contrast. The heart of a young man, a

dealer in Manchester goods, was inflamed by this make-weight lamp of love at Totness, from whence he pursued her so far as Marazion, where he stole her from her gigantic companion, by carrying her off under his great coat.

Bonner and Middleton's Bristol Journal
18 September 1784

Air-Balloon Bon Mot. When Lunardi was supposed to be at his highest ascent, with his balloon, on Wednesday last, a spectator observed, "If he did not pray now, he would never have such another opportunity of doing it so effectually."—"Why so," demands another?—"Because," replies the former, "he will never again have the same chance of being heard, by being so near Heaven."

Public Advertiser
18 September 1784

Last Wednesday one Adams, a blacksmith, was committed to Horsham gaol, for the murder of a labouring man, named Weston, on the Sunday before at Burwash. The prisoner and the deceased, who had been drinking together, went to the house of the latter, who soon after his arrival had words with his wife and struck her; upon which he received so violent a blow on the back part of his head from the prisoner, that he instantly dropped down dead on the spot. The murderer absconded, but was taken on Tuesday at Tunbridge-Wells, while he was playing at skittles.

Sussex Weekly Advertiser or Lewes Journal
20 September 1784

London, Sept. 21.
Last week George Fifield, of Romsey, was tried at Botley by the Botley law, for swindling, and found guilty; his

sentence to be whipped out of town with a post-chaise boy's whip, and a halter round his neck; which was put into execution, to the great joy of the spectators.

Bonner and Middleton's Bristol Journal
22 September 1784

Some of the morning papers puff the man who went up in the balloon as if he had done some signal service to this country; and even the cloathes in which he attended the Ambassador to Court are particularized, as if he was a person of the first consequence. This ascent was no more than a representation of what was often done in France, and which it was of no sort of good consequence to this kingdom to have performed here. Mr. Lunardi made a great number of idlers among both the low and high class of manufacturers, and thereby did an injury by his exhibition.

Parker's General Advertiser
24 September 1784

Yesterday Mr. Lunardi, accompanied by Sir James Wright, was at St. James's, and introduced to the nobility, by whom he was complimented on his safe return from his aerial tour.

His Royal Highness the Prince of Wales no sooner entered the drawing-room yesterday, than he addressed himself to Mr. Lunardi, with great affability and good humour, "Oh, Mr. Lunardi, (said he), I am happy to see you alive!"—His Highness continued in conversation with him for some time.

Bonner and Middleton's Bristol Journal
25 September 1784

A Gang of Footpads has infested Finchley Common, and the North Road for some Nights past. On Saturday Night, several Farmers Carts going from Town, were stopped by those fellows, who robbed the Drivers, &c. of their Money. Two Men who resisted were beat with the Butt Ends of their Pistols in a cruel Manner. On Sunday Evening two Gentlemen and a young Lady coming over the Common to London in a Post-Chaise, were attacked and robbed by three Men of their Watches and about 8 l. One of them, who had got into the Chaise to search under the Seats, told the Gentlemen, if they were again molested, to give the Pass-word *Bob!* Within Half an Hour after two other Footpads stopped the Carriage; but on receiving the above word, ran off, wishing the Gentlemen a good Night.

Jackson's Oxford Journal
25 September 1784

WHEREAS JOHN, alias BEDLAM FOX, stands charged with being concerned with JOHN WILLIAMS, a Hawker and Pedlar, of Retford, in Nottinghamshire, and another man named JOSEPH, in stealing on the 31st of May last, goods to the amount of 40 l. out of a waggon at Bolton.

Whoever will apprehend the said John, alias Bedlam Fox, and lodge him in any of his Majesty's Gaols in this kingdom, shall receive FIVE GUINEAS reward, from R. Langton Bankes, Esq; of Sleaford, Lincolnshire. The said Fox is about five feet six inches, of a black complexion, knock kneed, turns out his toes very much, generally wears a round hat with a ribbon and girdle, and frequents most horse races and fairs.

Newcastle Courant
25 September 1784

London, Sept. 21.
On Saturday, in the Dusk of the Evening, as Mr. Watkins, of Holborn, was crossing from the Dog and Duck, in St. George's Fields, to Blackfriars Bridge, he was stopped by two Footpads dressed in Soldier's Clothes, with Knives in

their Hands, who swore that if he did not immediately deliver, they would rip him up, and robbed him of Half a Guinea, 8 s. and his Handkerchief; and then told him if he called for Assistance to take them, they would return and murder him, and made off towards Westminster-Bridge.

Jackson's Oxford Journal
25 September 1784

London, Sept. 24.
Paris is at present crowded with young Englishmen of Fashion, who, as usual herd together, d——n the Monsieurs, and get drunk. Some go to Plays, and some to Dancing and Cards; but the main Purpose of Travelling is as little attended to by them as by their Horses.

Jackson's Oxford Journal
25 September 1784

Extract of a letter from Canterbury, Sept. 14

"The following remarkable circumstance may be relied on as a fact:– On Sunday se'nnight, in the Duke of Dorset's park at Knowle, near Seven Oaks, in Kent, a man and his wife who came into that country hopping, quarrelled; and being somewhat in liquor, they came to blows. After the heat of passion was over, the man was so much vexed with what he had done, that he hung himself on the arm of a tree with a cord which he had about his waist. The wife perceiving this, jumped from the ground, and going to her husband, said, "By the blessing of God; I'll do part of the hangman's office" and she pulled the legs of her husband with all her strength, ever and anon saying, "You shan't be disappointed deary." The force with which she pulled, broke the cord, and down he tumbled. After lying some time on the ground, he recovered, and his wife having related to him the assistance she gave he knocked her down, tied the cord together which his neck broke, and putting it about hers, he tied her up to the arm of the very same tree, where she hung until she expired. The man has since been taken up, and confessed the fact. Now the question of law is, "whether the attempt made on his life did not justify him in the act of retaliation."

Public Advertiser
27 September 1784

A few days since a young woman, servant to Mr. Woodnorth, at Chatham, in Kent, walked in her sleep into the garden, where she was caught by the leg in a man-trap. The trap being old, and the spring having but little power, the wound she received is but slight; but the terror occasioned by the accident, threw her into violent convulsions, from which her life is still judged to be in great danger.

Morning Chronicle
27 September 1784

Madrid, August 27.
They write from Mexico, in their Gazette of the 19th of May last, that there is now living a man named Francis Saenz de la Rosa, who was born in 1662, and is now at Xalapa in the 122d year of his age; he was married in the 75th year, and has had ten children; he always travelled as a carrier; he enjoys strength and good health, and mounts and rides on horseback like a young man. It is said he sleeps only one hour each day.

Public Advertiser
28 September 1784

The following remarkable account we extract from a letter dated Paris, September 13, and received by yesterday's Dutch mail:

"A young man, about 17 years of age, was found by chance in the neighbourhood of Caen, in Normandy, and after having been taken great care of by Comte de Faudras, first Alderman of that city, was sent up to Paris, where he lately arrived. He speaks a language, or rather, jargon, which resembles none that have yet come to knowledge. He has been successively presented to Mons. de Vergennes, Baron Breteuil, Mons. de Calonne, and lastly to Madame de Bourton. All means have been tried, every linguist of any celebrity employed, to find out, if possible, the meaning of his particular dialect, but all in vain; yet he differs in nothing, either as to features, size, and behaviour, from the inhabitants of Europe, especially to the northward. His conduct is morally correct, and his manners such as bespeak a well-bred young man, whose education seems to have been shamefully neglected. As he cannot express himself in any intelligent manner, and that we are not sure whether we can make out any thing of our signs and dumb shews to him, it is impossible to learn any thing of his adventures, nor how he came to wander about the spot where he was found, in a situation nearly similar to the noted man of the woods, except the latter's wildness and ferocity. The celebrated actor La Rive, having had the curiosity to pay him a visit at a Mrs. Ballard's, where he lives, and who treats him in the same manner as her own children, assembled the Committee of the Comedie Francaise, where it was resolved to allow the foundling 63 livres per month, though the police pays a good price to the aforementioned lady, to provide him with every necessary. As he is now under the tuition of the most eminent masters, we have little doubt, notwithstanding his apparent incapacity, that he will soon be able to converse in French, and give such account of himself as may satisfy the curiosity of those whose conversation is entirely engrossed by the oddity of the adventure.

Morning Chronicle
29 September 1784

OCTOBER

Last Friday died, very poor and very old, at his lodging in Whitecross-street, one Forcer, who many years ago was a sheep-doctor in Leicestershire, and occasionally a Merry-andrew, descended from Frank Forcer, who succeeded Dick Sadler, the original proprietor of Sadler's Wells.

Morning Chronicle
1 October 1784

UNCOMMON MANNER OF SPENDING A LARGE FORTUNE

Mr. Rogerson, of Gloucestershire, gave his son the very best education that England could afford; he sent him abroad to make the grand tour, upon which journey young R. attended to nothing but the various modes of cookery, and methods of eating and drinking luxuriously. Before his return his Father died, and he entered into possession of a very large monied fortune, and a small landed estate. He was now able to look over his notes of epicurism, and to discover where the most exquisite dishes were to be had, and the best cooks procured. He had no other servants in his house but men cooks; his footmen, butler, house-keeper, coachmen and grooms were all cooks. He had three Italian cooks, one from Florence, another from Siena, and a third from Viterbo, for dressing one fish, the *docce piceante* of Florence.—He had a German cook for dressing turkey's livers: the rest were all French. He had a foot messenger constantly on the road between Brittany and London, to bring him the eggs of a certain sort of Plover near St. Malo. He has eaten a single dinner at the expense of fifty-eight pounds, though himself only sat down to it, and there were but two dishes. He counted the minutes between meals, and seemed to be totally absorbed

236

in the idea, or in the action of eating, yet his stomach was very small; it was the exquisite flavour alone that he sought. In nine years he found his table dreadfully abridged by the ruin of his Fortunes; and found himself hastening quickly to poverty. This made him melancholy, and brought on disease. When totally ruined (having spent near 150,000 l.) a friend gave him a guinea to keep him from starving, and he was found in a garret soon after, roasting an artolan with his own hands. He shot himself in a few days.

Bonner and Middleton's Bristol Gazette
2 October 1784

London, Oct. 1.
A Cabbage of the Long-Kele Species is now growing in the Garden of Peter Ferguson, near Dissington, which measures five Yards and three Quarters in Circumference: It was sown in the Spring of 1783, and remained in the Ground all last Winter.

Jackson's Oxford Journal
2 October 1784

London, Oct. 2.
Yesterday no less than 2,534 persons paid a shilling a-piece to see Mr. Lunardi, his dog, his cat, and his balloon, at the Pantheon.

Bonner and Middleton's Bristol Journal
9 October 1784

London, Sept. 18.
On Thursday last a lad about 12 Years old, Son of a Farmer near Edmonton, swallowed near two Ounces of White Arsenic, which he mistook for sugar. The circumstance being immediately discovered, an ingenious

237

Surgeon at Southgate was called in, and by repeated Draughts of a Solution of Tartar Emetic the poisonous Mineral was Thrown up, and the Youth is now in perfect Health.

Jackson's Oxford Journal
2 October 1784

On Saturday evening as one of Mr. Henshaw's apprentices was going up Fetter-lane, with two boxes of gun-powder, one of six pounds, the other of eight, to the White Horse Inn, a man very genteelly dressed, fell down, and pretending he had hurt his leg, very much requested the lad to buy him some sticking plaster to stop the blood, and he would take care of the boxes, with which he made off, notwithstanding his lame leg, to the great disappointment of the youth, who thought he was so hurt as not to be able to walk.

Morning Chronicle
4 October 1784

The reported hurricane in the West-Indies, turns out, for the most part, a mere artifice of the sugar dealers, to raise the price of that valuable necessary.

Morning Chronicle
7 October 1784

Thursday last as Mrs. Willerton, of Bond-street, was walking in the garden of Mr. Roberts at Paddington, a swarm of bees settled on her head and neck, which threw her into fits, and so much alarmed her that she has kept her bed ever since.

Morning Chronicle
7 October 1784

London, Oct. 7.
The Ladies of the Town have honoured Mr. Lunardi with many marks of their affection.—They adorn their heads with Lunardi's hat; they have got the Lunardi colour, Lunardi snuffers, and kitten muffs, in honour of his enterprising puss. A march has been composed called Lunardi's march; and there is an allemande called Lunardi's flight.

Jopson's Coventry Mercury
11 October 1784

One of the blind men at Chelsea College carrying his pitcher of beer from the Hall, on Monday evening, held in his other hand a lanthorn; he was accosted by a maccaroni to know of what use the lanthorn could be to him, as he had no eyes. "It is not for my own use," replies the veteran, "but for your's; it is to prevent hare-brained fellows running against me, and overturning my pitcher."

General Evening Post
5–7 October 1784

Monday a quarrel arose between Mr. Death, butcher at Hargrave, near Bury, and one Samuel Salvage, formerly his journeyman, when Mr. Death was knocked down by his antagonist, and killed on the spot.

Norfolk Chronicle or Norwich Gazette
9 October 1784

On Tuesday night the dwelling-house of the Right Hon. Edmund Burke, at Beaconsfield, in Buckinghamshire, was broke open, and robbed of a quantity of plate, and other articles to a considerable value, with which the thieves got off.—The manner of committing this robbery was somewhat nouvelle. The gentlemen of the pick-lock society went to Beaconsfield, two in a phaeton dressed like

London Jackadandies, and two on horseback in the Livery of servants. Thus travelling in the disguise of gentlemen and servants, they were unsuspected in going to the house and in taking their booty from it. The horses and the phaeton were seen in the lawn by several of the town's people, who imagined the company to be different kinds of visitors than what they in reality were. They were seen to go through Beaconsfield in the same unsuspected manner, with several large bags in the chaise, early on Wednesday morning. In the hurry they left a large sack of linen behind them.

Norfolk Chronicle or Norwich Gazette
9 October 1784

An Architect of Paris named Berger, a Man of some Abilities, and who had very good Business in that City, enjoyed a decent Mediocrity, but unhappily for him he had a Fancy for picking Pockets, and in March last he was catched in the Fact, as he was taking a Gold Watch from a Gentleman going into the Opera-House. The Tribunal of the Tournelle sentenced him to be whipped, branded, and sent to the Galleys for nine Years.

Jackson's Oxford Journal
9 October 1784

London, Oct. 8.
We hear an old Man who was last week sentenced to be transported for stealing Alehouse-Pots, has confessed stealing no less than 1500 since last Christmas.

Jackson's Oxford Journal
9 October 1784

Yesterday morning as Mr. Hewet, pawnbroker in Leather-lane, Holborn, was standing at his door conversing with a neighbour, he suddenly exclaimed "I'm a dead man!" dropped down, and instantly expired.

General Evening Post
7–9 October 1784

London, Oct. 12.
Last Friday in the Afternoon one of those Vagrants stiled Gypsies, in a Field between Kentish Town and Copenhagen House, calling to a young man and asking him if he would have his Fortune told, and the latter foolishly agreeing to it, she took him behind a Hedge, where was another Woman, with a Man, who robbed the Youth of all the Money he had, stripped him to his very Shirt, and it was with some Difficulty he prevailed on them not to take even the Shirt also.

Jackson's Oxford Journal
16 October 1784

Friday the following singular occurrence took place: –
A seaman after being discharged from a vessel lying off Pickle Herring stairs, on account of his having rendered himself extremely obnoxious to the rest of the crew, was impudent enough to return on board the ship, upon which he was seized by some of the men, stripped, and tarred and feathered, with as much dexterity as ever that discipline was inflicted in the country where it was invented and first practised. In this situation he walked to the Public Office at Shadwell, followed by an immense concourse of people, not less anxious to gratify their curiosity by viewing this singular appearance, than were the multitude about the Artillery Ground to behold the aerial exaltation of the celebrated Lunardi, and exhibited his complaint before Peter Green, Esq. the presiding Magistrate, by whose order several pounds of butter and hog's lard, and some quarts of oil, were administered, to clear the man from this disagreeable covering. During the

above operation, proper persons were dispatched by the Magistrate in search of the delinquents, and in something more than an hour they brought to the office the mate and five of the seamen, belonging to the ship on board of which the fact had been committed, against whom a charge for assault, &c. was substantiated. The Captain bailed the mate and four of his men; but the other, a Negro youth about twenty, a native of Nevis, was committed to New Prison, Clerkenwell.

Morning Chronicle
12 October 1784

A circumstance of a most singular nature was last week brought to public view at the quarter-session held at Kingston, for the county of Surry. A select party of gentlemen and ladies, amongst whom were a pair of Benedicts and their spouses, some little time since paid a visit to a certain town in the county, and as they proposed spending the evening, and taking up their abode all night at the inn at which they had put up, it was necessary to secure beds. It so happened that the company could not be accommodated without making use of a two-bedded room, and in this room the married gentlemen and ladies agreed to repose themselves. After a joyous supper the glass flew merrily round, and the ladies withdrew to their apartments with the door unlocked, no doubt in expectation of their beloved partners. The gentlemen *kept it up*, and whilst they were quaffing and carousing, one of the company, a wag of the first class, no doubt on't, took an opportunity to slip into the ladies room, who had resigned themselves into the arms of sleep, and very dexterously interchanged the wearing-apparel from one of the beds to the other. The gentlemen, upon their approach to their respective beds, each of them seeing his wife's habiliments, and being unwilling to disturb her, immediately jumped into bed; and in this situation they actually continued *all night*; and it was not until the usual time of getting up in the

242

morning, that the mistake was discovered. The confusion that ensued is infinitely easier to be conceived than described. The ladies were transfused into blushes, and the gentlemen had no other resource but the brandy bottle, whilst the wag had decamped, and the rest of the company, the family, and attendants, were seen laughing, and tittering in every sly corner of the house. In order to obtain some revenge for this most extraordinary trick, a bill of indictment was preferred against the party for a misdemeanour; but here again fortune favoured this blade of fun and humour, for the Grand Jury threw out the bill.

General Evening Post
9–12 October 1784

Wednesday afternoon, about six o'clock, one of the most inhuman murders was committed that has been known for many years: That day, being a festival among the Jews, at which time it is customary for children to fire off squibs &c. a Mr. R. in Duke's Place, came amongst them, and desired them to desist from letting off the squibs; but upon their refusal, some words arose, upon which Mr. R. went up to his one pair of stairs window, and levelling a blunderbuss at them (when there were not less than 2000 Jews going to Synagogue), loaded with nails and shot, fired it off indiscriminately amongst them; by which two boys were shot dead on the spot, and three were wounded; one of whom died on being carried to the hospital. The person is secured and safely lodged in the Poultry Compter.

It seems on the evening the unfortunate circumstance took place, Mr. R. sent for a Constable, and took one of the boys into custody, for throwing squibs, crackers, &c. upon which many of them collected in a body and rescued him; this enraged Mr. R. so much that he went up stairs, loaded his blunderbuss, and putting up the sash, fired it off among them. It is reported that Mr. R. had been offended some time since by a young man of the sect of the Jews having debauched his sister.

243

The Vestry belonging to the synagogue have taken up the prosecution at the expence of themselves; as the boys were very poor and had but few friends.

Norfolk Chronicle or Norwich Gazette
16 October 1784

The person charged with the murder of the Jew boy, we are assured, on Tuesday last, transferred upwards of 5000 l. stock.

General Evening Post
12–14 October 1784

Extract of a letter from Brighthelmstone

"While his Royal Highness the Prince of Wales was at this part of the country, he several times visited Heydown-hill, between this place and Arundel, remarkable as commanding a most beautiful and extensive prospect, being a landmark for mariners, and as being the place of residence of Mr. Clement Oliver. Of this singular, but worthy character the following are some particulars: On the declivity of the hill, about a quarter of a mile from Mr. Oliver's dwelling, is a square piece of ground, inclosed with a railing, a yew-tree standing at each corner, and in the middle is a tomb, an inscription on which expresses, that it was erected in the year 1766 by Clement Oliver, miller, for the reception of his body when deceased; and the top and sides are inscribed with divers quotations from scripture, and some pieces of poetry, the production of Mr. Oliver's Muse. About ten yards from the tomb stands an alcove, painted within and without with death-heads, with a plantation of flowering shrubs, where the honest miller, when the weather permits, retires to regale himself with his pipe and jug of ale, after the fatigues of the business of the day. Another circumstance is expressive of the whimsical disposition of this extraordinary man: he many years since provided a coffin for the reception of his remains, which runs upon castors, and is every night wheeled under the bed of its future tenant: on the coffin is a plate, with the words *memento mori*. Mr. Oliver is about 66 years of age, but strong, active, healthy, and cheerful."

General Evening Post
12–14 October 1784

Yesterday se'nnight Mr. Hargreaves, attorney at Law, at Bradford, was seized with an apopleptic fit, while gathering thyme in his garden, and expired immediately.

Public Advertiser
15 October 1784

On Saturday last in the afternoon, a well-dressed person called at the house of a gentleman on Blackheath, and with all the easy behaviour of an acquaintance, asked the footman if his master was at home; being answered in the affirmative, he got off his horse, and was conducted by the servant to the parlour where his master was sitting alone. The gentleman, after the footman had withdrawn, civilly asked the person to sit down; but instead of doing so, he immediately locked the door, and observing that the business he was come about required no preface, instantly drew a pistol from his breast pocket, and demanded 200 l. The gentleman could not answer that he had such a sum in the house; then, said the villain, give me a draft on your banker, or you are a dead man. This, under the circumstances, the gentleman was obliged to comply with. The villain then ordered the gentleman to see him to the door, when he immediately mounted his horse, and rode full speed to town; the servant was ordered to pursue him, but unfortunately arrived in town about five minutes after the draft had been paid.

Norfolk Chronicle or Norwich Gazette
16 October 1784

On Tuesday last, at two o'clock in the afternoon, was launched out of —— Wilson's garden at Chelsea, for the amusement of his friends, one of the most curious balloons that ever went off in this country. It had sixteen beautiful variegated stripes, made of paper, and filled with rarefied air, twelve feet in diameter; and to try the experiment, it took up a large white Pomeranian dog, fastened on a car. About four o'clock the same afternoon it was taken up by a labourer in a vale near Epping in Essex, about eighteen miles distance, and was brought back the next morning for the reward of one guinea. The dog was in perfect safety; but in his flight he received a few drops of volatile spirits on fire, which makes him resemble as if he had been beautifully spotted by the pencil of a curious artist.

Norfolk Chronicle or Norwich Gazette
16 October 1784

A very curious marriage was lately celebrated in Drury-lane, which strongly marks the progress of folly and dissipation.—A man of some considerable fortune was kept for a week in a bagnio in a state of intoxication, and became so infatuated as to promise immediate marriage to one of the most common prostitutes of the place. Care was taken that he should be kept as devoid of reason as possible, until the business was finished, which was done with all the splendour of Old Drury. He gave a grand dinner to the mother abbess, and as many nuns as she pleased to invite—and thus a gentleman who perhaps deserved a better fate, was hurried by intoxication and proportioned infatuation, into a life of shame and misery.

Morning Chronicle
16 October 1784

Extract of a letter from Exeter, October 10
"Within these few days a duel was fought in the neighbourhood, occasioned by the following singular

246

incident. At a village, a short way from this city, a young clergyman from London preached a sermon which gave great satisfaction to most of the congregation. Coming from divine service, an old gentleman observed to his companion, 'that it was an excellent discourse.' On this a third person behind them, who is more remarkable for fortune than manners, said 'he thought it a d——d bad discourse.' Words from hence arose, and the latter insulting the gentleman upon his age, was told that should be no bar to his affording him satisfaction. In short, the parties went out, discharged a case of pistols, and the impertinent commentator received a slight wound in the cheek, which, it is supposed will put a stop to his criticisms for the future."

General Evening Post
14–16 October 1784

BLANCHARD'S BALLOON

The attention of a thinking and speculating nation, will ever be attracted by grand and important philosophical experiments; and the metropolis is more likely to be agitated upon such interesting occasions, than any other part of the kingdom. Exactly in that state were the various parts of the west end of the town on Saturday morning, when every mind seemed bent towards the spot, where Mr. Blanchard was to exhibit his grand aerostatick experiment. At ten o'clock, St. James's Park, Pall Mall, Hyde Park, and the several leading streets and avenues were crowded with inhabitants of all ranks and descriptions, and at eleven, the throng was increased so as to form one continued string of people in Hyde Park, particularly in the extensive transverse line, which leads from Oxford-street to Kensington Gate. In the meantime the turnpike roads were covered with carriages, from the ducal gilded coach and chariot to the humble city gig. Horsemen innumerable filled up the smaller vacancies, and the cut leading from the great western road to Little Chelsea, was well filled from one end to the other. The fields and orchards, for a considerable distance round the spot, were crowded with anxious spectators, and the very trees loaded with a new species of bipeds, whose impatient clamours and sounds were extremely dissonant and disagreeable. In Mr. Bryan's turnip field alone, which commanded an exceeding fine view, there were at least five hundred horsemen at one time; and the barriers of private property, hedges, mud walls and fences, were not considered as obstacles against the coaches, horsemen, &c. who drove and rode over rich and valuable grounds with the greatest heedlessness.

A few moments after eleven, a very handsome balloon, with a suspended gallery and a dog in it, was sprung from an adjoining piece of ground; its direction was north west and by west; by its size and rapid progress, it was for some time mistaken for the Blanchard, and in twenty minutes it was elevated beyond human sight. The half guinea tickets were admitted at Mr. Lochie's front gate; the humbler subscribers of crowns and half crowns were obliged to take a circuit to the back part of the academy, and were admitted through the riding house. Upon entering the ground, which was utterly inadequate to the business, both in point of extent and convenience, our correspondent found it divided into four compartments, viz. a passage or gallery, for the convenience of a tolerable good band of musick, consisting of wind instruments, drums, &c. a part railed off in a very rude manner for the crown tickets, and another part for the half crown visitants, to roam in at pleasure. The apparatus occupied that part of the ground next to the house, and consisted of two large casks, fixed in tubs of water, with twelve smaller casks surrounding them, in which the inflammable gas was excited, conducted to the receivers, and from them, conveyed by means of two silken hose, or tubes to the balloon, which was suspended by two strong poles and a rope, that ran through a noose at the top, fastened to the netting. The windows of the academy were taken out, and the rooms were filled with an

248

assemblage of the first personage in this kingdom, the Prince of Wales, Duke of Richmond, &c. &c. &c.

At twenty minutes before twelve, notice was given, that the balloon was filled, and the whole apparatus completed, by the firing of a gun. Shortly afterwards, the French and English standards were erected, and saluted with a gun. Another signal gun preceded a small gilt balloon, which was thrown up, to try the current of air. Mr. Sheldon next took an affectionate leave of his lady, and a fourth gun was fired as a signal, that the navigators had taken their seats. At this moment, the subscribers, to the amount of near a thousand, pulled off their hats, out of respect to the adventurers, and pressed forward on the machine, expressing their warmest wishes for the safety of the aerial passengers. A fifth gun announced, that the machine was ready to ascend, and a sixth, that the fastenings were loosened.

Immediately the balloon arose in majestic pomp, and the minds of the spectators were agitated with every nobler passion of the soul; hope, fear, joy, and terror, alternately possessing them. The balloon raised itself about ten feet, and was saluted with the acclamation of the spectators; it seemed to threaten the five shilling gallery, but luckily it came to the ground, upon which Mr. Blanchard and Mr. Sheldon threw over several bags of ballast and it again ascended about the same height, and passing over the wall, was precipated to the ground, a second time, in Mr. Carl's garden, where they disburthened themselves of the remaining ballast, together with several other trifling articles, such as musical instruments, &c. The balloon then arose a third time, with a majestic steadiness, cleared the grove of trees, behind the gardens, and pressed upwards into the atmosphere. The travellers threw over a great coat, some bladders of gas, and continued to salute the immense concourse of people with the flags, who in return made the air resound with acclamations of approbation and joy. The elevation continued to an immense height, taking its rapid progress at first due west, but in a few minutes it inclined two points towards the south, in a direction towards Windsor, and in about twenty minutes was lost to the most piercing sight. Previous to their departure, the gentlemen both declared, they would proceed as far as the light would permit. The balloon was of two colours; the superior half green, and the lower hemisphere yellow, which when it rose, being chiefly opposed to the spectators eyes below, caused it to be sooner out of sight than Mr. Lunardi's. A dark coloured car in the form of a boat, was suspended, in which sat Mr. Blanchard, accompanied by Mr. Sheldon. Their apparatus of wings, of different colours, made a lively appearance, from the reflection of the sun, which shone bright the whole time.

From the most authentick information, which could be obtained at ten o'clock last night, our correspondent learns, that after every effort had been exerted to raise the impending weight (in which even their coats and waistcoat did not escape) the machine was so much depressed, that Mr. Sheldon dismounted at Sunbury, a small village between Staines and Inglefield, sixteen miles from the place of departure, where they arrived in forty minutes, from whence he sent an express to his Lady, and immediately took post horse to follow his fellow aerial adventurer. Mr. Blanchard pursued his journey, elevated it, and arrived at Rumsey, an incorporated town in Hampshire, seventy-eight miles from London, situated on the river Test, in the direct road from Winchester.

At eleven last night there was no further accounts received in town either from Mr. Sheldon or Mr. Blanchard.

Mr. Jean Pierre Blanchard is, we understand, a native of Andley, a village in Normandy, and had rendered himself much known in France, long before the discovery of aerostation, by inventing a machine for flying. It seems he tried his project at Paris, which did not succeed, as he could not raise himself to any considerable height; but although he failed in this attempt, it did not discourage him, for we find he made a second experiment, by sending off a criminal in the machine, from the top of the church of

250

Notre Dame at Paris. The criminal who had been condemned for robbery was informed he should be pardoned if he would venture himself in it; he consented, the day was fixed, and the event proving successful, he was liberated. Spurred on by this little advantage, Mr. Blanchard again exerted his abilities, and soon after, during the late war, formed a flying boat, which he intended for carrying the dispatches from Brest to Paris, but as this did not answer his expectations, he was obliged to give up his design, and relinquish the idea of elevating himself above the clouds. Not long after this the invention of aerostation arose and Mr. Blanchard could not let pass so favourable an opportunity for his former pursuits, and when Mess. Charles and Robert ascended from the Thuilleries, he formed a balloon with wings or oars of his own invention, and on the second of last March arose to the altitude of 1500 fathoms, steering his course amidst the solitary paths of air, an heighth that no mortal *ever* before attained, in his boat, from the Cham de Mars, near Paris, amidst an incredible number of people. An accident happened which had like to have proved fatal to the expedition; a young gentleman of consequence of the Ecole-Royal-Militaire at Paris, insisted on ascending with Mr. Blanchard, and on his refusal, drew his sword, and cut the balloon in several places, but it was soon mended, and the gentleman taken into custody. The success of this expedition answered his wishes, and being determined to go onward in his career, he again ascended in the month of May, at Rouen, in hopes that he should be able to find a method to direct the boat at will; this likewise proving satisfactory he resolved on a third, in July, the result of which, with the whole account of his journey, observations, &c. we refer to this paper of September 28.

On the 20th of July, on his arrival at Rouen, from the third voyage, he was crowned at the publick theatre.

Morning Chronicle
18 October 1784

[The "young gentleman of consequence" is sometimes

stated to be Napoleon Bonaparte; his name in reality was Dupont de Chambon.]

Yesterday afternoon Messrs. Blanchard and Sheldon arrived safe in town from their aerial expedition. The boat in which they traversed the air was fixed on the top of the carriage they rode in, and were ushered into London with musick and colours flying.

Mr. Blanchard's ascension, as might be supposed, should have the effect of dividing the public attention, and detracting from that general monopoly Mr. Lunardi has made of popular favour; but whoever was present at the Pantheon yesterday must have seen an instance of unalterable constancy, of which nature, perhaps, never exhibited a stronger proof. Literally speaking, Mr. Lunardi was devoured; the crowd was so great about him, that he was almost in danger of suffocation; the apartment resounded with the loudest acclamations, and the clapping of hands were so violent and repeated, that for almost the space of three hours, every ear was deaf even to the shrill note of clarinet and hautboy. The very skirts of Mr. Lunardi's coat was kissed by those who could not reach his hand, with an enthusiasm which bordered on idolatry. Never to be sure was there a spectacle which spoke so incontrovertibly and emphatically the reigning and unequivocal sentiments of the publick, or does more honour to the natural character of Englishmen, who are as constant when their affections are once placed as they are cautious in bestowing them.

Morning Chronicle
19 October 1784

Mr. Blanchard could easily have prolonged his voyage to double its extent, as he had still all the ballast which he had taken in at Sunbury. His reason for coming down was that he saw the sea at a very little distance, and as he was

252

going on with astonishing rapidity, must very soon have been over it. This is a misfortune which our insular situation subjects us to, and tends in some measure to check the progress of aerostation in England.

Morning Chronicle
20 October 1784

When Mr. Blanchard's balloon came down in the garden adjacent to Mr. Lochee's, he was very urgent with Mr. Sheldon to alight, and suffer him to make his voyage alone. Mr. Sheldon would not comply, and a short dispute took place. "If you are my friend, says Mr. Blanchard, you will alight. My fame, my all, depends on my success." Still Mr. Sheldon was positive—On which the little man in a violent passion swore that he would starve him—point du chicken—"You shall have no chicken by Gat" says Blanchard; and saying this, he threw out every particle of their provisions, which lightening their machine, they ascended. It was a grand French notion, that the best way to get rid of an Englishman was to throw out the victuals.

Morning Chronicle
20 October 1784

Barrington, the noted pick-pocket, was detected on Saturday at the going up of Mr. Blanchard's balloon, and instantly handcuffed by the peace officers in waiting. Another of the tribe was detected at the same place.

Public Advertiser
20 October 1784

Saturday five well-dressed young men had fixed a telescope in a tree near the spot from whence the balloon was to ascend, and after having looked through it themselves, genteelly offered several well-looking spectators an opportunity of doing the same, and in helping them to get up, as genteelly picked their pockets.

Public Advertiser
20 October 1784

At Rumsey Mr. Blanchard saw himself very near the sea, and the new forest just before him, which induced him to come down where he did; but he was very much distressed from not being understood by the people who came up to him, and he was on the eve of launching himself again into the air.

Morning Chronicle
21 October 1784

A letter from a young gentleman at Dieppe in Normandy, to his relation, dated October 13, brings the following article: "A short time since two gentlemen went to fight a duel with swords, about a girl of the town, in the Tuileries gardens at Paris, in which place it is forbidden that any body should fight. They were therefore consequently taken up and tried; but being gentlemen, their sentence was mitigated to the confinement of a year and a day in prison. Whilst in prison they by some means procured fire-arms, with which they murdered the gaoler and another man. On the second of this month they were tried for the murder and convicted; and on the fourth were broke on the wheel."

General Evening Post
19–21 October 1784

Thursday being the day for the removal of the prisoners from the different gaols to Newgate, in order for trial at the Old Bailey, a sailor got up behind a hackney coach in which one of his old messmates was in custody, and placing one foot on each of the rails rising from the footboard, kept waving his handkerchief and hallooing as he rode; but the carriage turning sharp out of Berkley-street into St. John's-lane, by a sudden jolt the unfortunate tar was thrown over the hind wheel, which passing over his head, his skull was fractured in a terrible manner, and by the violence of his fall his shoulder was dislocated. He was taken to St. Bartholomew's Hospital.

Norfolk Chronicle or Norwich Gazette
23 October 1784

NORWICH

At a Court of Mayoralty, held the Ninth Day of October, 1784. WHEREAS many AEROSTATIC MACHINES ascending by means of Fire attached to them, have been seen in the Night over several Parts of this City, and there is Reason to apprehend that great Mischief may accrue from the further Use of such Machines. The Magistrates of this City hereby declare, that they will prosecute, with the utmost Rigor of the Law, any Person or Persons that shall send up, or cause to be sent up, any such Machine, by which Danger shall accrue to the Inhabitants of this City.
By the Court   DE HAGUE.

Norfolk Chronicle or Norwich Gazette
23 October 1784

Dishonesty punished.—An usurer, having lost an hundred pounds in a bag, promised a reward of ten pounds to the person that should restore it. A man having brought it to him, demanded the reward. The usurer loth to give the reward, now that he had got the bag, alledged after the bag was opened, that there was an hundred and ten pounds in it when he lost it. The usurer being called before the judge, unwarily acknowledged, that the seal was broke open in his presence, and that there were no more, at that time, but an hundred pounds in the bag. "You say," says

255

the judge, "that the bag you lost had an hundred and ten pounds in it." "Yes, my Lord." "Then," replied the judge, "this cannot be your bag, as it contained but an hundred pounds. Therefore the plaintiff must keep it till the true owner appears; and you must look for your bag where you can find it."

Public Advertiser
23 October 1784

We can assure the Public, from good Authority, that Mr. O'BOURNE, the noted and most wonderful astonishing IRISH GIANT; likewise the WARWICKSHIRE YOUNG LADY, will arrive at the SWAN WITH TWO NECKS, in this city in a few days.

MR. O'BOURNE is a Curiosity certainly more astonishing than any other Giant or tall Man ever exposed to public View in this or any other Kingdom since the Days of GOLIAH: he measures very nearly Eight Feet high; his Foot measures Sixteen Inches long; his Hand Twelve, and so in Proportion: He is of athletic Make, a great Exactness of Proportion, and high beyond all Conception, he being the most extraordinary Production of Human Nature ever seen.

Likewise Miss HAWTIN, the celebrated WARWICK-SHIRE YOUNG LADY, born without Arms, and will mark with her Toes, in as complete a Manner as with Arms and Hands. She is perfectly agreeable in her Countenance, of a fine Presence, and amazingly ready and sensible in her Discourse. This little Artist or Phaenomenon of Human Nature, by the help of her Toes and feet only, is capable of many curious Performances. She cuts curious Watch Papers, threads a Needle, Sews, picks Pins or Needles from a Pincushion, and sticks them in again; uses the Scissors dexterously in cutting out Devices in Paper; picks up Money, puts it in her Pocket, takes it out again, feeds herself, drinks out of a Glass with Ease, and exhibits sundry other Fancies too tedious to mention.

Several eminent Physicians, Surgeons, and Man-Midwives, have accurately examined this young Lady, particularly Francis de Valangin, M.D. and Member of the Royal College of Physicians, Thomas Unfreville, M.D., Mr. Horsley, Surgeon and Man-Midwife, as also that diligent investigator of Nature, Thomas Fisher, Gent. who all agree that she is *Natura Lusus quam maximi mirabilis*, or a most wonderful Sport of Nature, and a convincing proof that the DIVINE BEING can supply any Defects he permits in the Animal Formation, and unanimously recommend this Human Rarity, (as remarkable for its ripe understanding as its Make) to the serious Attention and Observation of the Public in general, and the *Anatomists* and *Virtuosi* in particular.

Any of the Nobility, Gentry, &c. willing to be satisfied of the Merits of this young Lady, by giving timely Notice, shall be waited upon.

Norfolk Chronicle or Norwich Gazette
23 October 1784

On Sunday afternoon as Lucas, a Constable, and an officer belonging to the Police, was coming thro' Chick-lane, observing a woman with a bundle, he accosted her with "Well, mistress, what have you got there." To which she replied, with seeming confusion, "What is that to you." This brought on some strong reasons that increased his suspicions; he insisted on searching her, and for that purpose conveyed her into a public-house. On opening her bundle, it was found to contain three thousand and upward forged stamps for receipts; and on more strict examination were also found a wedge of silver, weighing about six ounces, and two smaller pieces, which had evidently been in a crucible.—From many circumstances, there is great reason to believe she is an accomplice with the man frequently advertised in the Public Papers for having put off forged Bank Notes in different disguises, and is known in Bow-street under the appellation of Old

Patch. She is about forty years of age, and has the appearance of a Jewess.

Norfolk Chronicle or Norwich Gazette
23 October 1784

It is confidently reported that Lunardi has challenged Blanchard to a balloon-race, in three heats: the first with the wind, the second across the wind, and the third, which looses least against the wind. The betts on Monday and Tuesday night in the neighbourhood of St. James' were very considerble in favour of each adventurer, and great odds were laid on both sides, and it is positively declared that above 50,000 l. is depending.

Norfolk Chronicle or Norwich Gazette
23 October 1784

London, Oct. 23.
Three different attacks were made on Wednesday night last by the river pirates on the Westminster-side above the bridge, but fortunately all without success. They first attempted Mr. Heeker's yard, the stone-mason, but being disturbed by the brave defence of a fine dog, they killed him, and took to their boat. They next endeavoured to get into the premises of Mr. Gaunt, a little farther up the river, but he owed his safety to a few terriers, who kept a noise, while the villains could not get at them. The family were immediately roused, and the thieves desisted. Having failed in these enterprises, they assaulted a lime barge, which had taken in a valuable cargo of goods, and lay at anchor just above the bridge, in hope of finding her unguarded, but they were mistaken, for a blunderbuss was fired among them, and it is probable not without wounding some of them. They then sailed down the river.

Gloucester Journal
25 October 1784

Extract of a letter from Paris, Oct. 14

"It is said that *Monsieur* has asked the King his brother's permission to *oblige* the Carthusians to cede him their monastery and garden, contiguous to the promenade of Luxembourg; and that he offers to build a fine house for them in the forest of Brunoy; but that his Majesty had said in answer—'*I cannot, nor would it become me to grant your request: my maxim is, to let things remain as they are.*'"

General Evening Post
21–23 October 1784

John Stogdell was indicted for receiving various goods to the amount of 620 l. which John Hewlett, a servant boy to Mr. Priestman, Pawnbroker, of Princess-street, Soho, had stolen from his master, and who is now under sentence of death for the above robbery. Stogdell was tried last session as a principal with Hewlett, and acquitted, but directed by the Court to be prosecuted as a receiver. It appeared on this trial, that the prisoner had acted in capacity of pretended Valet to Hewlett, for the purpose of disposing of the property, the produce of which was distributed in a nominal Coffee-house in Charles-street, Covent-Garden, which Hewlett and Stogdell frequented. The record of Hewlett's conviction was read, and another pawnbroker's servant having proved the prisoner's having some of the property, and Mr. Shelley, silversmith, in the Strand, proving his purchasing a diamond ring for 35 l. of the prisoner, the property of Mr. Priestman, he was found guilty. His punishment is only 14 years transportation, whilst the deluded lad, 16 years of age, who has fallen a sacrifice to more artful villainies, must answer with his life for a crime of less magnitude.

General Evening Post
23–26 October 1784

Anecdote. Budé, the French author, being once informed in his study, that the house was on fire, coolly told the servant to tell his mistress, *that he never concerned himself in house affairs.*

Public Advertiser
29 October 1784

Friday at noon the trial of Mr. Porter Ridout, the keeper of a coffee-house in Dukes-place, for firing a blunderbuss, which killed a lad; on the 7th instant came on before Lord Loughborough. The Counsel for the prosecution were, Mr. Rous, Mr. Morgan and Mr. Sheppard—for the prisoner, Mr. Sylvester, Mr. Fielding and Mr. Garrow. The proof which seemed to bear the hardest against Mr. Ridout was that given by Saul Mordecai and David Levi, as to some expressions of being prepared for the Jews, who were celebrating their annual rejoicings, which epoch, in plain meaning, is their harvest home. On this occasion, they assemble and shew every token of transport, by way of returning thanks to the Supreme Being for the summer crop of fruits and corn. The day this unfortunate transaction happened, a great mob met, and fired squibs, &c. Mr. Ridout desired them to desist – they would not, and became outrageous. Mr. Ridout sent for peace officers – the Jews were then more outrageous, fell upon him, threw Mr. Ridout upon the ground, and picked his pocket: he fearful of his life, sought shelter in his own house – they were rushing in – the door was shut, and Mr. Ridout in an unhappy moment went up stairs, and fired the piece amongst the rioters.

This was the substance of the trial, and several Jews corroborated Mr. Ridout's defence, that his house was beset, and his life in danger.

Lord Loughborough gave a learned and elegant charge to the Jury: he defined all the legal distinctions in cases of murder. Amongst other doctrines he laid down this position, that a man might be guilty of this crime without having any particular object in view; and that it was not necessary he should take aim at A to kill him. If he fired

260

with malice amongst an assembly of persons, whoever fell a victim was clearly murdered. Also, if by firing at A he should miss him and kill B, it was murder, although the party aimed to destroy A without a design to injure B. The noble Lord then touched upon the doctrine of alleviation, through the weakness of human passions; and observed that if the Jury thought the prisoner, Mr. Ridout, was so led to fire the piece, when his mind was agitated, and had no time to cool, they undoubtedly acquit him of the charge of murder. His Lordship after going over all the evidence, with his discrimination, concluded with delivering his opinion, that he considered the Jury could not find more than manslaughter.

The Jury, without going out of Court, acquitted Mr. Ridout.

Norfolk Chronicle or Norwich Gazette
30 October 1784

London, Oct. 29.
In divers parts of the Country, the Windows have been stopped up in the Proportion of four, and in many Places, five out of twelve. There is a Village in Warwickshire, in which are resident two rural 'Squires, one of whom has blocked up nineteen, and the other the trifling Number of thirty-five!

Jackson's Oxford Journal
30 October 1784

London, Oct. 30.
A most melancholy accident happened last week at Ardleigh, near Colchester: A young man, who went to see his brother, being at dinner, a knife fell from the table, and attempting to catch it on his knees, nipped it horizontally with the edge downwards between his thighs,

and cut the arteries so that he bled to death, notwithstanding every assistance was given by the faculty.

Bonner and Middleton's Bristol Journal
6 November 1784

Extract of a letter from Dublin, Oct. 20

"You of course, in a letter from this side of the water, will expect news; I wish I could send you any that was pleasing. People now say every thing is quiet. What it was before my arrival a month go, I know not; but at present it appears very far from my ideas of peace and tranquillity. Every day the papers are full of scandal, and abuse of government, to call it by no other name. Some years ago it would have been deemed treason.—People in power seem afraid to act. No civil magistrate dare execute his duty without a military guard, for which both are generally grossly insulted and vilified in the papers. I wish the volunteers, who certainly have been of service, may not in the end prove the ruin of this country. The better sort of people being tired, have withdrawn, and now many entire corps are composed of Papists. At first none but Protestants were allowed to carry arms; but at present neither the one nor the other will be easily prevailed upon to give them up. The people here in general have been so long accustomed to idleness, that they do not care to do the little work that is for them; therefore, every street is crowded with beggars without number, and wretched beyond description."

Whitehall Evening Post
30 October 1784

The celebrated Dr. Graham who is figuring away at Manchester, has till very lately, buried himself every morning in the earth! He has stood, at least, up to his chin in it; then ran nimbly round a large field, attended by numerous spectators, to whom he advised the adoption of "this sure and happy means of preserving health, and of obtaining longevity!"—He dresses in a light suit of cotton, in compliment to the manufacturers of that place, and lives principally upon potatoes.

The above excentric character, who in lectures which he gives at Manchester recommends *Balloon-flying* as very conducive to health, says that in the course of years this mode of travelling will, he doubts not, be so much improved, and rendered familiar, that it will be "as common to hear a man call for his *Balloon* when he is going on a journey, as it is now for him to call for his *boots!*"—The art of flying he considers as one of the greatest desiderata of mechanics, attempted in divers ages, and now bringing to perfection.

Public Advertiser
30 October 1784

NOVEMBER

Two genteel young women were on Monday brought from the Compter, and committed for trial by the sitting Alderman at Guildhall, for assisting Stockdale, now under sentence of transportation in Newgate for fourteen years, to make his escape. It appeared that on Saturday afternoon, they went to the above gaol on a visit to the prisoner, and dressed him in woman's apparel so very speciously, that he and one of the parties passed the man at the first gate, but on their hastily demanding the second to be opened, Pitt, the turnkey, suspected a deceit and on pulling the bonnet off Stockdale, immediately discovered him; and at the same time securing the ladies, conducted him back to his old apartment, where he was double-ironed, and lodged in the cells.

General Advertiser
November 1784

[John Stockdell or Stogdell was "a convict and accessory of Hulet, lately executed for plundering Mr. Priestman" (*Whitehall Evening Post*, 20–23 November). "His female friends were committed to take their trial."]

A gentleman of Padua fell desperately in love with the Marchioness d'Obizzi; but despairing of possessing her by fair means, he contrived, in the absence of her husband, to conceal himself in the bedchamber where the Marchioness, and her child, about five years of age, usually slept; where, after using the gentlest means without success, he became furiously frantick, and stabbed to death the object of his love. The lady being found murdered, the gentleman's passion for her being notorious, and one of his shirt buttons being found in the bed, he was taken up, and suffered the torture ordinary and extraordinary, but still denied the fact; and after fifteen years imprisonment he was discharged. However, before he had enjoyed his liberty many weeks, the Marchioness's bedfellow and son took an opportunity to shoot him; and then retired into Germany. A monument is erected to record such an instance of virtuous courage. . . .

Morning Chronicle
2 November 1784

We observe with pleasure that steps are already taking by the civil power to prevent those mischiefs which almost always happen on the fifth of November, by throwing squibs and fireworks in the public streets; and we earnestly recommend it to parents and masters to promote this good purpose by confining their children, apprentices and servants to their houses on Friday evening next.

Public Advertiser
2 November 1784

ROBBERY EXTRAORDINARY

The Minister may be considered as having *lost a division*, in a business of an extraordinary kind which took place the other night. The whole service of plate, just finish'd for him as his official perquisite, was stolen, and left not a wreck behind.

The particulars of the above-mentioned event as they have come to our knowledge, are to this effect: Mr. Hemings, who has for the most part retired from business, and does not concern himself with any thing but very important strokes in trade, had, according to the order given to him, prepared the service of plate for Mr. Pitt, and it was all delivered to Mr. Hemings in Bond-street, from the different workmen on Friday or Saturday. On the evening of the following Sunday *it was all taken away again* nobody can tell where. The only circumstances at all appearing collaterally to be connected with this extra-

265

ordinary occurrence are as follow: That a hackney coachman has been found, who deposes that he was called off a stand in Oxford-street, by three men, whom he set down toward the west end of Conduit-street; that the coach was kept for them in waiting, and that in the course of about half an hour they all three returned, with bundles of a very large size, and as they seemed of great weight; that on the three men getting, thus loaded, into the coach, the man was ordered to drive to Old-street road. That in his way thither he was bid to stop at a house in Long-lane, where one of the men got out, and after staying a few minutes in the house, he returned, and said to the men, "We need go no farther;" on this they all got out, and the bundles were carried into the house. The time in which this happened was at the same time that the robbery was committed, viz. between the hours of seven and nine in the evening!

The loss sustained by this incident is valued at near 3000 l. sterling.

Whitehall Evening Post
30 October—2 November 1784

The freaks of dame Fortune are now and then very apposite; Lord Palmerston was one of Blanchard's particular patrons, and Blanchard descended on his Lordship's estate at Rumsey.

Morning Chronicle
1 November 1784

On Thursday morning last, a very melancholy accident happened to a child, about four years old, the son of Mr. Robinson, of East Harding-street. A friend of Mrs. Robinson came out of the country and slept at their house, in bed with the child, he had taken a peach out of his pocket, and gave to the child before he went to bed; the child waked early in the morning, and felt in the person's coat pocket, which was on the bed, and took out a bladder, wherein was a quantity of arsenick, which the person had used in the country to poison rats. The child eat some of the arsenick before the person waked, and with every assistance that could be given, the child, to the great grief of its parents, continued in great agonies all the day, and died the same evening.

Morning Chronicle
1 November 1784

A very melancholy, and most uncommon accident happened last week, at a village near Highgate. Miss G. a young lady of fortune, being thwarted by her friends in her affections for a deserving man, shot herself with a pistol. The ball passed through her brain and she died in an instant.

Morning Chronicle
3 November 1784

[The *Public Advertiser* (3 November) continued: "This melancholy event ought to be a warning to the hearts of parents, and a lesson how they suffer cold prudence to tyrannize over the generous ardour of passion."]

The thieves have lately adopted, or rather revived, a new method of depredation, by getting down chimneys; several houses in the borough have been entered and pillaged by this mode.

Public Advertiser
3 November 1784

Yesterday afternoon a Jew, who travels with hardware, was accosted by six or seven boys, who were attending some asses at feed upon Islington Common, between Ball's Pond and Kingsland turnpikes, and after asking the price of several articles, they overset his box of goods into a pool of muddy water, and snatching up several articles to the value of about twelve shillings, while the poor Israelite was scrambling up the rest of his property, the villains mounted their asses and rode off.

Whitehall Evening Post
2–4 November 1784

Sunday night some villains broke into the house of Mr. Lawrence Crow, master of the Sun alehouse at Wood's Wharf, Greenwich, and stole a silver watch and about four pounds in money out of Mr. Crow's bed-chamber, besides stripping other apartments of property to a considerable amount. The above robbery is supposed to have been committed by the fresh water pirates who have of late become so numerous and daring.

Whitehall Evening Post
2–4 November 1784

This day being the anniversary of the famous Conspiracy, the same will be observed as usual.

Public Advertiser
5 November 1784

Among the addresses presented upon the accession of that Solomon of Great Britain, James the First, was one from the ancient town of Shrewsbury, wishing that he might reign as long as the sun, moon, and stars endured. "Faith, mon, said the King to the Sheriff who presented it, if I do, my son must reign by candle-light."

Public Advertiser
6 November 1784

The following melancholy affair happened on Monday evening last: – Mr. Warren, of the Six Clerks Office, went with a lady to see Mr. Holman's first appearance in the character of Romeo. The Pit being much crowded, the lady complained that a person who stood near her had trod on her toes, upon which Mr. Warren remonstrated with him; but instead of desisting, he continued the same unjustifiable behaviour, which irritated Mr. Warren to an unusual degree, and very high words passed upon the occasion. No blows however ensued, and at the end of the play Mr. Warren left the house. The conduct of the person above mentioned still running in his mind all the way home, he gave great vent to his passion, threatening him with the most severe chastisement if ever he met with him again. When he had nearly reached his own house, he complained much of a violent pain in his head. When arrived at the door he knocked violently, and the servant maid not opening it so soon as he wished, he called out to her to be as expeditious as possible in letting him in, which she had no sooner done, than he ran into the parlour, sat down in a chair, and expired almost immediately. The next day Mr. John Hunter opened his head, and it appeared that from the violent passion he had been thrown into, several blood-vessels of the brain had burst.

Mr. Warren lived in Berners-street.

Norfolk Chronicle or Norwich Gazette
6 November 1784

[Holman was playing at Covent Garden.]

Letters from Avignon, dated October 24, mention that Mr. Joseph Montgolfier has made several ingenious and useful experiments on the resisting power of air. After having thrown a sheep six times from the top of a tower in that neighbourhood, upwards of 100 feet high, by the aid of a machine called a parachute, without the animal receiving any damage; he prevailed on a man, condemned to suffer a long imprisonment, to try the experiment, which was performed with the utmost safety to the satisfaction of many thousand spectators. In consequence of which the magistrates remitted the adventurer's punishment. The machine, we hear, is in many respects similar to an umbrella.

Morning Chronicle
6 November 1784

Paris, Oct. 22.
Our last letters from St. Malo mention a youth losing his life by the following accident; he was pealing an apple and balancing himself in his chair at the same time; unfortunately the chair slipped from under him, and he fell upon his knife, which entered into his side, and he died in a few hours.

Whitehall Evening Post
4–6 November 1784

Wednesday night some thoughtless youths, apprentices in Clerkenwell, committed an act of indiscretion that had well nigh been attended with serious consequences to them. They took away part of the bench and porter's block at the Baptist's Head in St. Johns-lane, and took from the yard of Mr. Barber in the same lane, several pieces of mahogany and some other wood, on some of which a good deal of time had been employed in workmanship, and the spoil thus obtained, they deposited in a cellar against this evening, for the purpose of celebrating the anniversary of Gunpowder Treason with a bonfire. However, a discovery taking place, seven of the lads were yesterday evening taken before William Blackborow, Esq; who very properly considering the offence as proceeding rather from youthful wantonness, than a deliberately bad design, advised the complaining parties to be content with receiving back their property, to which they chearfully consented.—The Magistrate then pathetically admonished the lads, explaining to them the consequences that might have ensued, had the persons they had injured proceeded against them with the severity which the law would have authorized, and cautioned them against indulging themselves in many practices not strictly justifiable, which, he remarked, had but too often the effect of leading young people, as it were insensibly, and step by step, from what are called acts of boyish folly to daring outrages; and after making several observations on the late melancholy event in Duke's-place, and enumerating the many mischievous effects likely to be occasioned by the use of fireworks in a populous town, the Magistrate dismissed the lads, observing, that from the contrition they expressed, he had hopes the advice he had given them would not be totally useless.

Whitehall Evening Post
4–6 November 1784

On Friday night as some boys were making a bonfire in Bedford-street, in commemoration of the anniversary of Gunpowder Treason, a barber's apprentice fired off a pistol, which being loaded with gravel stones, shot a youth dead on the spot, who happened unfortunately to be a partaker in the boyish caprices of the evening.

On Friday night a man received a violent blow from a person at a bonfire in Claremarket, which killed him on the spot; the deceased man was endeavouring to extinguish the bonfire when he received the fatal blow.

General Evening Post
6–9 November 1784

The dog-tax bill, it is said, has passed in the Cabinet, and we apprehend will be carried into the House at the ensuing meeting of Parliament. Greyhounds and lurchers are to be paid for at the rate of twenty shillings each; pointers and all other dogs of sport, ten shillings each; and dogs of different descriptions, such as mastiffs, lap-dogs, &c. five

271

shillings each; blind men's dogs *only* excepted. It was proposed that shepherds' dogs should be exempted from the tax, but overruled, from a suggestion, that a person who keeps a flock of sheep can very well afford to pay for his shepherd's dog.

Whitehall Evening Post
6–9 November 1784

On Wednesday James Braid, about 24 years of age, William Braid, near 20 years, (brothers) and Jean Lindsay, condemned at last Circuit for house-breaking and theft, were hanged in the Castle-yard, Glasgow. They appeared to be penitent, and their behaviour was decent. W. Braid addressed the populace in a speech of some length, in pathetic language, to avoid such courses as had brought him and his fellow-sufferers to so untimely an end, after which he prayed. The brothers shook hands, before they were turned off. They were attended by five ministers. The gibbet and scaffold on which the malefactors stood, were constructed on the plan of the London scaffold, with springs, and it sunk down with ease, so that the unhappy criminals were launched into eternity without any apparent struggle. The uncommon sight of three fellow-creatures suffering at once, drew together an immense croud of spectators.

Whitehall Evening Post
6–9 November 1784

The following inscription is to be placed on the stone erected by William Baker, Esq; in Hertfordshire, in honour and commemoration of Lunardi, where he finally descended:

Let Posterity know
And knowing be astonished!

272

That,
On the 15th day of September, 1784,
VINCENT LUNARDI
Of
Lucca in Tuscany
The first Aerial Traveller in Britain,
Mounting from the Artillery Ground
In London,
And traversing the Regions of the Air
For two Hours and fifteen Minutes,
In this Spot
Revisited the Earth.
On this rude Monument
For Ages be recorded
That wonderous enterprize, successfully
achieved
By the power of Chymistry,
And the fortitude of Man;
That improvement in Science,
which,
The Great Author of all Knowledge,
Patronising by his Providence
The Inventions of Mankind,
Hath graciously permitted,
To their Benefit
And
His own Eternal Glory.

Whitehall Evening Post
6–9 November 1784

On Saturday a Hackney-coachman was carried before Mr.
Alderman Le Mesurier for wilfully driving against a corpse
carrying up Fetter-lane, by which the coffin was thrown
from the bearers shoulders, and the undertaker endeavouring to keep the coach off, the wheels ran over his foot, and
he was so much hurt that he was unable to attend the
funeral. On the coachman paying two guineas and costs,

asking pardon, and promising not to be guilty of the like again, he was discharged.

Whitehall Evening Post
6–9 November 1784

Madrid, Oct. 15.
The Infanta Louisa Maria, consort to the Prince of the Asturias, was yesterday safely delivered of a Prince, who was baptized the same day with the usual ceremonies, and received the names of Ferdinand – Marie – Francois – de – Paule – Doninick – Vincent – Ferrier – Anthonio – Joseph – Joachim – Pascal – Diego – Joannes – Nepomcene – Januarius – Francois – Xavier – Raphael – Michael – Gabriel – Calixto – Cayetan – Faustus – Louis – Raymond – Gregory – Laurence – Gerome. The whole City was illuminated upon the above joyful event.

Whitehall Evening Post
6–9 November 1784

A few nights ago the bodies of the two Dunsdons, lately hung in chains in Wichwood Forest for murder were taken down from the gibbets, and carried off. The same night the lodge of one of the keepers was broke open, and robbed of a quantity of deers skins.

Morning Chronicle
10 November 1784

A young lady at Margate this summer, reading that the Ten Commandments were stolen from King-street Chapel, enquired of Dr. Parry, who stood near her, what the thief could mean by stealing the Commandments? The Doctor gravely replied, "Why, to break them immediately, to be sure, Madam!"

Public Advertiser
11 November 1784

The frequent accidents that happen from the overflow of outside travellers upon stage coaches, has been long complained of, as a very great nuisance. This was sadly experienced by the passengers in the Hertford coach on Monday evening last, between Kingsland and Hounsditch. There being *twenty-five* persons outside, and the road being lately considerably raised in the middle, the horses being wickedly lashed by the whips of a couple of drunken horsemen, they flew on the extremity of the road, and by the weight of the outside load, the coach immediately overturned; happily no lives were lost, nor were any limbs broken, but many of the passengers were very much hurt and bruised.

Morning Chronicle
11 November 1784

A whimsical circumstance occurred at the Ball, at Guildhall on Tuesday night,—Some wag circulated a report, that Barrington, the notorious pick-pocket, was in the Hall, dressed in brown and gold; in this identical dress was Mr. Pitt, and it is actually a fact, that some of the Marshall-men were about to convey the *virtuous* young Minister to one of the City Compters.

Morning Chronicle
11 November 1784

[Fate finally caught up with Barrington, who was ultimately transported to Botany Bay and a new life. He may have been the author of the lines
"True patriots we, for be it understood
We left our country for our country's good".]

FOR HORSES
Dr. Steers's Opodeldoc

The following letter from Mr. COWLING, Master of the

Riding-house, Moorfields, will be a further Proof of the superior Efficacy of this Medicine.

To Mr. H. Steers

SIR,

HAVING often known the good effects of your Opodeldoc in the human species, I was induced to try it on horses; and I have found it so superior to every other application in bruises, sprains, rheumatisms, and other external complaints, that I think it but justice to give you this testimony.—In treads through the coronet, if the wound is immediately filled up with it, and covered with a little bandage, so as to keep the cold out for a day or two, the cure will be perfected, without fettering, or any other inconvenience. In strains, from leaping or any other violence, where the seat of them could be ascertained, I have, by rubbing in very hard, half a bottle at a time, morning and evening, removed the complaint, though ever so bad, in a few days . . . I have also found it equally serviceable when horses have been wrung in the shoulders or bruised by the saddle, if immediately applied. Any gentleman may be further satisfied by writing to, or calling upon me at the Riding-house, Moorfields.

I am, Sir, &c.

WILLIAM COWLING.

May 17, 1781.

Racing Calendar
11 November 1784

GOULARD'S
The True Original Extract of Saturn,
from Montpellier.
Horse Medicines;
Sold only by Mrs. Turmeau, (Successor to Dr. Arnaud)

Removed from Little Compton-street, to
No. 48, Greek-street, Soho.

THE Extract of Saturn, 10s 6d a bottle, which makes a large quantity of the Vegeto Mineral Water, at 2s 6d a pint, or 4s 6d a quart, for speedily curing of sprains, bruises, swellings, ulcers, and other disorders of horses and dogs.

The Saturnine Pomatum, for old sprains, old sores, for ripening and dispersing any swellings, at 5s 3d, or 10s 6d a pot.

The Eye Water for inflammations, contusions, &c. 4s a bottle.

Goulard's Vegeto Mineral Water, prepared for horses, for curing sprains, bruises, &c. 2s 6d a pint.

Dr. Arnaud's Elixir for racing, hunting and other horses, it cleanses the blood and juices, it prevents and opens obstructions in the lungs, thereby enabling such horses to keep their wind when in action, 3s 6d a bottle, or 7s a pint.

Stomachic Purging Balls, 12s a dozen.
Pectoral Balls, for curing the most obstinate coughs, and epidemical colds, 9s a dozen.
Goulard's Vegeto Mineral Water, prepared for the human species, for curing of sprains, bruises, ulcers, burns, cuts, &c. 2s 6d a pint.

Dr. Arnaud's Vinegar of the Four Thieves; a sure preservative against contagions and epidemical disorders, fevers, &c. 3s a bottle, or 6s a pint.

Horse Medicine Chests, 3 1. 3s.

Racing Calendar
11 November 1784

On Saturday evening a man much in liquor coming out of a public-house by Millbank, Westminster, missed the footway, fell over the rail into the Thames, and was drowned.

Whitehall Evening Post
13–15 November 1784

277

Yesterday morning the malefactors were executed on a scaffold erected for that purpose before Newgate: They came upon the scaffold about half past seven, and after joining the Ordinary in the usual devotions, with every appearance of the most earnest and unaffected piety and contrition, the executioner put a cap upon the head of each, when Drummond and Hulet desired him to turn their caps above their eyes, which being complied with, they prayed aloud in a fervent manner, and with a very impassioned gesticulation, at intervals addressing themselves to the spectators, and admonishing all young persons to avoid the evil courses which had brought them to a premature and disgraceful fate. Hulet, a slim lad, about eighteen, kicked and struggled surprisingly, and continued to do so for several minutes after his fellow-sufferers were motionless. On this occasion the executioner, by order of the Lord Mayor and Sheriffs, for the first time, wore a black baize gown. The concourse of people was astonishingly great, and many were much hurt, particularly a woman, who was taken to the hospital, and a girl about twelve or thirteen years old, who after fainting was moved over the heads of several hundreds of people into Fleet-lane, where she was taken into a house. So great a number of people got upon Mr. Sheriff Hopkins' chariot, standing at the gate of the Sessions House, that the axletree broke.

General Evening Post
16–18 November 1784

Tuesday morning, about one o'clock, a man was discovered digging up a newly-interred corpse from the King's Road burying-ground in Chelsea. Offences of a similar nature having lately been committed upon the same spot, a guard was set to prevent it, who, upon finding the wretch at his trade, shot at him, when the ball went through his head, and killed him on the spot.

Norfolk Chronicle or Norwich Gazette
20 November 1784

Mr. Blanchard arrived on Monday from Dover, where he has been to choose a spot to ascend from: it is from the interior of the Castle, surrounded by a very high wall, that he proposes to take his flight. The masts for suspending the Balloon are fixed, and the vitriolick acid and iron filings are on the road. As soon as he has made his fifth voyage with Dr. Jefferies, which will be in a few days, he will return to Dover, to wait for a favourable wind, when his Balloon will be filled with the utmost expedition, and in thirty minutes afterwards, he is expected to land on the coast of France. It is supposed, there will be more boats assembled about Dover on this occasion, than have been seen in those parts, since the landing of Julius Caesar.

Morning Chronicle
20 November 1784

One day last week, Mr. Brookes, master of the menegery at Tottenham-court, being on the road from Tyburn, with one of his younger sons in a one-horse chaise, fell into conversation with a stranger, who, after riding with him about an hour, drew a pistol and presented it to his breast; on which Mr. Brookes desired him to remove his pistol, and said, his attack was unluckily timed, having just paid for a number of cattle he had been buying, but that he would give him what he had left, and delivering to him about four pounds, the fellow rode off; but Mr. Brookes calling after him, that he had no money to pay the turnpikes, he returned, and gave him a shilling.

Public Advertiser
23 November 1784

London, Nov. 23.
Yesterday the following extraordinary affair came before the Bow-Street Magistrates: – Count D——r, who has made so much noise about town, some little time since got

acquainted with a gentleman of the law, who lent him his assistance to extricate him from difficulties he was involved in: having access to his friend's table, who was married to a young lady of some accomplishments, the Count, by his attentions, insinuated himself so far into her affections, as to prevail upon her to elope with him to France. He sent off his baggage to Dover, whither he was to follow in a day or two. The husband, by a laconic letter from the lady, received the first intimation of her infidelity. After a very minute enquiry, he discovered, that the lady and her paramour were at a bagnio in Leicester-fields, whither he went on Sunday night, accompanied with some friends, and being guided to the room, desired admittance, which was refused; upon this he forced open the door, and the moment he entered the Count fired upon him; the ball went through his hat without doing him any mischief. The Count's conduct appeared in so extraordinary a light to the Magistrates, that for the purpose of more security he was committed to Newgate.

Jopson's Coventry Mercury
29 November 1784

On Monday two women were confined in St. Clement's workhouse for stealing a fine boy, of about three years old, and very genteelly dressed: They were discovered in Claremarket by falling out about which way they should go home; and one word bringing on another, they at last reciprocally accused each other with having no relation to the child, which its dress evidently confirmed; and a number of spectators being gathered round them, some of them questioned the child; and though they could not learn from him to whom he belonged, or where his friends resided, they discovered enough to convince them he had been stolen; which was no sooner known than the Knights of the Clever took the ladies in hand, and, after treating them some time in the same tender manner as they usually do lame and jaded cattle, consigned them over to the care of a beadle, who confined them as above.

Public Advertiser
25 November 1784

On Monday last was married Charles Aplin Fowey, Esq; of Grosvenor-street, to Miss Englis, of Worcestershire. The match was occasioned by a highwayman stopping a stage-coach, in which the gentleman and lady happened to be passengers, and the gallant behaviour of the former won the heart of the latter.

Public Advertiser
25 November 1784

The following curious case came before the Court of Conscience, Guildhall, a few days ago: A Jew taylor summoned a Jew priest for a guinea. The taylor stated, that the priest had agreed to give him a guinea for a pair of breeches, which were accordingly made and delivered, but not paid for. The priest in his defence answered, that he allowed the debt, but pleaded a *set off*; which was, that, by desire of the taylor, he had, in the capacity of a priest, attended the taylor's friend, who lay under sentence of death in Newgate, five times; and that the common price of attendance was four shillings a time. The taylor replied, he admitted the attendance: but that there was another Jew under sentence of death, with whom the priest prayed, and to whom the priest specially came, so that his friend had prayers but at *second-hand*, and should of course pay but half-price; besides, as his friend has been respited, he thought his promise void. The Court ordered the taylor half a guinea.

Public Advertiser
25 November 1784

Mr. England, who was so unfortunate to kill Mr. Rolls in a late duel, we are assured is arrived in Dover in order to surrender himself to take his tryal.

General Evening Post
23–25 November 1784

The gentleman charged with wilfully firing a pistol at Tuxley Sandon, Esq; in the Long-Acre Bagnio, committed to Newgate, by Sir Sampson Wright, is Louis Henry Scipio Duroure, Esq; of a noble family in France, and an officer in his Majesty's service.—The offence he is charged with is capital by what is called the *Black Act*, but from a variety of circumstances in his favour, it is supposed he will obtain bail for the offence.

General Evening Post
23–25 November 1784

Much has been said concerning the family of the unhappy youth now in Newgate, Lieut. Duroure, late of the Horse Guard Blues, who stands charged with firing a pistol at —— Sandon, Esq; . . . . Upon collecting the most authentic information, we learn that he is the son of Lieutenant-General Scipio Duroure, in the service of the King of France. This worthy veteran, who has been greatly distinguished by his military talents, is, as we are assured, at this time Governor of Fort d'Esprit, near Avignon, in the South of France, and has the command of a corps of 3000 men.

General Evening Post
4–7 December 1784

Those who are so attentive in imitating the slightest variations in the dress and appearance of the Heir-apparent, should devote themselves to participate in all his accidents and misfortunes. Diodorus Siculus says, that when the Prince or Sovereign of Ethiopia had lost the use of any part of his body by malady, or any other cause, they inflicted the same infirmity on themselves; deeming it shameful for instance, to walk straight after a lame King. They thought it absurd not to share with him in corporal inconveniences, when they deemed it their duty to die with their King, or the Heirs to their Kings. What a lesson for that *reputable* body who now surround an English Prince.

Public Advertiser
26 November 1784

Monday night a foreign gentleman, in a state of intoxication was decoyed into a house in Chick-lane by a black woman, who after stripping him of a gold watch, six guineas and some silver, and some other property, left him asleep. When he awakened and discovered his loss, he procured a constable, who took into custody two black women in a house communicating with that where he had been robbed; but being unable to ascertain which of the sable charmers had made the conquest of his person and property, he took no further measures for obtaining a refund of the latter.

Norfolk Chronicle or Norwich Gazette
27 November 1784

Last Wednesday a considerable corn-dealer in the neighbourhood of Leeds, returning from Tadcaster-market, took up a horse on the road, that he supposed to be the property of an acquaintance, and left it at a public house upon Clifford Moor; the corn dealer pursued his journey, and the beast he had just left, got loose and followed him. The noise of a horse on full speed at his heels alarmed him so much, that he clapped spurs to his horse, and went upon the Weatherby road till he reached the Granby's Head, near Weatherby-bridge; where he had not been

283

many minutes, before he was in the midst of a dreadful tale of the danger he had escaped, when the imaginary highwayman arrived. The laugh was much against the corn-dealer; however, the fright he received overcame him to such a degree, that he could not proceed home until the next morning.

Norfolk Chronicle or Norwich Gazette
27 November 1784

A caution against street charity.—Mr. Gainsborough some time since was accosted in the street by a woman, who had a remarkably fine boy with her; he relieved her, and desired her to call with the child next day at his house in Pall-Mall, which she accordingly did.—He had the child cloathed, and discovering some marks of genius, he told the mother that if she consented he would take the boy entirely under his care, and provide for him; the woman took a few days to consider of this humane and generous offer, when she returned and informed this eminent artist that she could not think of parting with her boy, for upon average for the last twelve months he earned by begging in the street seven shillings a day.

Norfolk Chronicle or Norwich Gazette
27 November 1784

London, Nov. 25.
Yesterday, at High Water, a Man who plies at Westminster Bridge, for the trifling Wager of two Shillings and sixpence, two Pounds of Beef-Steaks, and a Gallon of Porter, jumped from the centre arch of Westminster-Bridge, and swam to the Palace-Stairs at Lambeth.

Jackson's Oxford Journal
27 November 1784

Extract of a letter from Cork, Nov. 15

"Mr. ——, in this neighbourhood, who a short time since married Lady ——, daughter of Lord ——, having reason to suspect her fidelity with his cousin german, an officer in the army, who had been entertained at his house in the most hospitable manner, placed some spies upon their actions, and yesterday received the most convincing proof of his wife's infidelity. She had frequently made a practice of retiring into the garden, at the extremity of which were the ruins of an old abbey, which her Ladyship pretended to greatly admire. This was the place of their rendezvous, and she and her paramour were actually detected by her injured husband in a stone coffin in one of the aisles of this venerable building. Mr —— attempted to run his treacherous relative through the body; but he made his escape. The lady passed through this city yesterday. You may depend upon the truth of the above."

Public Advertiser
27 November 1784

Extract of a letter from Reading, Nov. 10

"On Saturday night last, the driver of one of the Glocestershire stage waggons was found dead in the turnpike-road near the Fleece inn, on Maidenhead-hill. On examination it was found, that he had three ribs broken, from which it was at first conjectured he had been murdered; but it appearing that he had left a public-house in Maidenhead, a few minutes before the accident happened, very much intoxicated, he is supposed to have fallen down, and being unable to help himself, was suffocated by the great quantity of liquor he had drank. The coroner's inquest brought in their verdict *accidental death*. His ribs were broken by falling on the lanthorn, which was found under him, squeezed quite flat."

Gloucester Journal
29 November 1784

On Saturday night Count Duroure, who was confined in the prison of Newgate on a charge of felony, for firing at Mr. S. with a loaded pistol, dispatched himself with a similar instrument.

Public Advertiser
30 November 1784

Mr. Lunardi on Saturday last settled his accounts with the proprietors of the Pantheon, when his share of the profits amounted to exactly two thousand eighty-five pounds five shillings and eightpence, exclusive of what he may have received from subscriptions; the above sum arises from the one shilling admittance to the Pantheon.

Public Advertiser
30 November 1784

A chairman of the name of Green, who plies at the Unicorn in Jermyn-street, has got the fourth of the 20,000 l. in the present lottery.

Public Advertiser
30 November 1784

A few days since Mr. Hankey, a gentleman of considerable fortune in Harley-street, Cavendish-square, swallowed, by an unfortunate mistake, a tea-cup full of Goulard's extract of lead, one of the most destructive and certain poisons in nature. Mr. Hankey, it seems, sustained himself with an uncommon firmness under this alarming situation, expecting immediate death, from which, however, he has been preserved by the skilful assistance of Dr. Rowley, an eminent physician of the same street; and we have the pleasure to inform the public, Mr. Hankey is now perfectly recovered.

Public Advertiser
30 November 1784

Friday last as Mrs. Hemmings, wife of Mr. Hemmings, Gardener, near the church at Battersea, was gathering some herbs near the dwelling-house, a fellow rushed through the hedge, and pointing a knife at her breast, demanded her money, which having delivered, to the amount of about six shillings, he seized her by the hand, and forced off her wedding ring, and then escaped by the way he had entered the garden.

General Evening Post
27–30 November 1784

DECEMBER

A daily paper says, that the following is the manner in which the retreat of a lady was lately discovered by her husband:—passing by a shoemaker's at the other end of town, he took notice of something wrote on a card on the inside of a woman's shoe, which, on nearer inspection, he discovered to be his wife's name. On enquiry, he found it had been sent to the shoemaker to make a pair of boy's shoes of the same size. The husband, and the lady's father, by agreement with the shoemaker, accompanied him when he carried the shoes home: and the lady, when she saw them, drew a brace of pistols, but was prevented doing any mischief by her father's striking them out of her hands. Her enamorato was at their entrance looking out at the window, and was secured by pulling the sash down upon his back; notwithstanding which, he found means to discharge a pistol, the ball from which went through the brim of the husband's hat. They are now both safely confined.

Morning Chronicle
2 December 1784

Last Saturday —— Reade, Esq; of Bedford-Row, dropped down dead in the Banking Shop of Boldero and Co. while a large sum of money was counting out to him.

Public Advertiser
3 December 1784

An *intimacy* has been discovered within this day or two between a certain Countess and one of her *domestics*, which will surprize the fashionable world more than any

288

circumstance in the annals of gallantry that has taken place for a considerable time.

Public Advertiser
3 December 1784

One quarter of the 20,000 l. prize, drew last week, is the property of two stage-coach men, who drive the Brighthelmstone machine. In consequence of their having often driven Fox, the Brighton Manager, backward and forward, they on Wednesday last ordered a genteel dinner, at the tavern he keeps, in Bow-street; and, as they are both very sober, honest, and respectable characters, their proprietors did them the honour to partake of it. Their plan is to put the money out to interest, to enjoy one week's holiday, and then to continue driving their old coaches, as before.

Public Advertiser
3 December 1784

Extract of a letter from Monaghan, November 23
"A few days ago, the following curious marriage happened near Newtownbutler, in the county of Fermanagh. The bridegroom and bride were Philip Beggin, of Bohofet, and Bridget Maguire, of Darrylce, at which place the marriage should have been celebrated. The dinner and every thing was ready, and waited only for the appearance of the bridegroom; but by the uncommon delay, the company grew hungry, ate up the dinner, and after waiting for the bridegroom till their patience were tired, they proposed a match for the bride among themselves, so as she might not be altogether disappointed. One of the company proposed two brothers, then present, to take her choice of them, Edward and Patrick Kierman, which the bride listened to, but upon Ned's asking her seriously, which of the two would she make choice of, as either of them would take her, she chose Paddy, though blind of an eye. They set off

289

that moment for Newtownbutler, were married, and returning to the company, ended the wedding with their friends."

Public Advertiser
4 December 1784

London, Nov. 30.
Remarkable instance of Honesty and its effect. George Dade was a poor parish boy, in a country village near Nottingham, and received some instruction in reading and writing, at a very mean village school, through the charity of an old lady, who had a regard for his mother. He was a foot-boy to a gentleman at 16, and soon afterwards, being 20 years old, was the only man servant kept by a family of small fortune in the country, to whom he behaved so well, that they recommended him as a secretary and butler to a man of large fortune in that neighbourhood. In a severe illness of his master, it happened that Dade had all the money in the house at command, and in recourse to, for physicians, &c., the sums were very considerable, the illness lasting some weeks; he had to receive also, as well as to pay. On his master's recovery, he gave so clear and exact account, that his scrupulous honesty was conviction itself. It happened that Dade was a remarkable handsome man, and that his master's single sister coming with a married one on a visit to the house, noticed him in such a manner as convinced that she was in love with him. The young lady was elegant, pleasing, accomplished, and with a good fortune. Dade drew very well, and her copying some of his drawings which hung in an anti-room, led to opportunities which convinced him, her heart was affected, which gave his own disquiet, which he had little notion of. A sense, however, of his duty, got the better of inclination and ambition; he opened his suspicion to his master, and desired that the lady might be sent away under some proper pretence. Struck at so generous and liberal a sense of his condition, the master removed his sister; and

290

as a reward for Dade, got him a very eligible appointment in a public office; Dade's talents and industry raised him rapidly. The lady's passion had not changed and she wrote to her brother, requesting his consent to an union necessary to her happiness. He agreed, and Mr. Dade is now in possession of above Twenty Thousand Pounds.

Shrewsbury Chronicle
4 December 1784

READING GAOL, Nov. 30, 1784.
WHEREAS the following Prisoners made their Escape from the above Gaol, between the Hours of Seven and Eight o'Clock this Evening, viz.
JAMES BECKET, about six Feet high, stout made, round-shouldered, wore his own dark Hair, and of a dark Complexion; had on a Bath striped Surtout Coat.
JAMES HADEN, about five Feet six Inches high, and has light Hair; had on a blue close-bodied Coat, with a Cape.
THOMAS BARNSLEY, about five Feet six Inches high, dark Hair tied behind, and of genteel Appearance; wore a light-coloured Drab close Coat, and Surtout, with Metal Buttons.
WILLIAM BLAKEMAN, about five Feet six Inches high, with dark Hair tied behind, thin Face, and has a genteel Look; had on a black close Coat, red Waistcoat, and Drab-coloured Surtout.
JOSEPH HAWKINS, near six Feet high, dark Hair, rather pale, stout made, and pitted with the Small-pox; had on white-ribbed Cotton Stockings, a Canvas Frock, and white Swan-skin Waistcoat, with Drawers.
—— HUMPHREYS, about five Feet, seven Inches high, very round-shouldered, wore his own dark Hair, and is slim made; had on a brown Drab-coloured close-bodied Coat, with Metal Buttons.
THOMAS WEST, about six Feet high, stout and genteel made, with long black Hair; had on a light Drab-coloured close-bodied Coat, dun-coloured double-breasted Shag

Waistcoat, black Stockings and Breeches.

GEORGE INGRAM, about five Feet, nine Inches high, black strait Hair, sallow Complexion, round-shouldered; had on a Drab-coloured close-bodied Coat, light Surtout, and Leather Breeches.

WILLIAM MULLEN, about five Feet, eight Inches high, a pale Visage, pitted with the Small-pox, is remarkably thin, and walks stooping; had on a light-coloured Horseman's Coat, and blue striped Trowsers.

THOMAS WESTON, five Feet high, well made, dark brown strait Hair, fair Complexion, about 25 Years of Age; had on a white Canvas Gaol Frock, Swan-skin Waistcoat, drill Breeches, dark-brown Stockings, and came from Farnborough, in this County.

ROBERT BALES, six Feet high, a strait, raw-boned Man, light Hair, pitted with the Small-pox, pale Complexion, being troubled with a Tertian Ague, aged about 21 Years, lately belonging to the Foot Guards; had on a Gaol Frock, Swan-skin Waistcoat, White Soldiers Breeches, and white Yarn Stockings.

GREGORY WILLOUGHWAYS, five Feet high, thin made, dark Complexion, black strait Hair, 20 Years of Age, has a Mole on his Chin, and a lounging Gait; had on the Gaol Frock, Swanskin Waistcoat, old greasy Leather Breeches, dark-brown Stockings, and a lopped Hat.

Whoever will apprehend the above Persons, so that they may be brought back to their former Place of Confinement, or secured in any of his Majesty's Gaols, shall receive Ten Pounds Reward for each of them so apprehended, by applying to

DANIEL BUSHNELL, Gaoler.

Public Advertiser
4 December 1784

Oxford, Dec. 4.
Tuesday evening the felons in the county jail at Reading seized the turnkey at the time he was about to lock them

up, and having secured him in the apartment intended for themselves, and being provided with pick-lock keys, they opened all the doors in their way, and offered a jail delivery.—Mr. Bushnell, the Jailer, being from home, they drove his wife up stairs, and with the bitterest imprecations threatened destruction if she gave the least alarm: Mrs. B. nevertheless got to the window of a one pair of stairs room, and cried out murder, which brought in a neighbour, who running up stairs, heightened her fears to such a degree, apprehending it had been some of the prisoners, that she threw herself out, and in the fall broke her arm; and the twelve following prisoners got away, viz. James Beckett, James Harden, Thomas Barnsley, William Blakeman, Joseph Hawkins, Thomas West, George Ingram, William Mullen, Thomas Weston, Robert Bales, Gregory Willoughways, and —— Humphreys.—Several of them are supposed to have taken the road towards Wallingford, and being immediately pursued, the following afternoon Ingram was apprehended under a hedge near Shillingford, in this county, who had not been able to get rid of his fetters.—The rest, it is hoped, will also be apprehended, there being among them several very desperate fellows.

Public Advertiser
6 December 1784

Yesterday a young man speaking to another with cheerfulness, on the subject of the Lottery, instantly dropt down dead in the Broadway, Blackfriars!

Public Advertiser
4 December 1784

EDUCATION
At Cheltenham, Glocestershire

YOUNG GENTLEMEN are boarded and educated in the

293

CLASSICKS, WRITING, ACCOUNTS, &c. by the REV. H. FOWLER, A.M. and ASSISTANTS.

The classicks are taught after the method of the capital schools; particular care is taken to inculcate a thorough knowledge of the rudiments of grammar; and a strict regard is had to the morals of the pupils. – Terms, 18 guineas per annum and one guinea entrance.

☞ Mr. FOWLER takes this opportunity of acquainting the public, that, on account of the advanced prices of meat, and other articles of house-keeping, he cannot afford to take young gentlemen in future under 18 guineas per annum; and flatters himself, that the parents of those now under his care, will not object to a small additional charge, to compensate those unforeseen expences.

An assistant is wanted to teach English, Writing and Accounts. He must be at least 30 years of age, used to the employment, thoroughly qualified, and well-recommended.

The salary is 20 l. per ann. board and lodging. – Letters (post paid) will be duly answered.

Gloucester Journal
6 December 1784

A farmer in Cheshire, who keeps a good team of horses, but had not entered one as a hackney, having occasion to attend Stockport market on Friday, actually saddled a cow, and rode her in triumph to and from the market, attended by a numerous concourse of laughing spectators, who enjoyed the joke.

Gloucester Journal
6 December 1784

Thursday morning Humphreys was taken near Kingsclere, in Hampshire; and in the afternoon, Bales and Willoughways were found secreted in a barn at Lambeth-hill in the parish of Shinfield.—The other eight are yet at large; it is hoped they will soon be secured, as several of them are very desperate fellows, particularly West, who was under sentence of transportation to Africa for life, for horse-stealing.

Whitehall Evening Post
4–7 December 1784

London, Dec. 8.
Yesterday morning a most remarkable murder was perpetrated in the following manner, by a journeyman barber that lives near Hyde-park-corner, who had been for a long time past jealous of his wife, but could no way bring it home to her: a young gentleman by chance coming into his master's shop to be shaved and dressed, and, being in liquor, mentioned his having seen a fine girl home to —— street, from whom he had certain favours the night before, at the same time describing her person; the barber concluded it to be his wife, and in the height of his phrenzy cut the gentleman's throat, and absconded.

Jopson's Coventry Mercury
6 December 1784

[The *Gentleman's Magazine* (vol. 44, p. 953) copied this "well imagined fable", "not perhaps inferior to any of modern invention", and added the *Moral*: "This is meant as a caution to young sparks of the town, how they boast of the favours they receive of the fair sex while under the Berbars hands."]

On Saturday last four prisoners, who made their escape from Reading gaol, were taken up at Brentford, and sent back to Reading, who will be brought in a few days to London, in order to be transported to Africa, agreeable to their sentence.

Public Advertiser
8 December 1784

Monday morning the son of a publican at Islington was taken drowned out of the New River. He had wrote on his chamber-door, If you want me, you will find me in the New River.

Public Advertiser
8 December 1784

Dr. Johnson is so dangerously relapsed, that there are little hopes of his getting over the winter. His disorder is dropsy of the legs, which are swelled to a prodigious circumference; and which, to men of his time of life, is generally fatal.

Public Advertiser
8 December 1784

Many doubt the authenticity of the anecdote respecting the intrigue in the Stone Coffin, near the Earl of G——'s seat in Ireland;—but the circumstance in question is a fact. Such is the *heat* of love in some Females, that nothing less than a *Coffin* can cool the passion!

Public Advertiser
9 December 1784

London, Dec. 11.
Wednesday evening the following singular affair happened at the theatre in Covent-Garden. After the third act a person came into the stage-box with dirty boots, and clothes exceedingly shabby. He wore a star and blue ribband. There were two ladies in the box, to whom he behaved with so much rudeness, that they got up, and left the box. After the play was finished this singular person went into the Lobby, and strutted about for some time. He was not recognized by any person in the house, though there were several gentlemen of fashion in the boxes. One of the servants of the theatre called to the company, and

296

desired them to guard their pockets, for he was sure the man with the star and garter was a pick pocket. This drew the attention of the company more particularly to our adventurer, who was instantly bustled out of the Lobby.

Gloucester Journal
13 December 1784

Winchester, Dec. 11.
Monday a man was found frozen to death on Waltham-Common.—he was seen to run through this city on Sunday evening without any clothes. He is supposed to have been a lunatic, and to have broken from some place of confinement.

Bonner and Middleton's Bristol Journal
18 December 1784

A detection has taken place in Hertfordshire of an unpleasant kind. The Lady of a Peer, distinguished for his figure and pride, has indulged herself, it seems, in an intrigue with her footman — and her Lord, though a Courtier, is so unpolite as to take the matter in so surly a mood, that it is imagined a divorce will be the issue.

Public Advertiser
13 December 1784

The roads were never known to be in worse condition than on Thursday last; out of ten coaches belonging to one set of partners on the Bristol road, two only reached London, and they got in at five o'clock in the evening, instead of seven in the morning. The mail coach was twice dug out of the snow, and was in so much danger upon Marlborough Downs, that the passengers would venture no further than Marlborough, from which place, by the active zeal of the drivers, and an additional number of horses, it reached

Lombard-street about half past eleven o'clock in the morning. Drifts of snow have in many places rendered the roads impassable, and carriages were obliged to drive at random through ploughed fields on Thursday night; but as the frost is likely to set in, these obstructions to travelling will cease, at least till a general thaw comes on.

Gloucester Journal
13 December 1784

England, who unfortunately killed Mr. Rowles in the duel, is not coming over to take his trial, but is said to have offered himself a volunteer in the Emperor's service.—It may easily be supposed how the Emperor would receive such an offer.

Public Advertiser
13 December 1784

On Saturday se'nnight one Samuel Bower, a sailor on board a trow coming up the Severn from Bristol swore a horrid oath that he would have some beef and potatoes before he got to Gloucester, for he knew he should then be discharged; and instantly stooping to take a bucket of water out of the river he fell overboard and was drowned, altho' one of his comrades jumped into the river, and made every effort to save him.

Gloucester Journal
13 December 1784

On Sunday, November 28 the following accident happened at Eton: As a boy of eleven years of age was reading a book at school, which another, fifteen years old, observing, reprimanded him for, and said, the work was unfit to be perused; the boy who was reading, insisted upon the contrary; a scuffle ensued, and the elder of the two got the youngest down, and knelt on him, declaring

that he would keep him in that position till he acknowledged the book to be a very improper one to be read; after
a struggle, the young one got the better, and put the other
in the same position that he had been himself. They were
soon after interrupted; upon which they agreed to fight it
out on the next day. They accordingly met on the Monday,
and the boy of eleven years of age beat the other so
violently that his death was the consequence. The
surviving boy now lies in a very dangerous state. The Jury
have sat upon the body, and brought in their verdict
Accidental Death. The deceased was the son of Mr. Wade,
an eminent Attorney in the country, the other the son of
Mr. Masters at Exeter.

On Monday night the corpse of the above young
Gentleman was interred in Eton College Church. All the
Gentlemen of the school attended the funeral.

Jopson's Coventry Mercury
13 December 1784

*An Account of the Trial of Capt. Kenneth Mackenzie,
yesterday, by a Special Commission at the Old Bailey*

The prisoner was indicted, for that he having the
command of the garrison and fort of Moree, on the coast of
Africa, did fasten one Murray Mackenzie to a gun, which
he ordered to be fired, whereby the man was blown into
pieces.

The evidence for the prosecution clearly proved the fact
charged in the indictment. By their testimony it appeared
that McKenzie (the same person related to the domestic of
a noble Lord, then at the head of Administration, by
whose interest he was three times respited from capital
punishment) was sent from England with other convicts,
who, to the number of seventeen, formed, together with a
few volunteers, the whole garrison of Moree—That the
deceased was first an Adjutant under the command of
Capt. Mackenzie, but deserted twice, and was reduced to
the ranks—He was then a prisoner at large, and deserted a

third time—The Captain sent a party in search of him, after a most severe and inhuman correction of 1500 lashes, which was inflicted for an hour upon the centinel who suffered the deceased to pass—the prisoner thinking the deceased was secreted by the Blacks, fired into one of their settlements, which had the desired effect. When the deceased was surrendered, the Captain ordered him to be tied to a gun, and the poor wretch begged a small space of time to say his prayers; with the utmost difficulty he was allowed *twenty minutes*—just before the fatal signal he cried out, "You tyrant, you have your will of me, my comrades farewel." He also accounted for his absence, and said, he went only to get a little brandy, and fell asleep.—One or two of the men offered their mediation; the prisoner threatened to blow out *their* brains, and held a pistol; he gave the signal, and the gun was fired, which scattered his body into instant dissolution.

Upon cross examination it turned out, that the deceased, three days before this execution, had sent his cloaths to the Dutch fort, and betrayed a disposition to desert.

Some witnesses were called on behalf of the prisoner to justify the act from necessity, and in defence of the fort, which was intended to be given up by the deceased and his confederates, who meditated to murder the Captain; but it was insisted on by the Counsel for the Crown, that the Captain should have sent the deceased to Cape Coast, and called a Court Martial. On the other hand it was allowed that there were no Officers to compose a Court Martial. Why then he should (they contended) have been confined and sent to England. At Moree there was not a place of safety, but at Cape Coast there was.

Judge Willes in his charge said, the case rested on two questions; first, Was the prisoner justified by Martial law? Secondly, Was it an act of necessity?—Most clearly it was indefensible by Martial law; the prisoner would not hear the man, but without any form of law put him to death. If the Jury found him guilty, he deserved a severe condemnation.

As to the other point, the Jury would maturely consider.

They withdrew for above two hours, and brought in their verdict *Guilty*, with a recommendation. Sentence of death was immediately pronounced by the Recorder.

In consequence of the recommendation of the Jury, Judge Willes respited the prisoner for a week, to lay his case before his Majesty.

The unfortunate Murray Mackenzie, alias Jefferson, for whose murder Capt. Mackenzie was convicted, has been bred a drummer in the third regiment of Foot Guards, but falling in, about twelve years since, with a gang of shop-lifters, he was no less than *three* times *capitally* convicted at the Old Bailey; twice for stealing diamonds, and once for horse-stealing; but always found friends to obtain a mitigation of his sentence for transportation.

Jopson's Coventy Mercury
13 December 1784

The Ladies insist, that in this age, men have carried the passion of jealousy to such a pitch, as it never reached before; formerly they were content to examine closets, cupboards, and dark corners; to look in the bed, under the bed, and over the bed; to peep behind fire-screens, and into clothes-presses, and chests of drawers; but now, dreadful improvement! they suppose that their wives can carry their gallantry to the grave, and are afraid even to trust them in their coffins!

The expression, "I had rather be buried alive" was never rightly understood till a late event explained it, and brought it into universal fashion. Now, every woman who has an accidental *fracas* with her husband, exclaims—"I had rather be buried alive," and really means it too.

Public Advertiser
13 December 1784

London, Dec. 14.
On Friday as a Coachman who drove one of the long

301

Stages, was coming from Gloucester to London, he was so affected by the intenseness of the Cold, that he was found dead on the Coach Box near Windsor.

Jackson's Oxford Journal
18 December 1784

We are happy to have it in our power to assure the public, from the best authority, that the absurd and malicious story circulated with so much industry, and which found its way into the Public Advertiser of Thursday last, and calculated to disturb the domestic peace and happiness of a noble and repectable family in Ireland, is absolutely devoid of foundation. The utmost diligence is using to trace out the scandalous author of the report, who no doubt will meet with the punishment such calumny deserves.

'Tis with equal pleasure we can assure our readers that the late scandalous reports, relative to a noble lady in Hertfordshire, have no foundation, but in the malice of those base calumniators who invented them.

Public Advertiser
14 December 1784

A melancholy affair lately happened at Pontesbury, in the county of Salop. Three men went to a publick house, and called for some drink; but as they appeared very much intoxicated, a young woman (who was the only person in the house) refused to draw them any; whereupon one of them used very opprobrious language to her in a menacing posture, she struck him on the temples with a hatchet, which fractured his skull, and he died before the morning. On Monday the Coroner's Inquest sat on the body, and brought in their verdict manslaughter. The girl is bailed.

Morning Chronicle
14 December 1784

We hear from Darlington, that the following trick was lately put upon one of the principal inn-keepers at that place:—The inn-keeper about the middle of last month received a letter with the Carlisle postmark and signed by a person who pretended he was the gentleman to the Duke of Norfolk, and acquainted the inn-keeper that his Grace, with a large retinue, would be at the said inn-keeper's house, on the 20th ult. ordered him to provide the best supper in his power, some good claret and other wines, as his Grace, &c. would sleep with him, for which purpose he was to provide at least a dozen beds, and have in readiness several horses for the next morning. The inn-keeper exulted not a little at having so noble a guest, provided a most elegant supper with great alacrity, which consisted of the greatest dainties he could procure, and on the morning of the day was big with expectation, and waited with impatience for the appointed time to receive his most noble visitor;—but O grief of griefs! his Grace never arrived, to the unspeakable disappointment of the inn-keeper. This it is hoped, may serve to caution others how they obey the orders of persons they are not well acquainted with.

Leeds Intelligencer
14 December 1784

With the truest concern we inform our readers, that at seven o'clock on Monday evening, the great and good Dr. Samuel Johnson breathed his last, aged 74 years and three months. This death has been expected and feared by his nearest and dearest friends for some days past; and it is some consolation, that he has not left the world, distressed in circumstances.

The Morning Post included the following eulogy from a bookseller:

The Doctor was a great *original*, he is *translated* into a heavenly language, he was a *folio* among men, he is now *out of print*, and we shall never have a *new edition* of him.

Morning Chronicle
15 December 1784

London, Dec. 16.
This day at eleven o'clock came on at the Old Bailey the trial of Henry Scipio Duroure, Esq. (commonly called Count Duroure) for feloniously firing a loaded pistol at Huxley Sandon, Esq. in the Long acre Bagnio, a short time since.

Mr. Erskine was Counsel for the prisoner.

The first and only witness was a female servant at the above Bagnio, who deposed that she heard the pistol discharged; but was in doubt whether it was fired by Capt. Duroure, or Mrs. S——, who was in the bed-chamber in boy's cloathes, armed with a brace of pistols.

The Counsel then discovered A FLAW in the indictment, the Christian name of the keeper of the Bagnio being a MISNOMER.

On this, after a short consultation, the Court ordered the prisoner to be discharged.

Capt. Duroure was elegantly dressed in a suit of black. He is a handsome figure, about 24 years of age.

The above gentleman is detained for a prisoner, upon two actions for debt, to a considerable amount.

Jopson's Coventry Mercury
26 December 1784

Saturday while a gentleman in the neighbourhood of Warwick-lane was having his hair dressed by an apprentice barber in Paternoster-row, whom he suspected to have twice robbed him, he pretended to fall asleep, when the lad picked his pocket of seventeen shillings, which being found in his hand, he was taken to Wood-street Compter. Upon his examination at Guildhall, he offered to enter as a soldier into the service of the East-India Company, to which the prosecutor consented.

Morning Chronicle
16 December 1784

The following is a remarkable instance of intrepidity in an old Woman.—A Mrs. Wilcox, aged 78 years, who some time ago resided in Little Holland-house, made it her general rule, every night, to go round her gardens, in order to discover, if possible, whether any thief was lurking about them; she would never suffer any person to accompany her, but taking a loaded gun over her shoulder, with a lanthorn in her hand, attended by her faithful mastiff, the constant companion of his mistress in these nocturnal visits, would make the whole tour of the gardens, as above described. She happened, after her usual round in the gardens, to be disturbed out of her sleep, one morning, about three o'clock, by some thieves, who had set a ladder against her chamber window, for the purpose of robbing her; but she fortunately waking out of her sleep at the time, immediately jumped out of bed, and, seizing her musket, which she always kept loaded by her bedside, flung open her chamber window, when to her great astonishment she discovered one man already advanced very near her chamber window, and the other preparing to ascend the ladder. At that instant she presented her piece to them, and said, "Do I ever turn any of you away from my doors, without relieving you? Why, then, will you break in upon my peaceful slumbers, and disturb my repose at this late hour? Begone this instant or I'll blow your brains out." They retired immediately, muttering, although we are disappointed to night, we'll visit you again soon.

Norfolk Chronicle or Norwich Gazette
18 December 1784

The acquittal of Count Duroure has given great satisfaction to all the parties concerned in the trial.—"Why (says Figaro in the new Comedy) should a man fancy you do him an injury, when you are endeavouring to oblige his wife!"

Public Advertiser
18 December 1784

It is well known that Dr. Johnson supported in his family an indigent old lady who was stone blind, and not in any way qualified to be his companion; on being one day asked by an intimate friend what reason he had for having done so, he replied, "because he believed if he had not, that nobody else would."

Public Advertiser
20 December 1784

A most extraordinary *prelude* to the comedy of *The Follies of a Day* was performed this night at the Theatre of Covent-Garden. A Lady and gentleman, both young and elegant in their appearance, stepped into a front row in the green boxes, where a servant was keeping places for his master. When the gentleman came with his company, the box-keeper civilly begged the couple to yield the seat; but the lady who by her dialect appeared to be a Caledonian said she would not remove, as the servant told her he was only keeping one place for his master, and there was a place reserved for him. The box-keeper told her this was a mistake, as the row was kept, and the gentleman being peremptory to have his places, the keeper hoped they would not drive him to the necessity of making them forcibly withdraw. The lady was positive, and a constable was sent for, who laying hold of the husband, the lady gave him a blow, which, in the phrase of boxing, was literally a black eye. The Constable retreated, and brought in a soldier.—The matter now became serious—The lady placed her husband behind her, and now declared that no man should strike him, and that since they used these means they would not yield. The soldier struck both gentleman and lady, but he was himself thrust out by the company. In the end, however, the lady and gentleman were dragged out by superior and collective strength—The lady's cloak, head-dress, gown, and everything were first torn from her shoulders, and she was conveyed to the lobby spent with fatigue, but not subdued in spirit. The proper company then took their places, and Mr. Davies came on to speak the prologue; but the house rose in such a clamour, that he was forced to retire. Mr. Lewis came on, and endeavoured to quiet the disturbance by explaining the matter to the house—that is, by telling them that the lady and gentleman who had usurped the places previously engaged were taken out, and that the proper company now being in their seats, he hoped the house would suffer the play to proceed. The house exclaimed, that that was not the cause of their discontent – it was the appearance of a soldier to which they objected, and because that soldier had struck the lady. Mr. Lewis retired – Mr. Davies tried again to speak the prologue, and was driven off. They then strove to begin the play without the prologue, and Miss Younge came forward, and after some minutes was suffered to speak. She begged they might understand the house. What was the offence, and to what did the audience object? A gentleman from the side-boxes said, "Our complaint is shortly, that with your French play you are introducing French manners. This is an English Theatre, and we will suffer no soldiers to be employed here. The intruders should have been withdrawn by the servants of the house."

After some time Mr. Davies came on again, and was again driven off. Mr. Lewis then advanced, and assured the audience "that the soldier was indiscreetly brought in by the peace-officer without the orders and without the knowledge of any person engaged in the Theatre. We disclaim all share in the act; we are very sorry that it has happened, and we hope you will believe that we shall never countenance the introduction of soldiery to this house."—This address was received with great pleasure, and the play went on with great good humour.

Bonner and Middleton's Bristol Journal
25 December 1784
[*The Follies of a Day* is *Le Mariage de Figaro, ou la Folle Journée*, by Beaumarchais.]

London, Dec. 21.
Yesterday the remains of the much lamented Dr. Samuel Johnson were interred in Westminster-Abbey. The procession, consisting of a coach and six with the corpse, and ten mourning coaches and four, set out from Bolt-court, Fleet-street, a few minutes after 12, being followed by several gentlemen's carriages, most of the company in which were in mourning. At one o'clock the corpse arrived at the Abbey, where it was met by Dr. Taylor (who read the funeral service) and several prebends, and conducted to the Poet's Corner, and laid close to the remains of David Garrick, Esq. The principal mourners on this solemn occasion were Sir Joshua Reynolds, Mr. Edmund Burke, Sir John Hawkins, Mr. Colman, and the deceased's faithful black servant; there were present besides, Dr. Priestley, Dr. Horsley, Gen. Paoli, Mr. Stevens, Mr. Malone, Rev. Mr. Strahan, Mr. Hoole, Mr. Nichols, and other distinguished persons. A great concourse of people were assembled, who behaved with a degree of decency suitable to the solemn occasion.

Gloucester Journal
27 December 1784

The Amazon who fought so desperately in the green boxes at Covent-garden, on Saturday evening, exceeds in her feats all the heroines that we ever saw within the pale of a theatre. Sir John Brute, in woman's apparel, knocking 'down watchmen, fell short of her prowess, when she made the soldier with his *fixed bayonet*, retreat!

Public Advertiser
21 December 1784

A gentleman of rank and fortune was on Wednesday night last seized by a soldier in St. James's Park, and delivered over to an officer of the guard, on a charge of having manifested brutal propensities. The gentleman accounted for his being out in so inclement a night by saying, that he had a letter to deliver to a lady at Buckingham House, of so much importance, that he chose to be himself the messenger—that the centinel attempted to rob him, and failing in that, seized him under the pretence of an abominable accusation. This is the short recital of a story which is now a topic of discussion. We think it improper to enter into the particulars, for among other fatal consequences resulting from the frequent report of these unnatural vices in the Newspapers, one is, that it encourages obscure villains to charge gentlemen with the crime, for the sake of composition. We fear the practice is too common.

Public Advertiser
21 December 1784

In order to prevent for the future complaints of disorderly behaviour among the soldiers in St. James's-park, we are assured the officers of the foot-guards have, with great propriety, ordered that no private soldier, unless on duty, shall frequent the park after sun set.

General Evening Post
25–28 December 1784

CROSSING OF THE CHANNEL IN A FLYING BOAT

MR. BLANCHARD has the honour to inform the Nobility and Gentry that in company with his late companion DR. JEFFRIES, he intends to ascend from Dover Castle, on Thursday next, the 23d instant, if the wind proves favourable, and to cross the Channel with that Gentleman in his Flying Boat.

Whitehall Evening Post
18–21 December 1784

[This feat was accomplished by Blanchard and Jeffries, a rich American backer, on 7 January 1785. The balloon was twice the size of anything yet sent up and carried barometers, compasses, cork jackets, lifebelts, warm clothing, flags, anchors, silken oars, sheaves of pamphlets, bottles of brandy, boxes of provisions, crates of fruit, bags of sand and Blanchard's *moulinet*, a kind of revolving fan eight feet across, to sail him against the wind. Most of these were thrown overboard, including Blanchard's trousers, to gain height. They eventually landed safely in the forest of Guines (L. Gardiner, *Man in the Clouds*, p. 67).]

The late Dr. Johnson drank a great deal of tea, as a strengthener of the stomach and bowels. He used to say that it refreshed his spirits, and "kept him awake"—When writing at a late hour, he had always a bason of tea near him. He extolled it as the greatest of all medicines, if not drank to excess.

Public Advertiser
22 December 1784

Reading, Dec. 18.
A person unknown was found frozen to death at Culham-heath, near Abingdon, the beginning of this week. It is

thought he was one of the felons that escaped from our gaol a short time since.

Public Advertiser
23 December 1784

DUELLING

An appeal to the lists is inconsistent with the rules of honour, when it usurps the office of the law. It becomes a nuisance to society, when it is made in cases for which the statute of the law of the land has provided ample justice. Matters of bargain and traffic cannot honourably be referred to the Court. They would be ridiculous as well as incompatible. Let us for a moment indulge the idea of substituting the practice of Duelling in the place of legal process, and see how contemptible as well as unproductive the means would be. How must the feelings of gentlemen be affected, if after the institution of this new tribunal for the recovery of debts, they should read paragraphs in the newspapers to the following purport!

Last week a haberdasher of small-wares sent in the bill of a lady to her husband, and having twice called for payment in vain, he challenged the gentleman to fight, and yesterday they met in Hyde Park when the haberdasher shot the gentleman through the body. The haberdasher has decamped, and his shop is shut up.

A shoemaker of eminence called at the house of an officer of the guards to receive his bill; but the officer thinking that his spatterdashes were overcharged, told the tradesman that he would not be imposed on, and insisted on deducting half a guinea. The shoemaker took fire at the imputation, said his honour was engaged, and demanded satisfaction. The officer laughed at him, upon which the shoemaker pulled him by the nose. The officer could not bear this indignity even from a dealer in cordwain, and they accordingly adjourned to Hyde Park, where they fought. At the second shot the shoemaker was wounded in

311

the groin, but the ball was happily extracted, and he is in a fair way of recovery.

We are sorry to inform our readers, that a very unhappy duel took place yesterday morning. The circumstances were as follow: a milk-woman in Bond-street, after dunning Sir Highflight for a bill of two years standing, sent him a message, that if he did not pay it that evening, her cousin Bob, of the Lincoln militia, should fight him; Bob, who is a smart lad, with a good box lobby figure, accordingly wrote Sir George a letter, and called him a scoundrel for not discharging his milk-score. Sir George, in consequence of this, challenged Bob to meet him the next morning. They met and after discharging three brace of pistols without effect, Sir George wounded Bob in the side; Bob instantly returned, and the Baronet fell. After lingering two days in great agonies he is since dead; and Bob, who is too ill to fly, is in custody.

Can any thing be more ridiculous than such instances of duelling abused?

Or is there any necessity for a comment?

Whitehall Evening Post
21–23 December 1784

[A box lobby was the lobby leading to the boxes in a theatre.]

RULES TO BE OBSERVED IN THE CHRISTMAS HOLIDAYS

The Lord Mayor is recommended to take especial care, that the kennels near the Mansion House are properly overflowed, and that the snow be piled up in the present form, to prevent crossing before his door.

Housekeepers will be cautious not to throw sawdust before their doors, because it may prevent people from falling; and as it is a season of festivity, the more laughing there is at accidents the better.

All apprentices who go out to collect Christmas boxes

must be sure to get drunk as early in the day as they can, because as Christmas comes but once a year, they may not have so good an opportunity to enjoy themselves for a year to come.

Maids must not neglect to hang a sprig of mistletoe in the middle of their kitchens, because, though they may be kissed in private all the year round, at this season, the more publicly it is done the more they conform to a good custom.

If a gentleman's butler has saved a dozen or two of superior wine, to any his master has got in his cellar, this is the best time in the world to treat his friends with it; besides, it is for the honour of the house to make an hospitable appearance at this season.

Let no lady's maid play a pool at quadrille for less than half a crown a fish, for if friends come to see us in large parties only once a year, we cannot make too much of them.

Those that market for genteel families, and people of fashion, must be sure to renew their contracts with the poulterer, butcher, &c. &c. and take care to proportion the fine to the extra charges in the last year's bills.

It is recommended to city sportsmen, who parade with a gun in St. George's and Islington Fields, never to fire at a sparrow that is at a greater distance than five yards, and if they can, to rest the gun on a gate, and shut their eyes.

The clergy are particularly recommended not to be bashful, and refuse to take a good dinner with their parishioners on Christmas Day.

Public Advertiser
24 December 1784

The Parade at the Horse-guards was on Wednesday morning one entire piece of ice. After the Adjutant had examined the King's guard, and delivered them over to the officer for duty, when the word was given for close Ranks, the centre and rear ranks, in their attempts to obey, found

themselves on such slippery footing, that there were scarce
ten in either ranks but were laid prostrate, to the no small
amusement of the be-powdered and be-scented Ensigns.

Public Advertiser
24 December 1784

The high hills of Malvern, in Glocesteshire have, this
season, struck travellers with an awe, by the heaps of snow
covering them; and in the valleys great numbers of cattle
have been lost.

Yesterday morning a man was found frozen to death in
Newgate Market. He had the preceeding evening been
seen begging alms. 'Tis shocking to hear of a fellow
creature thus perishing.

At this season Dr. Steer's Opodeldoc is recommended to
the use of families, and in particular to those that have the
care of children, being the best application for Chilblains
or Chaps in the hands and feet, which it removes very
speedily, and if used in time will prevent the Chilblains
from breaking: It is equally efficacious in the Rheumatism,
and in Bruises, Sprains, and other external complaints.—
Sold by H. Steers, at No. 45, St. Paul's Churchyard,
London, in bottles, price 1s. 9d. each, or seven for half a
guinea; and to prevent counterfeits the Public will observe,
that on the cork of each bottle is a label with the following
words: "Dr. Steers's Opodeldoc, prepared by H. Steers."

Public Advertiser
24 December 1784

Lusus Naturae. A few days since, the wife of a porter in
the service of Mr. Dixie, master of the Windmill-Inn, St.
John's-street, Clerkenwell, was delivered of a still-born
child, perfect in all its parts but the extremity of one leg,
which terminated in the exact resemblance of the shank of
a lamb's leg with the foot and hoof, a hole appearing
through the leaders, like that made in a leg of lamb by

314

hanging it upon a butcher's hook. Only a few days before her delivery the mother asked the price of a leg of house-lamb, and was very urgent for the butcher to cut her off what he could afford for a shilling or eighteenpence, but was refused.

Public Advertiser
24 December 1784

Tuesday night was brought to the New Jail, Southwark, from Battersea, and fully committed, a gardener, for the wilful murder of William Draper, another gardener, by striking him over the temple with a spade, who died immediately.

Morning Chronicle
24 December 1784

Several of the public papers having been led to insert reflections on the conduct of the Dean and Chapter of Westminster, in relation to the funeral of Dr. Johnson, we have authority to inform the public, that the service upon that occasion was agreeable to the constant practice at the Abbey; that the Choir would have been summoned to assist if Dr. Johnson's Executor, who settled the business of the funeral, had chosen that it should; that the Dean's not officiating was owing to illness; and that every Prebendary who could, which were six in number, voluntarily attended, in order to pay all the respect, which the occasion admitted, to so uncommonly distinguished a character as that of Dr. Johnson.

Public Advertiser
24 December 1784

The river was so frozen up last night, that the navigation above bridge was entirely put a stop to; and at King's stairs, Rotherhithe, and many other publick stairs, there was no approaching the shore, and the ships hauled ashore. This will naturally deprive some thousands of industrious men from following their daily occupations, and greatly increase the publick distress.

Morning Chronicle
25 December 1784

William Prince, a petty larceny thief, was committed from the Public Office in Bow-street, for robbing a public-house at Kilburn-wells of some knives and forks. It is somewhat remarkable, in the conduct of this pitiful wretch, that there is not a public-house from Edgware to Tyburn turnpike, but has been robbed by him of some trifling thing or other, such as pewter pots, plates, spoons, old shoes, saws, &c. Five detainers are lodged against him for the above offences.

Whitehall Evening Post
23–25 December 1784

A very extraordinary case has lately been read before the Society for promoting Medical Knowledge. A widow, named Ann Liddel, at Carlisle, was about two years since admitted a patient in the Dispensary there, for a most excruciating pain in her face, and on the right side of the head. Many medicines were given her without relief.

After several months torment, Dr. Heysham directed the maxillary antrum (or hollow part of the cheek bone) to be opened, where her pain was seated; after injecting some decoction of bark for a few days, a frightful insect was extracted about an inch long, and thicker than a goose-quill—She had a remission of her complaint for several hours—but it returned, and another insect was seen at the orifice, but could not be extracted. Two days after this the second insect was discharged, in form and size like the first; and some time from thence the fragments of a third,

316

which procured her long intervals of ease, though the last accounts of Mrs. Liddel do not say she is perfectly recovered.

The above narrative, however wonderful, we are assured is strictly true. The substance of it was transmitted by Dr. Heysham, a physician of character at Newcastle, to Mr. Latham, F.R.S., at Dartford, in Kent. Mrs. Liddel is near 60 years of age, and has been accustomed to take large quantities of snuff.

General Evening Post
23–25 December 1784

As Christmas-time is the watchmens jubilee, the city patrole ought to be considerably increased, to check their intemperance.

Public Advertiser
26 December 1784

A certain nymph who figures in the high ranks of Cyprian votaries, found herself some time ago in a state of *delicate* perplexity, out of which she extricated herself in a manner equally *delicate*. One of her paramours hearing her complain for the want of a pair of diamond ear-rings, thought this opportunity excellent to enforce his suit; accordingly next morning *Mercury* was dispatched to the lady with a couple of pairs, requesting her choice of either. The brilliant toys were laid before her, examined, and admired; and after some hesitation, the following polite answer was returned:

"Mrs. B——'s compliments to Mr. C——; has received the ear-rings. Both pairs are so well set, the brilliants of so perfect a water, they are altogether so elegant and tasty, that she cannot possibly determine a preference. Therefore rather than make a partial or injudicious choice, she intends with Mr. C——'s leave, to keep them both." And she was as good as her word.

Public Advertiser
27 December 1784

CAUTIONS TO ALL WHOM THEY MAY CONCERN

THE Bishops are earnestly requested not to distribute much money among the poor this hard weather.

Those who receive bills of seven or ten years standing are desired not to set a bad example by paying them, as it may encourage troublesome applications.

Porters of great men should have a strict charge at these times, not to give away either beef or bread to the poor, because, though they are more particularly in want of relief, hospitality is now quite out of fashion.

Those who never felt distress of any kind themselves, should be very careful, at this hard season, not to give a farthing to a beggar, but rather apologize to themselves for not doing it, by observing, that the money will be spent in gin.

If old and infirm people tumble into a kennel, don't help them up, because what business have those abroad, who can't walk as well as their neighbours?

Let those Members of the City Committees who have large sums given them from the Chamber of London to distribute abroad, not do it too publicly, lest it look ostentatious; like pride as it were; the more privately these things are done the better.

If you can afford a good dinner on a Sunday, never ask a poor friend or relation to dine with you; it may make them too familiar, and they will expect it another time.

All good citizens should be cautious not to study the bellman's verses lest they insensibly grow poetical and neglect their trade.

Public Advertiser
27 December 1784

The floating cakes of ice in the river are so thick and heavy, that the Gravesend boats lost their passage on Thursday afternoon, and in two tides were only able to make Blackwall.

Public Advertiser
27 December 1784

The Hertfordshire stage coaches have been busily employed this week past in transporting the works of milliners, mantua-makers, and taylors into that country, against Lady Salisbury's intended ball. It is much on the plan of the famous one given on the late King's birth-day in Ireland, by the present Duchess Dowager of Leinster. Every body is invited, great and small, and it is supposed there will be near three thousand persons present.

A gang of desperate fellows infest the neighbourhood of Charing-cross, which makes it dangerous being out even at an early hour. About a week ago a gentleman at Holborn was knocked down and robbed at the corner of Craig's-court; and on Tuesday evening a gentleman and his son were robbed and ill-treated, as supposed, by the same villains, on the same spot.

Public Advertiser
27 December 1784

Edinburgh, Dec. 22.
Last week a party of soldiers in Buchan being sent out in pursuit of smuggled goods, some of them were so imprudent as to take off their shoes, and walk in their stockings, to prevent them slipping on the frost; the consequence was that one soldier died in a few hours after, and another lies dangerously ill.

Public Advertiser
27 December 1784

A Correspondent recommends Mr. Lunardi to have the following lines painted on his new balloon, as he thinks them very a-propos:

"On vent'rous wings, in quest of praise I go,
And leave the gazing multitude below."

Public Advertiser
29 December 1784

The grand farm annual dinner, at Mr. Waller's, Hall barn, in Bucks, is to be given on Thursday next; to which seven hundred neighbouring farmers and cottagers are invited. This is the true spirit of benevolence, and does honour to the memory of our old English hospitality.

General Evening Post
25–28 December 1784

We have long complained of the extravagance of the present times, and not without reason. The refinements of dissipation have arisen to such a pitch of late, that what was luxury to our forefathers does not now even comprize the ordinary necessaries of life. Were this folly confined to titled and fashionable fools alone, the evil would be less dangerous; but it runs through almost every station, and reaches even the lowest mechanic. The trader, who some years since thought it a piece of unwarrantable extravagance to go once in the twelve months with his wife and devour beef or ham at a shilling an ounce at Vauxhall, thinks it now inconsistent with his dignity not to repair to one of the polite watering places for some weeks, to wash away the plebeian scent of Thames-street. The consequence often is, that the summer levies an *extra* tax of some score of pounds upon his pocket, without including the article of gaming, in which his dear *rib*, at least, will not bear being behind-hand with her betters; so that, probably, before the close of the winter, he appears a *Whereas* in the Gazette.

Public Advertiser
29 December 1784

We hear that an officer of high rank in the army has given the sum of three hundred guineas to the proprietor of an air balloon for permission to ascend with him; articles of agreement are signed by the parties, and if after three days notice the officer should think proper to decline going upon the aerial voyage, then he is to forfeit his money. This has been undertaken by the officer in consequence of a conversation held with a certain Great Personage, on the use that might be made of a balloon in reconnoitring a country, which he was of opinion the voyager could not possibly attend to after he had ascended: to satisfy his —— in this particular the officer has undertaken the experiment.

General V—— is said to be the officer who is to go on a reconnoitring party to the clouds: above twenty thousand pounds are laid already upon this undertaking in the sporting-houses in St. James's-street.

Public Advertiser
29 December 1784

Copy of a PAINTER's Bill, presented to the Vestry, for Work done in a *Country Church*.
TO filling up the Chink in the Red Sea, and repairing the Damages of Pharaoh's Host.
TO a new Thief on the Cross.
TO cleaning six of the Apostles and adding an entire new Judas Iscariot.
TO a new Pair of Hands for Daniel in the Lion's Den, and a Set of Teeth for the Lioness.
TO a new Alteration in the Belief, mending the Commandments, and making a new Lord's Prayer.
TO repairing Nebuchadnezzar's Board.

TO mending the Pitcher of Jacob's Daughter.

TO a Pair of Sleeves for Susannah's Shift, and repairing the Breeches of one of the Elders.

TO cleansing the Whale's Belly, varnishing Jonah's Face, and mending his left Arm.

TO a new Skirt to Joseph's Garment, and a lascivious Eye for Potiphar's Wife.

TO a new Sheet-anchor, a Jury-mast, and a Long-boat for Noah's Ark.

TO adding some Scotch Cattle to Pharaoh's lean kine.

TO making a new Head for Holophernes, and cleaning Judith's Hands.

TO making perfect the Eunuch attending on Esther.

TO giving a Blush to the Cheeks of Eve, on presenting the Apple to Adam.

TO mending the Net in the miraculous Draught of Fishes.

TO a perspective Glass for David viewing Bathsheba, and mending his right Eye.

TO painting a new City in the Land of Nod.

TO cleansing the Garden of Eden after Adam's Expulsion.

TO finishing the Tower of Babel, and furnishing most of the Figures with new Heads.

TO painting a Shoulder of Mutton and a Shin of Beef in the Mouths of two of the Ravens feeding Elijah.

Public Advertiser
29 December 1784

Extract of a letter from Dover, Dec. 24

Amidst the great preparations now making for aerial excursions by Lunardi, Blanchard, and Count Zambaccari, whose exploits are to out-wonder wonders, our ingenious English aerial traveller Mr. Sadler, is now here, and is determined to make another effort for the honour of his country. He has prepared an apparatus for filling a Balloon, with which he intends to take an excursion to the Continent so soon as a vessel arrives with some materials, which is expected every hour. Mr. Sadler has already soared higher than either Lunardi or Blanchard, and, to the honour of Old England, is the only person who has been his own projector and chymist in this or any other country.

Public Advertiser
29 December 1784

A letter from Amboise on the banks of the Loire, has the following article. On the 8th of last month, a woman named Rose Darc, wife of a fruiterer of this town, was delivered of four children, namely a boy and three girls: the boy came into the world with all his teeth, and each of the girls had two. The boy refused the breast, but eats heartily of soup, boiled meat, and puddings, and drinks freely of either wine or water. This child is of a disposition so singularly untractable, that he scratches and otherwise so strenuously opposes those who have the care of him, that they find it impossible to swathe or dress him like other infants, and therefore he is kept in a Hamper, the edges of which are three feet from the ground, the inside being properly guarded with sheep-skins. All the children have been baptized; and of the boy it is remarkable, that he is named Jean-Berlin Darc, which three words form the following anagram: Diable incarne.

Public Advertiser
30 December 1784

A few nights since the House of Mr. Crow, one of the officers belonging to the Court of Conscience in Fulwood's Rents, Holborn, was broke open and robbed of property to the amount of between twenty and thirty pounds. The Robbers came into the Chamber where Mr. Crow was in bed, and stole from his breeches pockets a silver watch, and about five pounds in money, without disturbing him.

Public Advertiser
30 December 1784

THE LONDON GENERAL BILL OF
CHRISTENINGS AND BURIALS
From December 16, 1783, to December 14, 1784

Christened Males 8778 Buried Males 9229 Decreased
       Females 8401   Females 8599 in the
                                       Burials
                                       this Year
                                       1201

Died under 2 Years	– 5729	80 and 90	– 391
Between 2 and 5	– 1711	90 and 100	– 48
5 and 10	– 683	100 –	1
10 and 20	– 636	101 –	1
20 and 30	– 1417	102 –	0
30 and 40	– 1599	103 –	1
40 and 50	– 1781	104 –	0
50 and 60	– 1523	105 –	0
60 and 70	– 1359	106 –	2
70 and 80	– 917		

DISEASES.

Abortive & Stillborn	528	Diabetes	0
Abscess	1	Dropsy	830
Aged	1240	Evil	13
Ague	8	Fever, malignant Fever,	
Apoplexy & Sudden	207	Scarlet Fever, Spotted	
Asthma & Phthysic	377	Fever, and Purples	1973
Bedridden	12	Fistula	4
Bleeding	4	Flux	9
Bloody Flux	1	French Pox	32
Bursten and Rupture	17	Gout	63
Cancer	43	Gravel, Strangury, and	
Canker	2	Stone	35
Chicken Pox	3	Grief	3
Childbed	133	Head-Ach	1
Cholic, Gripes, Twisting		Headmouldshot,	
of the Guts	8	Horshoehead, and Water	
Cold	3	in the Head	15
Consumption	4540	Jaundice	62
Convulsions	4219	Imposthume	4
Cough and Hooping		Inflammation	198
Cough	467	Itch	0

Leprosy	0	Worms	11
Lethargy	0		
Livergrown	4	CASUALTIES	
Lunatick	46	Bit by a mad dog	2
Measles	29	Broken limbs	3
Miscarriage	3	Bruised	2
Mortification	136	Burnt	14
Palsy	66	Choaked	1
Pleurisy	15	Drowned	97
Quinsy	4	Excessive Drinking	8
Rash	0	Executed	11
Rheumatism	8	Found Dead	5
Rickets	0	Frighted	0
Rising of the Lights	0	Killed by Falls and	
Scald-head	0	several other Accidents	39
Scurvy	4	Killed themselves	23
Small Pox	1759	Murdered	4
Sore Throat	6	Overlaid	0
Sores and Ulcers	13	Poisoned	2
St. Anthony's Fire	0	Scalded	5
Stoppage in the Stomach	10	Smothered	0
Surfeit	1	Starved	1
Swelling	1	Suffocated	3
Teeth	369		
Thrush	6		————
Tympany	1	Total 220	
Vomiting and			————
Looseness	2		

*Gentleman's Magazine
Vol 2. (LIV) 1784*

ANNUAL BILL

A General List of the DISEASES and CASUALTIES; from December 18, 1783, to December 18, 1784.

Abortive – undertakings 528
Aged – in iniquity 30,000
Ague – at great men's levees 50
Bedridden – by the fair sex 1,000
Bleeding – to sharpers 1,051
Rupture – between friends 164
Child-bed – in the rehearsals 10
Cholic, gripes – after Lord Mayor's Day 500
Cold – in broken love 60
Consumption – of the purse 1,500
Convulsions – of laughter at a wit 1
Evil – communications 5,000
Fever – on the first night of a new piece 5
Flux – of money 1,000
Grief – for the loss of a wife ....
Headach – in a morning 500
Jaundice – in poets 50
Inflamation – of libels 61
Lethargy – the House of Lords 230
Lunatic – of balloons 1,000
Miscarriage – of comedies 3
Mortification – of vain hopes 63
Rash – promises 30
Rising of the lights – the window-tax 1
Scurvy – behaviour 124
Stoppage in the stomach – of authors 40
Surfeit – in city companies 56
Swelling – of pride 600
Looseness – of carriage 350
Worms – in booksellers garrets ....
Poisoned – by bad books 10,000
Killed themselves – by dullness 6
Frightened – by the critics 10

Morning Post
8 January 1785

LIST OF SOURCES

NEWSPAPERS AT BLOOMSBURY: BURNEY COLLECTION, BRITISH LIBRARY

London

Gazeteer and New Daily Advertiser
General Evening Post
London Chronicle
Morning Chronicle
Morning Herald
Morning Post
Parker's General Advertiser
Public Advertiser
Racing Calendar
Whitehall Evening Post

Bath

Bath Chronicle

NEWSPAPERS AT COLINDALE: BRITISH LIBRARY, NEWSPAPER LIBRARY

Adam's Weekly Courant, Chester
Bonner and Middleton's Bristol Journal
Cambridge Chronicle and Journal
Canterbury Journal
Jopson's Coventry Mercury
Magee's Weekly Packet, Dublin
Caledonian Mercury, Edinburgh
Edinburgh Evening Courant
Gloucester Journal
Gentleman's Magazine 1784
Scots Magazine 1784
Annual Register 1784
Dictionary of National Biography
Ipswich Journal
Leeds Intelligencer
Newcastle Courant
Norfolk Chronicle
Jackson's Oxford Journal
Shrewsbury Chronicle
Sussex Weekly Advertiser
Berrow's Worcester Journal
York Courant

327

INDEX

accidents: shooting 46, 118, 181, 193,
    215–16; on River Trent 33–4;
    greenhouse 126
adders, in the mouth 159–60
adultery 288
advertisements
    Master Crotch 20
    perfumery goods 25
    deal box lost 45
    dentists 48–9
    concave razors 50–1, 176
    hand washing 51–2
    Mr. Buzaglo 57, 161, 178–9
    estranged husband 84
    Olympian Dew 87, 176
    African cucumber 109
    gardener 112
    parish clerk 129
    lost dog 145, 202
    Richard England 152–3
    a man of light weight 154
    negroes 166
    young gentleman missing 170–1
    brick maker 171–2
    deserters 202–3
    perukes 217–18
    Bedlam Fox 232
    aerostatic machines 255
    education 293–4
America, emigration to 193–4
April Fool 81
arsenic 237–8, 267
anecdotes
    sailor 2
    foreign 15
    Sir Robert Henley 198
    judge 129
    superstition 164
    George Philipson 150
    strong exercise 165
    shooting of Daniel Bohely 180
    Duke of Cumberland 204
    Paddy 223–4
    honest stock broker 228–9
    Sir Philip Cravenleigh 227
    Mr. Rogerson 236

    Mr. Clement Oliver 244
    James I 268
    Piovano Arlotto 195–6

bagnio 102
    Drury Lane 246
    Leicester Fields 280
balloons
    at Aberdeen 73
    Adlington 166
    Bath 19
    Berkeley Castle 212–13
    Berwick 103
    Carlisle 142
    Chelsea 246
    London 218
    Paris 38
    Rouen 177
        mistaken for
            Last Trump 73
            whale's bladder 103
            Devil 142
    accident 220
    explodes 52
    diligences 2
    fox 104
    on fire 218
    Jew barber in 55
    flight 67
    ice-balloon 32
    mania 220
    reconnaissance 321
    Sadler's 55
    see Blanchard, Lunardi
balls
    Bath 94
    Mrs. Crewe's 115–16
bandits 24; in Ireland 132
Barrington, George, pickpocket
    trial 54
    in Dublin 146
    arrested 147–9
    and Mrs. Siddons 151
    free 180
    back in London 186
    at Blanchard's ascent 226

Pitt mistaken for 275
Bartholomew Fair 209
bathing
    Brighton 164
    Thames 168
Beaumarchais, beaten 162
    Figaro 308
bears, polar 184
bees
    cause death 163
    swarms at Burleigh 180–1
    Mrs. Willerton and 238
beetles
    plague of 145–6
    how to get quit of 162
births 28th 61
    triplets 62
    extraordinary 314–15
Bisset, Mr., beast teacher 23
Blanchard, Jean-Pierre
    balloonist, flight 247f.
    to race Lunardi 258
    lands on patron's property 266
    plans Channel flight 279
    Channel crossing 310
Boaz, Hernon, balloonist 183
Bray, Capt., and smugglers 105
Brown, Dr., and the toast 149
burglary 29, 68, 239–40
Burke, Edmund, house burgled
        239–40

Charing Cross, mob 319
charity
    Dublin 46
    required 135–6
    spurned 284
Charlotte, Queen
    birthday 20–1
    ill 91–2
Chartres, duc de, balloonist 175, 179
chilblains, cure for 314
Clarges, Thomas, miser 81–2
clergy
    suicide 190
    committed for theft 191
    robbed 216
    sermon controversial 247
    confirmation 229
    at Newgate 203
clothes, described 45, 153, 171, 197,
        202, 232, 291–2

coaches
    overturned 1
    stopped 12–13
    Emperor's 59
    arrest on 92
    stuck 297–8
    driver frozen 301–2
    25 outside passengers 275
    new mail coach 182
    tarred and feathered 213
    dangerous driving 273–4
coalition 110
coffee house
    quarrel 42–3
    shooting 149
    keeper shoots Jews 260
convicts
    Black Harry 92
    Bumper Smith 93, 170
    and handcuffs 103
    escaped
        from ship 104
        from Bridewell 157, 197
        from gaol 158
    hulks 163
    young 178
    small 178
    bound for USA 214
    captured 294–5
    frozen 310
Covent Garden
    riot 85, 100; in bagnio 102
    arrest 97
    ox in 97
    hustings 97
    affray 107
    Linton murdered 157–8
    death of crimp 111
    see Theatres
Crewe, Mrs., ball 115
cricket 119, 185
Cumberland, Duke of, and
        cold chicken 204

dancing 139, 141, 233
deaths
    of grief 91
    gentlewoman's 92
    of corpulence 166
    cow doctor's 184
    with 251 descendants 192
    of midget 192

of cold after dancing 216
of fright 226
Thomas Wilson 106
Dr. Johnson 303
of rage 269
diseases and casualties 1784 324–5
debt
  Sir Robert Henley 198
dentist 48–9
deserters 202–3
Devil 47, 132, 142
Devonshire, Duchess of
  gambling 38
  canvassing 85
  and Fox 113
  at Public Breakfast 114
  at ball 115–16
diving machine 28
divorce 33
dogs
  bite 67
  stolen 97, 202
  poisoned 124–5
  lost 145
  killed 258
  taxed 271–2
Donnellan, Nehemiah
  not dead 134
drowning, cure for 126
Dublin, news from 262
duels and fights
  at Norwich 35
  Clark v. Moyston 42
  in Hyde Park 48
  avoided 81
  Capt. C. and Mr. D. 53
  lessons for duellists 138
  Death v. Johnson 185
  over sermon 247
  Death v. Salvage 239
  in Tuileries 254
  ridiculed 311
  Rose/Rowlls v. England 142–5,
    152–3, 186, 282, 298
Dunsden brothers 62, 134–5, 177
Duroure, Count L. H. S. horse 92–3
  elopes 280; committed 282;
    suicide 286; acquitted 304, 306

Edinburgh, Siddonized 133–4
election
  meeting 39–40, 78

hustings 97
Fox brush 98
propaganda 98
result 113
elopements
  to Scotland 71–2
  Duroure 279–80
emigration, to America 193–4
Ethiopian satyr 195
Eton, boy killed 298–9
executions
  Mr. Lee 63–4
  Daniel Cato 69
  Henfrey and Rider 84
  Elizabeth Wood 94
  Dunsden brothers 177
  Glasgow 272
  Rich. Edwards 203
exercise, fatal 165
Exeter, Earl of, bees 180–1
explosions
  gunpowder 52
extravagance, of the times 320

fair, Bartholomew 209
  riots 216
fires
  anecdote 259
  balloon 218
  candle causes 197
fireworks 270–1
flying 8, 218–19; see also balloons
foreigners
  robbed 74
  English life explained to 105
forgery
  Mr. Lee 63–4
  genteel 137
foundlings
  Gt. Ormond Street 85
  Otaheite 173
  Caen 235
Fox, Charles James, M.P.
  on hustings 95
  bag thrown at 41
  toasted 75
  canvassing 80
  brush 98
  propaganda 98–9
  supporters riot 100
  election result 113
  chaired 113

331

public breakfast 114
ball 115–16
Derby celebrates 117
election for Orkney 123–4
niece dances with enemy 141
feted and robbed 227
footpads 72, 117, 148, 177, 231–2
Fortescue, Lord
reduces rents 8
fortunes
eaten 236–7
honesty makes 290
Franklin, Benjamin 155

Gainsborough, Thomas, painter
charity spurned 284
galleys
Frenchman sent to 240
gambling 34, 150, 233
£5000 lost 10
George III, King of Britain
cheered 109
opens parliament 115
birthday 156
polar bears 184
Graham, James, quack
lecture 78
in Newgate 107, 109
at Manchester 262–3
rolling in chariot 198
gossip 285, 288–9, 296–7, 301
proves false 302
gunpowder
explodes 52
stolen 238

hailstones 131
Handel, jubilee 121
profits 162–3
Harbord, Sir Harbord, not dead 67
harvest 167
Henfrey and Rider 28
executed 84
highwaymen 13, 41; shot 120; nr.
Tyburn 279
imaginary 284
honesty rewarded 290
Horse Guards parade 313
hospitality, old English 320
House, Samuel
honest Englishman 76
hunger strike 217

hunting 88, 207
hurricane 238

ice, see weather
impostors
Violet Chambers, courtesan 22
man is woman 64
James Jackson 39
inheritances
Thomas Nelson 14–15
Strasbourg Idiots Hospital 17
Irish Giant 256; married 229–30

Jews, accused 93
shot 243
robbed 268
and second-hand prayers 281
Johnson, Samuel
relapsed 296
death 303
anecdote 306
on tea 310
funeral 315

Katterfelto, Dr., quack
and Devil in London 47
kleptomaniacs
alehouse pots 240
knives and forks 316

Lady Holland's Mob 214
ladies, fashion 98
make up 132
in balloon 177
Lavater, Johann Kaspar
jilted 152
Londonderry
Quaker admonishes 136–7
lottery 293
winners 286, 289
Louis XVI, King of France 259
Loughborough, Lord 260
Lunardi, Vincenzo, balloonist
balloon exhibited 205, 237
aerial excursion 224f.
bon mot 230
belittled 231
meets nobility 231
and the ladies 239
to race Blanchard 258
monument 272–3
accounts 286

332

lunatics
  kill family 103
  suicide 137, 170
  recover 181

Mackenzie, Capt., accused 151
  trial 299
marriage
  promising 62, 152
  musical 157
  Mrs. Thrale 169
  remarkable 190
  curious 229–30, 246
  highway 281
  sudden 289–90
meals and food
  extempore 32
  at Grocer's Hall 56
  at Bath 94
  at Derby 117
  physicians' dinner 167
  and Mr. Rogerson 236
medicines and cures
  for drowned persons 126–7
  prescriptions 133
  against viper's bite 191
  for hooping cough 207
  for ague 207
  Dr. Steers' Opodeldoc 275–6
  Buzaglo, cures without medicine 57,
    161–2, 178–9
  Goulard's extract of lead 286
  Mrs. Liddel of Carlisle 316–17
Mesmer, Franz Anton 104, 185
meteor 178
Mexican, aged 234
Milkmaid's Frolic, origin of 193
misers
  Thomas Clarges 81–2
  Wm. Thatcher 107
mob
  take sides 9
  law 118–19, 179–80, 189, 199
  Lady Holland's 214
Montgolfier, Jacques-Etienne, French
  balloonist, 269
Morocco, Emperor of 35–6
Mountmorres, Lord, dancing 141
Muddle, hunger striker 217
murder
  of Edward Kelsall 29
  of Thomas Rosser 69

of mother-in-law 77
body in church 155
of Mr. Linton 157
of waterman 208
of Weston 230
Muskerry, Lord
  coach tarred 213

Newgate, prison
  death in 25, 151
  number of prisoners 49
  convicts transported 76–7
  Dr. Graham in 107
  executions 278
Newmarket
  Duroure's horse 92–3
  Prince of Wales at 91–2
Norfolk, Duke of, at Darlington 303
North, Lord, fox or pig 123

Obizzi, Marchioness d'
  murdered 264
Olympian Dew, perfume 87, 122, 176

Palmerston, Lord 266
parachute, early 269
parliament 3–4, 70, 73, 123
perfumes
  Olympian Dew 87, 122, 176
pickpockets
  warning against 212
  at Blanchard's ascent 254
  French 240
  see Barrington
pirates
  river 258
  Moorish 36
  Deal 105
  freshwater 268
Pitt, William (the Younger)
  freeman of the City 56
  return from 56–7
  toasted 75
  anecdotes of 138–9
  burnt in effigy 168
  lost and shot at 187
  comment on 191–2
  plate stolen 265
  mistaken for Barrington 275
poisonings
  mother-in-law 77
  dog 124

333

arsenic 237
  master by servant 52
  James Simister 94
police 108
  arrests 97, 165–6, 257, 155
  insufficient 159, 314
Portland, Lady 85, 113
postmen
  lost 59
  frozen 53
practical jokes
  Duke of Norfolk 303
pregnancy, pretended 94
prescriptions 133
prisons, *see* Newgate, convicts
prostitutes
  black 283
  Covent Garden 102
  steal from client 124, 283
punishments
  whipping 17
  lashes 189
  see executions, murder

races
  Newmarket 92
  Epsom 117–18
razors
  C. Sharp's concave 50–1, 176
resurrection men 21
  and surgeon's sister 14
  shot 278
  and lascars' heads 141
  defended 144
  uncle sold 128
Reynolds, Sir Joshua 217
Ridout, Porter 243; trial 260
riots
  in brothel 102
  Covent Garden 82, 100, 107–8
  Smithfield 213
roads 297
  and old lady 24
robbery
  spoon 1
  pastry cook 6
  Dublin 14
  Henfrey and Rider 28
  Mrs. Hall 34
  near Pantheon 45
  at John Wiggins 49–50
  Dunsdens 61–2

of Great Seal of England 73
  at West Malling 174
  at Mr. Hett's 174
  at Mrs. Roe's 86
  Bumper Smith 93
  William Vandeput 93
  of boys fishing 108
  copper 112
  diamond pin 118
  shoes 119
  paymaster 124
  Joseph Radley 187
  at Blackheath 245
  at Mrs. Hemmings 287
  see Barrington, footpads
rules, for Christmas 312–13

Sadler, English balloonist 55
sailors
  riot 82–3
  tarred and feathered 241–2
  oath 298
Salisbury, Lady
  ball 319
schoolmasters/schools 63, 200; advert
    293–4
Seagood, Mrs., concubine 35–6
Sharp, C., perfumer 88, 176
Sheldon, balloonist 249f.
Sheridan, C. F., M.P.
  stone thrown at 130
sheep
  and calamity 110–11
  in parachute experiment 269–70
shipping 7, 22
shooting 207
Siddons, Sarah, actress
  fees 110
  in Edinburgh 133
  moving effect of 147
smallpox
  inoculation 172
Smith, Bumper
  trial 93; escape and return 170
smuggling
  Capt. Bray 105–6
  Angmering 182
  Galloway 37
  Framlingham 216
Soissons, Count de 34–5
soldiers
  frozen 29, 39

in scuffle 120
  in St. James's Park 309
  barefoot in frost 319
sugar, price of 238
suicide
  at Pickle-Herring-Stairs 16
  Dr. Staker of Bath 95
  footman's 95–6
  attempted 140
  at Calais 170
  Miss G. 267
  in New River 296
  clergyman's 190
skittles, murderer playing 230
snuff, and Mrs. Liddel 316–17
Stogdell/Stockdale
  committed 259
  escape 264
Sunday, in Dublin 169
swindler, whipped 230–1

tax, on ribbons 168
  windows 261
  dogs 271–2
tea, surfeit of 196
teeth 48–9
Ten Commandments
  stolen 274
tips 325
tourists, English 233
Thames, River
  frozen 35, 315
  pirates 258
  S. House jumps in 76
  suicide 140
  drunk drowned 277
  wager 284
  ice 319
  crossed on foot 35
theatres
  cats opera 23
  Covent Garden 109, 269, 296, 306
  pickpockets at 146–7, 186
thieves
  dead 37
  horse 61
  chimney 267
  child 280
Thrale, Hester (Mrs. Piozzi)
  married 169
Thurlow, Lord
  robbed of Great Seal 73

umbrellas
  20,000 lost 91
uncle sold 128

Vernon, Miss, match-maker 141

wagers re
  frost 1
  red hot poker 129
  walking 136, 189–90
  balloon race 258
  plum pudding 200
  jump into Thames 76, 284
wages 154, 217, 294
Wales, Prince of (George IV)
  windows broken 60
  at Queen's bedside 91
  bruised 153
  wet 154
  recovered 154
  public breakfast 114
  cricket match 119
  day return 176
  sea bathing 164
  and Duc de Chartres 175, 179
  meets Lunardi 231
  at Blanchard's ascent 248
  imitators 282–3
Wardrobe, Annabella
  banished 198
Warwickshire Young Lady
  exhibited 256
watchmen
  musical 201
  intemperance 317
weather
  backwardness of 94
  ball of fire 158
  change in 130
  floods 163–4
  frost 7, 47
  hailstones 131
  harvest 167
  ice 11–12, 313
  lightning 199
  meteor 178
  May 101
  Severn frozen 13
  snipes frozen 13
  snow 34, 50; leads to arrest 86–7
  temperature 160
  thunder, beneficial effect of 120–1

335

Westminster Abbey
   Handel's Jubilee 122
   thanksgiving for peace 172
wigs 217
wills
   John Angel 72
   re Spanish Liquorice 77
   Dr. Wilson's young ladies 106
windfalls
   button seller's boy 206

   poor girl's 222
window tax 261
wives
   advert for husband 84–5
   arm broken 125
   to borrow or for sale 139
   sold 219
   hanged 233–4
   toes trodden on 269